IN ACTION

Measuring Return on Investment

VOLUME 2

SEVENTEEN

CASE STUDIES

FROM THE

REAL WORLD

OF TRAINING

JACK J. PHILLIPS

SERIES EDITOR

ASTD

Linking People,
Learning & Performance

Ordering information: Books published by the American Society for Training & Development can be ordered by calling 703.683.8100.

Library of Congress Catalog Card Number: 94-78503
ISBN: 1-56286-065-8

Table of Contents

About the Series Editor..vi

Introduction to the *In Action* Series....................................vii

Preface...ix

How to Use This Casebook...xiv

The ROI Challenge: Developing a Credible Process 1
Jack J. Phillips

Preventing Sexual Harassment 17
Healthcare, Inc.
Dianne Hill and Jack J. Phillips

Transforming Supervisors Into Innovative Team Leaders 37
A Consortium of Companies
Darlene Russ-Eft and Kathleen Hurson

Measuring ROI in an Advanced Sales Skills Program.....................49
Apex Corporation
Wade A. Hannum

Evaluation of Techniques for an Empowered Workforce.................73
Eastman Chemical Company
Paul Bernthal and Bill Byham

Measuring the Impact of Sales Training 89
Big Apple Bank
Neil Rackham

Measuring the ROI for a Finance Course: An Evolution
    of Methods 103
Nortel
James A. Hite Jr. and Linda Trask

Using ROI Forecasting to Develop a High-Impact,
    High-Value Training Curriculum 113
Commonwealth Edison
Jim Graber, Gerry Post, and Rick Erwin

A Preprogram ROI for Machine Operator Training 129
Canadian Valve Company
Tim Renaud and Jack J. Phillips

An Information Technology Program Evaluation 141
NYNEX Corporation
Janet F. Chernick

Measuring ROI for Negotiation Sales Training 153
Texas Instruments Systems Group
Herb Graff and Rob Schriver

Training's Contribution to a Major Change Initiative 163
First Union National Bank
Ronnie D. Stone, Douglas R. Steele, Debra M. Wallace,
    and Wesley B. Spurrier

Computer-Based Training for Maintenance Employees.............................191
Bell Atlantic Network Services
Toni M. Hodges

Replicating a Performance Management ROI Evaluation 199
Speedy Telecommunications Company
William Wurtz

Evaluating Leadership Training for Newly Appointed
     People Managers 207
Global Technology Company
Jack J. Phillips

Measuring the Impact of Leadership Training 229
LensCrafters
Patricia Zigarmi and Frank Baynham

Workforce Transition Project 239
Pitney Bowes
Rändi Sigmund Smith

Measuring the Impact of Basic Skills Training 267
Otto Engineering
Edward E. Gordon and Boyd Owens

About the Series Editor

Jack Phillips has more than 27 years of professional experience in human resources and management, and has served as training and development manager at two *Fortune* 500 firms. In 1992, Phillips founded Performance Resources Organization, an international consulting firm specializing in human resources accountability programs. Phillips consults with his clients in the United States, Canada, England, South Africa, Mexico, Venezuela, Malaysia, Indonesia, Australia, and Singapore on issues ranging from measurement and evaluation to productivity and quality enhancement.

A frequent contributor to management literature, Phillips has authored or edited *Accountability in Human Resource Management* (1996), *Handbook of Training Evaluation and Measurement Methods* (2d edition, 1991), *Measuring Return on Investment* (Vol. 1, 1994), *Conducting Needs Assessment* (1995), *The Development of a Human Resource Effectiveness Index* (1988), *Recruiting, Training and Retaining New Employees* (1987), and *Improving Supervisors' Effectiveness* (1985), which won an award from the Society for Human Resource Management. Phillips has written more than 75 articles for professional, business, and trade publications.

Phillips has earned undergraduate degrees in electrical engineering, physics, and mathematics from Southern College of Technology and Oglethorpe University; a master's in decision sciences from Georgia State University; and a doctorate in human resource management from University of Alabama. In 1987, he won the Yoder-Heneman Personnel Creative Application Award from the Society for Human Resource Management. He is an active member of several professional organizations.

Jack Phillips can be reached at the following address: Performance Resources Organization, Box 380637, Birmingham, AL 35238-0637. Phone: 205.991.7627; Fax: 205.980.0671; e-mail: roipro@ wwisp.com.

Introduction to the
In Action Series

As are most professionals, the people involved in human resource development (HRD) are eager to see practical applications of the models, techniques, theories, strategies, and issues the field comprises. In recent years, practitioners have developed an intense desire to learn about the success of other organizations when they implement HRD programs. The Publishing Review Committee of the American Society for Training and Development has established this series of casebooks to fill this need. Covering a variety of topics in HRD, the series should add significantly to the current literature in the field.

This series has the following objectives:

- *To provide real-world examples of HRD program application and implementation.* Each case will describe significant issues, events, actions, and activities. When possible, the actual names of the organizations and individuals involved will be used. In other cases, the names will be disguised, but the events are factual.

- *To focus on challenging and difficult issues confronting the HRD field.* These cases will explore areas where it is difficult to find information or where the processes or techniques are not standardized or fully developed. Also, emerging issues critical to success in the field will be covered in the series.

- *To recognize the work of professionals in the HRD field by presenting best practices.* Each book in the series will attempt to represent the most effective examples in the field. The most respected organizations, practitioners, authors, researchers, and consultants will be asked to provide cases.

- *To serve as a self-teaching tool for people learning about the HRD field.* As a stand-alone reference, each volume should be a very useful learning tool. Each case will contain many issues and fully explore several topics.

- *To present a medium for teaching groups about the practical aspects of HRD.* Each book should serve as a discussion guide to enhance learning in formal and informal settings. Each case will have questions for discussion. And each book will be useful as a supplement to general and specialized textbooks in HRD.

The topics for the volumes will be carefully selected to ensure that they represent important and timely issues in the HRD field. The editors for the individual volumes are experienced professionals in the field. The series will provide a high-quality product to fill a critical void in the literature. An ambitious schedule is planned.

If you have suggestions of ways to improve this series or an individual volume in the series, please respond directly to me. Your input is welcome.

Jack J. Phillips, Ph.D.
Series Editor
Performance Resources Organization
Box 380637
Birmingham, AL 35238-0637

Preface

Since the publication of volume 1, the interest in measuring the return-on-investment has continued to escalate. By all measures, volume 1 was a success with practitioners, consultants, and professors. Published in 1994, it became the best-seller among the books the American Society for Training & Development (ASTD) sold in both 1995 and 1996, and it is well on the way to becoming ASTD's all-time best-seller. The book filled an important void in the literature. Readers found the cases to be extremely valuable in helping them tackle this important issue.

We hope to repeat the success of volume 1 with the new set of cases presented in volume 2. The authors, who reflect several viewpoints and have varied backgrounds, are diligently pursuing accountability of training, human resource development, and performance improvement programs. The cases cover a variety of programs in a diverse group of organizations, many of them global in scope. Collectively, they should add to the growing database of return-on-investment (ROI) studies and make an important contribution to the literature.

Target Audience

The book should interest anyone involved in training, human resource development (HRD), human resources (HR), and performance improvement. The primary audience is made up of the practitioners who are struggling to determine the value of programs and to show how programs contribute to an organization's goals. They are the ones who request more examples from what they often label the real world. This same group also expresses concern that there are too many models, methods, strategies, and theories, and too few examples to show if any of them has really made a difference. This publication should satisfy practitioners' needs by providing successful models of how the measurement and evaluation process works. Also, this book should encourage more practitioners to tackle this important topic and help them avoid some of the problems that are inherent in the process.

The second audience comprises instructors and professors. Whether they choose this book for use in university classes for students who are pursuing degrees in HRD, internal workshops for professional HRD staff members, or public seminars on HRD implementation, the casebook will be a valuable reference. It can be used as a supplement to a standard HRD textbook or as a complement to a textbook on measurement and evaluation, such as the third edition of the *Handbook of Training Evaluation and Measurement Methods* (Phillips, 1997). In my seminars on ROI in training and development, the handbook and casebook will be standard requirements. As a supplemental text, this casebook will bring practical significance to training and development, convincing students that the measurement and evaluation process does make a difference.

A third audience is composed of the researchers and consultants who are seeking ways to document results from programs. This book provides additional insight into how to satisfy the client with impressive results. It shows the application of a wide range of models and techniques, some of which are based on sound theory and logical assumptions and others of which may not fare well under the scrutiny of close examination. Unfortunately, the HRD measurement and evaluation process does not have a prescribed set of standards and techniques.

The last audience, but certainly not the least, is made up of managers who must work with HRD on a peripheral basis—managers who are participants in HRD programs to develop their own management skills, managers who send other employees to participate in HRD programs, and managers who occasionally lead or conduct sessions of HRD programs. In these roles, managers must understand the process and appreciate the value of HRD. This casebook should provide evidence of this value.

Each audience should find the casebook entertaining and engaging reading. Questions are placed at the end of each case to stimulate additional thought and discussion. One of the most effective ways to maximize the usefulness of this book is through group discussions, using the questions to develop and dissect the issues, techniques, methodologies, and results.

The Cases

The most difficult part of developing this book was to identify case authors for a process that does not exist in many organizations. Where it does exist, HRD staffers are not always willing to discuss it. In the search, letters were sent to more than 10,000 individuals who have an interest in evaluation. In order to tap the global market, 1,000 of the individuals contacted were outside the United States. ROI in HRD is a global topic, with no boundaries. We are pleased that more than 100 individuals requested copies of detailed case guidelines, and 45 made the commitment to develop a case. In the end, 17 case studies have been accepted for publication.

Cases for this publication had to meet some very tough guidelines. They had to focus on the business results of training, usually at Level 4 in

Kirkpatrick's evaluation levels (Kirkpatrick, 1975). More than 30 years ago Kirkpatrick developed what has become a popular framework for evaluating training at four levels: reaction, learning, behavior, and results. Most of the cases in this book use these levels of evaluation or some modified version of them. The selected cases for this book also had to have data that could be converted to a monetary value so that ROI could be calculated. This essentially creates a fifth level of evaluation, ROI (Phillips, 1996).

Although there was some attempt to structure cases similarly, they are not identical in style and content. It is important for the reader to experience the programs as they were developed and identify the issues pertinent to each particular setting and situation. The result is a variety of presentations with a variety of styles. Some cases are brief and to the point, outlining precisely what happened and what was achieved. Others provide more detailed background information, including how the need for the program was determined, the personalities involved, and how their backgrounds and biases created a unique situation.

There was no attempt to restrict cases to a particular methodology, technique, or process. It is helpful to show a wide range of approaches. We have resisted the temptation to pass judgment on the various approaches, preferring to let readers evaluate the different techniques and their appropriateness to their own particular settings. Some of the assumptions, methodologies, and strategies might not be as comprehensive and sound as others.

In some cases, the name of the organization is identified, as are the individuals who were involved. In others, the organization's name is disguised at the request of either the organization or the case author. In today's competitive world and in situations where there is an attempt to explore new territory, it is understandable why an organization would choose not to be identified. Identification should not be a critical issue, however. Though some cases are lightly modified, they are based on real-world situations faced by real people.

Case Authors

It would be difficult to find a more impressive group of contributors to an HRD publication than those for this casebook. For such a difficult topic, we expected to find the best, and we were not disappointed. If we had to describe the group, we would say they are experienced, professional, knowledgeable, and on the leading edge of HRD. Collectively, they represent practitioners, consultants, researchers, and professors. Individually, they represent a cross section of HRD. Most are experts, and some are well known in the field. A few are high-profile authors who have made a tremendous contribution to HRD and have taken the opportunity to provide an example of their top-quality work. Others have made their mark quietly and have achieved success for their organizations.

Best Practices?

In our search for cases, we contacted the most respected and well-known organizations in the world, leading experts in the field, key executives in HRD, and well-known authors and researchers. We were seeking examples that represent best practices in measurement and evaluation. Whether they have been delivered, we will never know. What we do know is that if these are not best practices, no other publication can claim to have them either. Many of the experts producing these cases characterize them as the best examples of measurement and devaluation in the field.

Suggestions

We welcome your input. If you have ideas or recommendations regarding presentation, case selection, or case quality, please send them to me at the above address. All letters will be not only appreciated, but also acknowledged.

Acknowledgments

Although this casebook is a collective work of many individuals, the first acknowledgment must go to all the case authors. We are grateful for their professional contribution. We also want to acknowledge the organizations that have allowed us to use their names and programs for publication. We realize this action is not without risk. We trust the final product has portrayed them as the progressive organizations interested in results and willing to try new processes and techniques.

Tammy Bush has served as my assistant for this project, and without her untiring efforts, this publication would not have been developed or delivered within a reasonable time frame. With her experience in human resources, she was able to make important contributions and offer useful input throughout the process. Thanks for a job well done. In addition, Libby Morris provided helpful assistance in coordinating the final stages of the project.

Finally, I owe continued appreciation to my spouse, Johnnie, who has tolerated my hectic and demanding schedule during the development of this book. She is a very understanding, thoughtful, and patient partner.

Jack J. Phillips
Birmingham, Alabama
October 1997

References

Phillips, J.J. *Handbook of Training Evaluation and Measurement Methods* (3d edition). Houston: Gulf Publishing, 1997.

Kirkpatrick, D.L. "Techniques for Evaluating Training Programs." *Training Programs,* D.L. Kirkpatrick, editor. Alexandria, VA: ASTD, 1975, pp. 1-17.

Phillips, J.J. "The Search for Best Practices." *Training & Development,* volume 50, number 2, February 1996, pp. 42-47.

How to Use This Casebook

These cases present a variety of approaches to measuring the return-on-investment in human resource development (HRD). Most of the cases focus on evaluation at the ultimate level: business results. Collectively, the cases offer a wide range of settings, methods, techniques, strategies, and approaches, representing manufacturing, service, and government organizations. Target groups for the programs vary from all employees to managers to technical specialists. Although most of the programs focus on training and development, others include organization development and performance management. As a group, these cases represent a rich source of information about the strategies of some of the best practitioners, consultants, and researchers in the field.

Each case does not necessarily represent the ideal approach for the specific situation. In every case, it is possible to identify areas that could benefit from refinement and improvement. That is part of the learning process—to build on the work of other people. Although the evaluation approach is contextual, these methods and techniques can be used in other organizations.

Table 1 presents basic descriptions of the cases in the order in which they appear in the book. This table can serve as a quick reference for readers who want to examine the evaluation approach for a particular type of program, audience, or industry.

Using the Cases

There are several ways to use this book. In essence, it will be helpful to anyone who wants to see real-life examples of the business results of training. Specifically, four uses are recommended:

- This book will be useful to HRD professionals as a basic reference of practical applications of measurement and evaluation. A reader can analyze and dissect each of the cases to develop an understanding of the issues, approaches, and most of all, refinements, or improvements that could be made.
- This book will be useful in group discussions, where interested individu-

als can react to the material, offer different perspectives, and draw conclusions about approaches and techniques. The questions at the end of each case can serve as a beginning point for lively and entertaining discussions.

- This book will serve as an excellent supplement to other training and development or evaluation textbooks. It provides the extra dimensions of real-life cases that show the outcomes of training and development.

- Finally, this book will be extremely valuable for managers who do not have primary training responsibility. These managers provide support and assistance to the HRD staff, and it is helpful for them to understand the results that HRD programs can yield.

It is important to remember that each organization and its program implementation is unique. What works well for one may not work for another, even if they are in similar settings. The book offers a variety of approaches and provides an arsenal of tools from which to choose in the evaluation process.

Follow-Up

Space limitations have required that some cases be shorter than the author and editor would have liked. Some information concerning background, assumptions, strategies, and results had to be omitted. If additional information on a case is needed, the lead author can be contacted directly. The lead authors' addresses are listed at the end of each case.

Table 1. Overview of case studies by industry, training program, design type.

Case	Industry	HRD Program	Target Audience
Healthcare, Inc.	Health care	Sexual harassment prevention	First-and-second level supervisors and managers, all employees
Consortium of Companies	Varied	Innovation training	Team leaders
Apex Corporation	Business products	Empowerment	Sales representatives
Eastman Chemical Company	Specialty chemicals	Sales training	All employees in the division

Table 1 (continued). Overview of case studies by industry, training program, design type.

Case	Industry	HRD Program	Target Audience
Big Apple Bank	Banking	Financial skills	Sales representatives
Nortel	Telecommunications	Varied	Finance managers
Commonwealth Edison	Electric utility	Machine operator training	Varied
Canadian Valve Company	Valve manufacturing	Information technology	Machine operators
NYNEX Corporation	Telecommunications	Three negotiation skills	Telecommunication managers
Texas Instruments	Electronics	Public training and jobs	Managers
First Union National Bank	Banking	Skills	Relationship managers, support team members, and sales managers
Bell Atlantic	Telecommunications	Computer-based maintenance training	Maintenance employees
Speedy Telecommunications Company	Telecommunications	Performance management systems	Managers
Global Technology Company	Technical products	Leadership training	New managers
Lenscrafters	Specialty retailing	Leadership training	Managers
Pitney Bowes	Postal equipment	Workforce transition	All employees
Otto Engineering	Specialty manufacturing	Literacy training	All employees

The ROI Challenge: Developing a Credible Process

Jack J. Phillips

Although the interest in return-on-investment (ROI) has heightened and much progress has been made in understanding and calculating ROI, it is still an issue that challenges even the most sophisticated and progressive human resource development (HRD) departments. Some professionals argue that it is not possible to calculate the ROI on HRD programs, but others quietly and deliberately proceed to develop measures and ROI calculations. Regardless of the position taken on the issue, the reasons for measuring the return are still there. Almost all training, HRD, and performance improvement professionals share a belief that they must eventually show a return-on-investment. If they don't show one, funding may be reduced, or the department may not be able to maintain or enhance its present status and influence in the organization.

The dilemma surrounding the ROI process is a source of frustration for many senior executives and for some people even within the HRD field itself. Most executives realize that training is a basic necessity when organizations are experiencing significant growth or increased competition. In those cases, training can prepare employees to perform the required skills while fine-tuning skills needed to meet competitive challenges. Training is also important during business restructuring and rapid change where employees must learn new skills and often find themselves doing much more work in a dramatically downsized workforce.

In addition to realizing the need for training and development, these same executives intuitively feel that there is value in training. They logically conclude that training and development should pay off in important bottom-line measures such as productivity improvements, quality enhancements, cost reductions, and savings in time. Also, they believe that training can enhance customer satisfaction, improve morale, and build teamwork. Yet the frustration comes from the lack of evidence to show that the process is actually adding value. Although the payoffs are assumed to be there and training appears to be needed, more evidence is needed or training and development funds may not be allocated in the future. The ROI process represents the most promising way to show this accountability following a logical, rational approach (Phillips, 1997).

The Concerns With ROI

Although progress is evident, the ROI process is not without its share of problems and concerns. The mere presence of the process creates a dilemma for many organizations. When an organization embraces the concept and implements the process, the management team is usually anxiously waiting for results, only to be disappointed when they are not quantifiable. For an ROI process to be useful, it must balance many issues such as feasibility, simplicity, credibility, and soundness. More specifically, three major audiences must be pleased with a specific ROI process to accept and use it—HRD practitioners; senior managers, sponsors, and clients; and researchers.

For years, HRD practitioners have assumed that ROI could not be measured. When they examined a typical process, they found long formulas, complicated equations, and complex models that made the ROI process appear confusing. With this perceived complexity, HRD managers could visualize the tremendous efforts required for data collection and analysis, and more important, the increased cost necessary to make the process work. Because of these concerns, HRD practitioners are seeking an ROI process that is simple and easy to understand so they can easily implement the steps and strategies. Also, they need a process that will not take an excessive amount of time to implement and will not consume too much precious staff time. Finally, practitioners need a process that is not too expensive. With competition for financial resources, they need a process that will not command a significant portion of the HRD budget. In summary, the ROI process, from the perspective of the HRD practitioner, must be user-friendly, efficient, and cost-effective.

Senior managers, sponsors, and clients who must approve HRD budgets, request HRD programs, or live with the results of programs have a strong interest in developing the ROI in training. They want an ROI process that provides quantifiable results using a method similar to the ROI formula applied to other types of investments. Senior managers have a never-ending desire to have it all come down to an ROI calculation reflected as a percentage. And, like HRD practitioners, they want a process that is simple and easy to understand. The assumptions made in the calculations and the methodology used in the process should reflect their point of reference, backgrounds, and level of understanding. They do not want, or need, a string of formulas, charts, and complicated models. Instead, they need a process that they can explain to others, if necessary. More important, they need a process with which they can identify, one that is sound and realistic enough to earn their confidence.

Finally, researchers will only support a process that measures up to their scrutiny. Researchers usually insist that models, formulas, assumptions, and theories are sound and based on commonly accepted practices. Also, they want a process that produces accurate values and consistent outcomes. If estimates are necessary, researchers want a process that provides the most accuracy within the constraints of the situation, recognizing that adjustments need to be made when there is uncertainty in the process. The challenge is to develop acceptable requirements for an ROI process that will satisfy researchers and, at the same time, please practitioners and senior managers. Sound impossible? Maybe not.

Criteria for an Effective ROI Process

To satisfy the needs of these three critical groups, the ROI process must meet several specific requirements. Ten essential criteria for an effective ROI process are outlined below:

1. The ROI process must be **simple**, void of complex formulas, lengthy equations, and complicated methodologies. Most ROI models have failed to satisfy this requirement. In an attempt to obtain statistical perfection and use too many theories, several ROI models and processes have become too complex to understand and use.

2. The ROI process must be **economical** and able to be implemented easily. The process should have the capability to become a routine part of training and development without requiring significant additional resources. Sampling for ROI calculations and early planning for ROI are often necessary to make progress with this concept without adding new staff.

3. The assumptions, methodology, and techniques must be **credible.** For an ROI process to earn the respect of practitioners and senior managers, it must have logical, methodical steps. This requires a very practical approach for the process.

4. From a research perspective, the ROI process must be **theoreti-**

cally sound and based on generally accepted practices. Unfortunately, this requirement can lead to an extensive, complicated process. Ideally, the process must strike a balance between maintaining a practical and sensible approach and having a theoretical basis for the process. This is perhaps one of the greatest challenges to those who have developed models for the ROI process.

5. An ROI process must **account for other factors** that have influenced output variables. Isolating the influence of the HRD program, one of the most often overlooked issues, is necessary to build credibility and accuracy within the process. The ROI process should pinpoint the contribution of the program when other factors have influenced the business measures.

6. The ROI process must be appropriate for use with a **variety of programs.** Some models apply to only a small number of programs, such as sales or productivity training. Ideally, the process must be applicable to all types of training and HRD programs, such as career development, organization development, and major performance improvement change initiatives.

7. The ROI process must have the **flexibility** to be applied on a preprogram basis as well as a postprogram basis. In some situations, an estimate of the ROI is required before the actual program is developed. Ideally, the ROI process should be able to adjust to a range of potential time frames for collecting data.

8. The ROI process must be **applicable with all types of data**, including hard data (typically represented as output, quality, costs, and time) and soft data (job satisfaction, customer satisfaction, grievances, and complaints).

9. The ROI process must **include the costs** of the program. The ultimate level of evaluation is a comparison of benefits with costs. Although the term *ROI* has been loosely used to express any benefit of training, an acceptable ROI formula must include costs. Omitting or underestimating costs will only destroy the credibility of ROI values.

10. Finally, the ROI process must have a successful **track record** in a variety of applications. In far too many situations, models are created but never successfully applied. An effective ROI process should withstand the wear and tear of implementation and should get the results expected.

Because these criteria are considered essential, an ROI process should meet most of these criteria, if not all of them.

The Ultimate Level of Evaluation: ROI

The ROI process adds a fifth level to the four levels of evaluation that Kirkpatrick (1974) developed almost 40 years ago. The concept of different levels of evaluation is both helpful and instructive in understanding how the return-on-investment is calculated. Table 1 shows the five-level framework used in this book.

Table 1. Characteristics of evaluation levels.

Level	Brief Description
1. Reaction and planned action	Measures participant's reaction to the program and outlines.
2. Learning	Measures skills, knowledge, or attitude changes.
3. Job applications	Measures changes in behavior on the job and specific application of the training material.
4. Business impact	Measures business impact of the program.
5. Return-on-investment	Measures the monetary value of the results and costs for the program, usually expressed as percentage.

At Level 1, "reaction and planned action," satisfaction from program participants is measured along with a listing of how they planned to apply what they have learned. Almost all organizations evaluate at Level 1, usually with a generic, end-of-program questionnaire. Although this level of evaluation is important as a measure of customer satisfaction, a favorable reaction does not ensure that participants have learned new skills or knowledge (Dixon, 1990). At Level 2, learning, a variety of assessment tools, like tests, skill practices, role plays, simulations, and group evaluations, measure what participants learned during the program. A learning check is helpful to ensure that participants have absorbed the material and know how to use it. A positive measure at this level, however, is no guarantee that the material will be used on the job. The literature is laced with studies that show the failure of learning to be transferred to the job (Broad and Newstrom, 1992). At Level 3, job applications, a variety of follow-up methods are used to determine if participants applied what they learned on the job. The frequency and use of skills are important measures at Level 3.

Level 3 evaluations are important to gauge the success of the application of the program, but they do not guarantee that there will be a positive impact in the organization. At Level 4, business impact, the measurement focuses on the actual results achieved by program participants as they successfully apply the program material. Typical Level 4 measures include output, quality, costs, time, and customer satisfaction. Although the program may produce a measurable business impact, there is still a concern that the program may have cost too much. At Level 5, return-on-investment, the measurement compares the monetary benefits from the program with the program costs. Although the ROI can be expressed in several ways, it is usually presented as a percent or cost-benefit ratio. The evaluation cycle is not complete until Level 5, or the ultimate evaluation, is conducted.

Almost all HRD organizations conduct evaluations to measure satisfaction, but very few conduct evaluations at the ROI level, perhaps because ROI evaluations are often characterized as difficult and expensive. Although business results and ROI are desired, it is very important to evaluate all the levels. A chain of impact should occur through the levels as the skills and knowledge learned (Level 2) are applied on the job (Level 3) to produce business results (Level 4). If measurements are not taken at each level, it would be difficult to conclude that the results achieved are actually caused by the HRD program (Alliger and Janak, 1989). Because of this, it is recommended that evaluation be conducted at all levels, when a Level 5 evaluation is planned. This practice is consistent with the practices of ASTD's benchmarking forum members (Kimmerling, 1993).

The ROI Process

The calculation of the return-on-investment in HRD begins with the basic ROI process model shown in figure 1, where a potentially complicated process can be simplified with sequential steps (Phillips, "Level 4," 1997).

The model provides a systematic approach to ROI calculations and meets all the criteria for an effective ROI process described earlier. It is the model of choice for most of the cases in this casebook. The model also emphasizes the fact that this is a logical, systematic process that flows from one step to another.

A step-by-step approach helps to keep the process manageable so that users can tackle one issue at a time. Applying the model provides consistency from one ROI calculation to another. Each step of the model is briefly described here.

Figure 1. ROI process model.

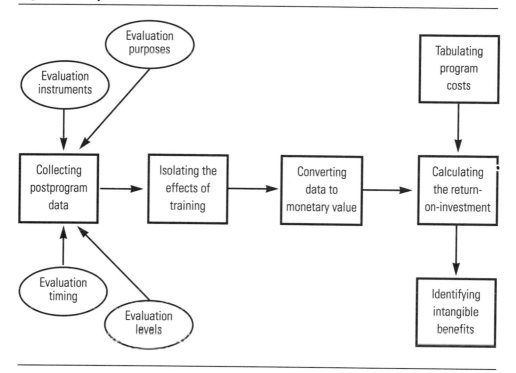

Preliminary Evaluation Information

Four specific elements of the evaluation process must be explained when developing the evaluation plan for an ROI calculation. First, evaluation purposes should be considered prior to developing the evaluation plan because the purposes will often determine the scope of the evaluation, the types of instruments used, and the type of data collected. For example, when an ROI calculation is planned, one of the purposes would be to compare the cost of the program with its benefits. This purpose has implications for the type of data collected (hard data), type of data collection method (performance monitoring), the type of analysis (thorough), and the communication medium for results (formal evaluation report). For most programs, multiple evaluation purposes are pursued.

Second, instrument selection should be considered in the early stages of developing the ROI. Questionnaires, interviews, and focus groups are common instruments used to collect data in evaluation. The instruments most familiar to the culture of the organization and appropriate for the setting and evaluation requirements should be used in the data collection process.

Third, the levels of evaluation are determined early. Training programs are evaluated at five different levels, as illustrated earlier. Data should be collected at Levels 1, 2, 3, and 4 if an ROI analysis is planned. This collection helps ensure that the chain of impact occurs as participants learn the skills, apply them on the job, and obtain business results.

A final piece of the evaluation plan is the timing of the data collection. In some cases, preprogram measurements are taken to compare with postprogram measures. In other cases, multiple measures are taken. When preprogram measurements are not available, follow-ups are still taken after the program. The important issue is to determine the appropriate timing for the follow-up evaluation. In some programs, such as a customer service skills training program for a major airline, data can be collected as early as three weeks. Five years may be required to measure the payback for an employee to attend a master's in business administration program sponsored by an Indonesian company. For most training, a follow-up is usually conducted in three to six months.

These four elements—evaluation purposes, instruments, levels, and timing—are all considerations in selecting the data collection methods and developing the data collection plan.

Collecting Data

Data collection is central to the ROI process. In some situations, postprogram data are collected and compared to preprogram situations, control group differences, and expectations. Both hard data (representing output, quality, cost, and time) and soft data (including work habits, work climate, and attitudes) are collected. Data collection methods include the following:

- Follow-up surveys are taken to determine the degree to which participants have utilized various aspects of the program. Survey responses are often developed on a sliding scale and usually represent attitudinal data. Surveys are useful for Level 3 data.
- Follow-up questionnaires are administered to uncover specific applications of training. Participants provide responses to various open-ended and forced-response questions. Questionnaires can be used to capture both Level 3 and Level 4 data.
- On-the-job observation captures actual skill application and use. Observations are particularly useful in customer service training and are more effective when the observer is either invisible or

transparent. Observations are appropriate for Level 3 data.

- Postprogram interviews are conducted with participants to determine the extent to which learning has been utilized on the job. Interviews allow for probing to uncover specific applications, and they are appropriate with Level 3 data.
- Focus groups are conducted to determine the degree to which a group of participants has applied the training to job situations. Focus groups are appropriate with Level 3 data.
- Program assignments are useful for simple, short-term projects. Participants complete the assignment, on the job, utilizing skills or knowledge learned in the program. Completed assignments can often contain both Level 3 and Level 4 data.
- Action plans are developed in training programs and are implemented on the job after the program is completed. A follow-up of a plan provides evidence of a training program's success. Level 3 and 4 data can be collected with action plans.
- Performance contracts are developed in which the participant, the participant's supervisor, and the instructor all agree prior to the program on specific outcomes from the training. Performance contracts are appropriate for both Level 3 and Level 4 data.
- Programs are designed with a follow-up session that is utilized to capture evaluation data as well as present additional learning material. In the follow-up session, participants discuss their successes with the program. Follow-up sessions are appropriate for both Level 3 and Level 4 data.
- Performance monitoring, in which various performance records and operational data are examined for improvement, is particularly useful for Level 4 data.

The important challenge in this step is to select the data collection method or methods appropriate for the setting and the specific program, within the time and budget constraints of the organization.

Isolating the Effects of Training

An often overlooked issue in most evaluations is the process to isolate the effects of training. In this step of the process, specific strategies are explored that determine the amount of output performance directly related to the program. This step is essential because there are many factors that will influence performance data after training. The specific strategies of this step will pinpoint the amount of improvement directly related to the training program. The result is increased accuracy and credibility of the ROI calculation. The following strategies have been utilized by organizations to tackle this important issue (Phillips, March 1996).

- A control group arrangement is used to isolate the impact of training. With this strategy, while one group receives training, a similar group does not. The difference between the two groups' performance is attributed to the training program. When properly set up and implemented, the control group management is the most effective way to isolate the effects of training.
- Trend lines are used to project the value of specific output variables as if training had not been undertaken. The projection is compared to the actual data after training, and the difference represents the estimate of the impact of training. Under certain conditions, this strategy can be an accurate way to isolate the impact of training.
- When mathematical relationships between input and output variables are known, a forecasting model is used to isolate the effects of training. With this approach, the output variable is predicted using the forecasting model with the assumption that no training is conducted. The actual performance of the variable after the training is then compared with the forecasted value to estimate the impact of training.
- Participants estimate the amount of improvement related to training. With this approach, participants are provided with the total amount of improvement, on a pre- and postprogram basis, and are asked to indicate the percent of the improvement that is actually related to the training program.
- Supervisors of participants estimate the impact of training on the output variables. With this approach, supervisors of participants are presented with the total amount of improvement and are asked to indicate the percent related to training.
- Senior management estimates the impact of training. In these cases, managers provide an estimate or "adjustment" to reflect the portion of the improvement related to the training program. Although their estimate may be inaccurate, there are some advantages in having senior management involved in this process.
- Experts provide estimates of the impact of training on the performance variable. Because the estimates are based on experience, the experts must be familiar with the type of training and the specific situation.
- In supervisory and management training, the subordinates of participants identify changes in the work climate that could in-

fluence the output variables. With this approach, the subordi-nates of the supervisors receiving training determine if changes in other variables in the work climate could have influenced output performance.

- When feasible, other influencing factors are identified and the impact is estimated or calculated, leaving the remaining unexplained improvement attributed to training. In this case, the influence of all of the other factors are developed, and training remains the one variable not accounted for in the analysis. The unexplained portion of the output is then attributed to training.
- In some situations, customers provide input about the extent to which training has influenced their decision to use a product or service. Although this strategy has limited applications, it can be quite useful in customer service and sales training.

Collectively, these 10 strategies provide a comprehensive set of tools to tackle the important and critical issue of isolating the effects of training.

Converting Data to Monetary Values

To calculate the return-on-investment, data collected in a Level 4 evaluation are converted to monetary values to compare to program costs. This step requires that a value be placed on each unit of data connected with the program. Ten strategies are available for use in converting data to monetary values, and the best strategy will depend on the type of data and the situation (Phillips, April 1996).

- Output data is converted to profit contribution or cost savings. In this strategy, output increases are converted to monetary value based on their unit contribution to profit or the unit of cost reduction. These values are readily available in most organizations.
- The cost of quality is calculated and quality improvements are directly converted to cost savings. This value is available in many organizations.
- For programs where employee time is saved, the participant's wages and benefits are used for the value for time. Because a variety of programs focus on improving the time required to complete projects, processes, or daily activities, the value of time becomes an important and necessary issue.
- Historical costs are used when they are available for a specific variable. In this case, organizational cost data are utilized to establish the specific value of an improvement.
- When available, internal and external experts may be used to es-

timate a value for an improvement. In this situation, the credibility of the estimate hinges on the expertise and reputation of the individual.

- External databases are sometimes available to estimate the value or cost of data items. Research, government, and industry databases can provide important information for these values. The difficulty lies in finding a specific database related to the situation.
- Participants estimate the value of the data item. For this approach to be effective, participants must be capable of providing a value for the improvement.
- Supervisors of participants provide estimates when they are both willing and capable of assigning values to the improvement. This approach is especially useful when participants are not fully capable of providing this input or in situations where supervisors need to confirm or adjust the participant's estimate.
- Senior management provides estimates on the value of an improvement when they are willing to offer estimates. This approach is particularly helpful to establish values for performance measures that are very important to senior management.
- HRD staff estimates may be used to determine a value of an output data item. In these cases, it is essential for the estimates to be provided on an unbiased basis.

This step in the ROI model is important and absolutely necessary for determining the monetary benefits from a program. The process is challenging, particularly with soft data, but it can be methodically accomplished using one or more of the above strategies.

Tabulating Program Costs

The other part of the equation on a cost-benefit analysis is the cost of the program. Tabulating the costs involves monitoring or developing all the related costs of the program targeted for the ROI calculation. Among the cost components that should be included are the following:

- the cost to design and develop the program, possibly prorated over the expected life of the program
- the cost of all program materials provided to each participant
- the cost for the instructor or facilitator, including preparation and delivery time
- the cost of the facilities for the training program
- travel, lodging, and meal costs for the participants, if applicable
- salaries plus employee benefits of the participants to attend the training

- administrative and overhead costs of the training function allocated in some convenient way to the training program.

In addition, specific costs related to the needs assessment and evaluation should be included, if appropriate. The conservative approach is to include all of these costs so that the total is fully loaded.

Calculating the ROI

The return-on-investment is calculated using the program benefits and costs. The benefit-cost ratio is the program benefits divided by cost. In formula form it is

$$BCR = \frac{\text{Program Benefits}}{\text{Program Costs}}$$

The return-on-investment uses the net benefits divided by program costs. The net benefits are the program benefits minus the costs. In formula form, the ROI becomes

$$ROI (\%) = \frac{\text{Net Program Benefits}}{\text{Program Costs}} \times 100$$

This is the same basic formula used in evaluating other investments in which the ROI is traditionally reported as earnings divided by investment. The ROI from some training programs is high. For example, in sales training, supervisory training, and managerial training, the ROI can be quite large, frequently over 100 percent, and the ROI value for technical and operator training may be lower.

Identifying Intangible Benefits

Most training programs will have both tangible monetary benefits and intangible nonmonetary benefits. The ROI calculation is based on converting both hard and soft data to monetary values. Other data items are identified that are not converted to monetary values and these intangible benefits include items such as
- increased job satisfaction
- increased organizational commitment
- improved teamwork
- improved customer service
- reduced complaints
- reduced conflicts.

During data analysis, every attempt is made to convert all data to monetary values. All hard data such as output, quality, and time are converted to monetary values. The conversion of each soft data item is attempted, but if the process used for conversion is too subjective or inaccurate and the resulting values lose credibility in the process, then the measure is listed as an intangible benefit with the appropriate explanation. For some programs intangible, nonmonetary benefits are extremely valuable, often carrying as much influence as the hard data items.

Targets

Because of the effort and costs of evaluation at Level 4 and Level 5, only a small number of program evaluations are taken to these levels each year. Setting specific targets for evaluation levels is a feasible way to make progress with measurement and evaluation without exhausting resources. The targets represent the percent of courses planned for evaluation at each level. Targets enable the staff to focus on the improvements needed at specific levels.

The first step to develop targets is to assess the present situation. The number of all courses, including repeated sections of a course, is tabulated along with the corresponding level or levels of evaluation currently conducted for each course. Next, the percent of courses using Level 1 reaction questionnaires is calculated. The process is repeated for each level of the evaluation.

After detailing the current situation, the next step is to determine a realistic target within a specific time frame. Many organizations set annual targets for changes. This process should involve the input of the HRD staff to ensure that the targets are realistic and that the staff is committed to the process. If the training and development or HRD staff does not buy into this process, the targets will not be met. The improvement targets must be achievable, and at the same time, challenging and motivating. These are the targets that a large telecommunications company set:

Level	Target
Level 1, reaction	100 percent
Level 2, learning	50 percent
Level 3, job applications	30 percent
Level 4, business impact	20 percent
Level 5, ROI	10 percent

In this organization, 20 percent of programs are targeted for Level 4 evaluations with half of them planned for Level 5, ROI. These numbers are ambitious. It is more common to target 10 percent and 5 percent for Levels 4 and 5. This process requires the organization to carefully select a few programs for Level 4 and 5 evaluations, using predetermined criteria.

Conclusion

Developing the ROI for a select number of programs is a challenging process, but a necessary one. The ROI issue can no longer be ignored. It must be implemented with a rational approach, using a process that is acceptable to practitioners, senior management, and evaluation researchers. The ROI model outlined in this chapter meets the criteria for an effective ROI process. Hundreds of organizations worldwide are using it, and it is the model used in most of the cases in this book.

References

Alliger, G.M., and E.A. Janak. "Kirkpatrick's Levels of Training Criteria: Thirty Years Later." *Personnel Psychology*, volume 42, 1989, pp. 331-342.

Broad, M.L., and J.W. Newstrom. *Transfer of Training*. Reading, MA: Addison-Wesley, 1992.

Dixon, N.M. *Evaluation: A Tool for Improving HRD Quality*. San Diego, CA. University Associates, 1990.

Kimmerling, G. "Gathering Best Practices." *Training & Development*, volume 47, number 3, September 1993, pp. 28-36.

Kirkpatrick, D.L. "Techniques for Evaluating Training Programs." *Evaluating Training Programs*, D.L. Kirkpatrick, editor. Alexandria, VA: ASTD, 1975, pp. 1-17.

Phillips, J.J. "Was It the Training?" *Training & Development*, volume 50, number 3, March 1996, pp. 28-32.

Phillips, J.J. "How Much Is the Training Worth?" *Training & Development*, volume 50, number 4, April 1996, pp. 20-24.

Phillips, J.J. *Return on Investment in Training and Performance Improvement Programs*. Houston, TX: Gulf Publishing, 1997.

Phillips, J.J. "Level 4 and Beyond: an ROI Model." *Evaluating Corporate Training: Models and Issues*, S. Brown, editor. Norwell, MA: Kluwer Academic Publishers, 1997.

Preventing Sexual Harassment

Healthcare, Inc.

Dianne Hill and Jack J. Phillips

Most organizations have sexual harassment prevention programs, but few are subjected to accountability up to and including a return-on-investment (ROI) analysis. In the setting in this case, a large health-care chain conducted a sexual harassment prevention workshop involving first-level managers and supervisors. Workshops were followed by meetings with all employees conducted by the same managers and supervisors. In all, 17 workshops were presented and the monetary impact was developed. Several unique issues are involved in this case, including the techniques to isolate the effects of training and convert data to monetary values. The analysis used a traditional ROI model and yielded significant and impressive results that surprised the evaluation team and senior managers.

Background

Healthcare, Inc. (HI) is a regional provider of a variety of health-care services through a chain of hospitals, health maintenance organizations (HMOs), and clinics. HI has grown steadily in the last few years and has earned a reputation as a progressive and financially sound company. HI is publicly owned and has an aggressive management team poised for additional growth.

The health-care industry in the United States is undergoing tremendous transformation and transition. The concern over health-care costs, the threat of additional government regulation, and the implementation of new technology and health-care delivery systems are

This case was prepared to serve as a basis for discussion rather than to illustrate either effective or ineffective administrative and management practices. All names, dates, places, and organizations have been disguised at the request of the author or organization.

radically transforming the health-care field. HI is attempting to take advantage of these challenges and carve out a significant market share in its regional area of operation.

Triggering Events

Sexual harassment continues to grow as a significant employee relations issue. Sparked in part by increased public awareness of the issue and by the willingness of the victims to report harassment complaints, sexual harassment claims have also been growing throughout the country and in the health-care industry. HI has experienced an increasing number of sexual harassment complaints, and a significant number of them have become charges and lawsuits. Executives considered the complaint record excessive and thought it represented a persistent and irritating problem. HI was also experiencing an unusually high level of turnover, which may be linked to sexual harassment.

Concerned about the stigma of continued sexual harassment complaints and the increasing cost of defending the company against claims, senior management instructed the vice president of human resources (HR) to take corrective and preventive action to significantly reduce complaints and ultimately rid the workplace of any signs of harassment. The HR vice president instructed the human resources development (HRD) staff to develop a workshop for employees or managers, or both, but only if there is a lack of understanding and knowledge of the issue.

Needs Assessment

In response to the request, the HRD staff conducted interviews with the entire equal employment opportunity (EEO) and affirmative action (AA) staff to explore the magnitude of the problem and the potential causes. Most of the staff indicated that there appeared to be a significant lack of understanding of the company's policy on sexual harassment and what actually constitutes inappropriate or illegal behavior.

HRD staff also examined the complaints for the past year for issues and patterns. An analysis of complaints showed that the typical person accused of sexual harassment was a supervisor and usually male, and the typical victim of harassment was nonsupervisory and female. The analysis also revealed that the type of sexual harassment typically experienced at HI was in the category of hostile environment, defined by the Equal Employment Opportunity Commission (EEOC) as "an individual making unwelcome sexual advances or other verbal or physical conduct of a sexual nature with the purpose of, or that creates the effect of, unreasonably interfering with an individual's work performance or creating an intimidating, hostile or offensive working environment." This type of harassment should be minimized by developing a clear understanding of HI's policy regarding harassment and by teaching managers to identify illegal and inappropriate activity.

Exit interviews of terminating employees for the past year were reviewed to see if there was a linkage to sexual harassment. Approximately 11 percent of terminating employees identified sexual harassment or a hostile environment as a factor in their decision to leave HI. Exit interview data were computerized and readily available. Because of the request to proceed with this program, the HRD staff did not conduct a full-scale needs assessment. Instead, staff members augmented the input from the EEO/AA staff and exit interviews with 10 randomly selected interviews with first-level supervisors to explore the level of understanding of the policy, inappropriate and illegal behavior, and the perceived causes of the increased complaint activity. As part of HI's policy, supervisors and managers were required to conduct a limited investigation of informal complaints and to discuss issues as they are uncovered.

Program Design, Development, and Implementation

Armed with input from 10 supervisor interviews, detailed input from the EEO/AA staff, and information from company records, HRD staff identified two major causes of the problem. There was an apparent lack of understanding of the company's sexual harassment policy and of what constitutes inappropriate and illegal behavior. In addition, there was an apparent insensitivity to the issue. As a result, the HRD staff designed a one-day sexual harassment prevention workshop for all first- and second-level supervisors and managers. The objective was that after participating in the program, participants would be able to do the following:

- understand and administer the company's policy on sexual harassment
- identify inappropriate and illegal behavior related to sexual harassment
- investigate and discuss sexual harassment issues
- conduct a meeting with all direct reports to discuss policy and expected behavior
- ensure that the workplace is free from sexual harassment
- reduce the number of sexual harassment complaints.

Because of the implications of this issue, it was important for the information to be discussed with all employees so that there would not be any misunderstanding about the policy or inappropriate behavior. Consequently, each supervisor was asked to conduct a meeting with his or her direct reports to discuss this topic.

The program design was typical of HI programs in that it used a combination of purchased and internally developed materials. The one-day program was implemented and conducted over a 45-day period with 17 sessions involving 655 managers. HR managers and coordinators served as program facilitators.

Why ROI?

HR/HRD programs usually targeted for an ROI calculation are those that are perceived to add significant value to the company and are closely linked to the organizational goals and strategic objectives. In those cases, the ROI calculation is pursued to confirm the added value. Based on the results of the ROI analysis, these programs may be enhanced, redesigned, or eliminated if the ROI is negative. Sexual harassment prevention training is usually different. If the ROI analysis yields a negative value, the program would not be discontinued. It may be altered for future sessions, particularly if behavior changes are not identified in the Level 3 evaluation.

The sexual harassment prevention program was chosen for an ROI calculation for two reasons. First, the HR and HRD departments were interested in the accountability of all programs, including sexual harassment. Second, a positive ROI would clearly show management that these types of programs, which are preventive in nature, can significantly contribute to the bottom line when they are implemented throughout the organization and supported by management.

With the decision to pursue the ROI calculation, HI engaged the services of Performance Resources Organization, a leading firm for ROI consulting. The model used in this project has been used in hundreds of ROI studies (Phillips, February 1996).

Data Collection

Figure 1 shows the completed data collection plan for the sexual harassment training program. A pretest, which is used later as a posttest, was administered to measure knowledge of HI's sexual harassment policy and inappropriate and illegal behavior. The 20-item questionnaire was evenly split on policy and behavior issues.

To measure the successful application of the program, three data collection methods were utilized. First, each supervisor and manager

Figure 1. Training program data collection plan.

Program: Preventing Sexual Harassment

Responsibility: _____   **Date:** _____

Evaluation Plan: Data Collection

Level	Program Objective(s)	Evaluation Method	Timing	Responsibilities
I Reaction, Satisfaction, and Planned Actions	• Obtain a positive reaction to program and materials • Obtain input for suggestions for improving program • Identify planned actions	• Reaction questionnaire	• End of session	• Facilitator
II Learning	• Knowledge of policy on sexual harassment • Knowledge of inappropriate and illegal behavior • Skills to investigate and discuss sexual harassment	• Pre- and posttest • Skill practices	• Beginning of session • End of session • During session	• Facilitator

Figure 1 (continued). Training program data collection plan.

Program: Preventing Sexual Harassment

Responsibility: _____   **Date:** _____

Evaluation Plan: Data Collection

Level	Program Objective(s)	Evaluation Method	Timing	Responsibilities
III Job Application	• Administer policy • Conduct meeting with employees • Ensure that workplace is free of sexual harassment	• Self-assessment questionnaire • Complete and submit meeting record • Employees survey (25 percent sample)	• Six months after program • One month after program • Six months after program	• Program evaluator • HRIS staff • Employee communications
IV Business Results	• Reduce internal complaints • Reduce external complaints • Reduce employee turnover	• Performance monitoring • Self-assessment questionnaire	• Monthly for one year before and after program • Six months after program	• Program evaluator

Jack J. Phillips, Ph.D., Performance Resources Organization. All Rights Reserved. Box 380637, Birmingham, AL 35238-0637 USA.

had to document their meetings with employees by recording the time of the meeting, duration, topics, and participants. Although the form did not address the quality of the meeting, it provided evidence that the meeting was conducted.

The second data collection method was a survey of the nonsupervisory employees, the typical target group for harassment activity. Although all employees could have been surveyed, it was felt that it was more important to examine behavior change from the perspective of those who were more likely to be victims of harassment. The survey was planned for administration six months after the program was completed. It provided postprogram data only, and thus each questionnaire had to be worded to measure behavior change since the training was conducted. The 15-item survey examined specific behavior changes and environmental changes related to harassment activity, including actions that might be considered inappropriate or offensive. The following are some typical questions:

In the Last Six Months	Strongly Disagree	Disagree	Neutral	Agree	Strongly Agree
I have noticed less offensive language at work.	☐	☐	☐	☐	☐
The company is more likely to take swift action against those who are found guilty of sexual harassment.	☐	☐	☐	☐	☐

The third data collection method was a self-assessment questionnaire that supervisors and managers would complete. This questionnaire would capture actions, behavior change, and results linked to the program. Although there were a variety of other data collection possibilities, including focus groups, interviews, and third-party observation, given the time and cost considerations, it was felt that these three methods would provide sufficient data to capture behavior change and show that the program had been successful.

Several measures were used to assess business results. Initially, it was planned that internal complaints, lodged formally with the Human Resources Division, would be monitored along with external charges filed with various agencies (primarily the Equal Employment Opportunity Commission). Because of the lag time between changes in behavior and a reduction in complaints, data would be collected for one year after the program and would be compared with data from one year before the program to determine specific improvements. Also, as alternative information, litigated complaints would be tracked along with the direct costs, including legal fees, settlements, and losses. In addition, annual employee turnover would be examined for the same time period because of the perceived link between a hostile work environment and turnover.

Figure 2 shows the completed document for the ROI analysis plan. Because of the relatively short time frame required to implement the program and the desire from top management to implement it throughout the organization quickly, a control group arrangement was not feasible. Because historical data are available on all complaint measures, however, a trend-line analysis was initially planned. Complaint activity would be projected based on 12 months of data prior to the program. Actual performance would be compared to the projected value, and the difference would reflect the actual impact of the program on that measure. Participants' estimation was planned to compare with trend-line data. In this situation, supervisors and managers (participants) are asked to indicate the extent to which the program influenced the changes in the number of complaints.

Trend-line analysis could not be used because of the other initiatives that were planned for implementation to reduce turnover. For the trend-line analysis to be accurate, no additional influences should enter the process during the postprogram evaluation period (Phillips, March 1996). Thus, a type of forecasting was used in which the percentage of turnover related to sexual harassment is developed for the 12-month period prior to the program The same percentage is calculated for the 12 months after the program.

To convert the data to monetary values, the cost of complaints would be derived from historical data, when available, and from estimates for other factors, such as the actual time utilized on harassment complaints. The estimates would be developed with input from the EEO and AA staff. For turnover, industry data would be used because HI had not calculated the actual cost of turnover for any employee groups. The specific cost items, intangible benefits, other influences, and communication targets were all identified and are presented in figure 2.

Figure 2. Training program ROI analysis plan.

Program: Preventing Sexual Harassment

Responsibility: _____

Date: _____

Strategy: ROI Analysis

Data Items	Methods of Isolating the Effects of the Program	Methods of Converting Data	Cost Categories	Intangible Benefits	Other Influences/ Issues	Communication Targets
Formal internal complaints of sexual harassment	• Trend-line analysis • Participant estimation	• Historical costs with estimation from EEO/AA staff	• Needs assessment program • Development/ acquisition • Coordination/ facilitation time • Program materials • Food/refreshments • Facilities • Participant salaries and benefits • Evaluation	• Job satisfaction • Absenteeism • Stress reduction • Image of HI • Recruiting	• Several initiatives to reduce turnover were implemented during this time period • Must not duplicate benefits from both internal and external complaints	• All employees (condensed information) • Senior executives (summary of report with detailed backup) • All supervisors and managers (brief report) • All HR/HRD staff (full report)
External complaints of sexual harassment	• Trend-line analysis • Participant estimation	• Historical costs with estimation from EEO/AA staff				
Employee turnover	• Forecasting using percent of turnover related to sexual harassment	• External studies within industry				

Copyright 1996 Jack J. Phillips, Ph.D., Performance Resources Organization. All Rights Reserved. Box 380637, Birmingham, AL 35238-0637 JSA.

Reaction and Learning Data

A typical end-of-program questionnaire was utilized to capture reaction data. Overall, the participants had a very positive reaction to the program and perceived it to be timely and useful. A composite rating of 4.11 out of a possible 5 was achieved. The vast majority of the participants (93 percent) provided a list of action items planned as a result of the program.

For a Level 2 evaluation, the preprogram test scores averaged 51 and the postprogram scores averaged 84, representing a dramatic increase of 65 percent. These results were significant and exceeded the expectations of program organizers. Two important points were underscored with the Level 2 assessment. First, the low scores on preprogram testing provided evidence that the program was necessary, validating the needs assessment. The participants did not understand the organization's policy or recognize what constituted inappropriate and illegal behavior. Second, the dramatic improvement in scores provided assurance that the content of the program was appropriate for both key issues as the participants learned much about policy and behavior. As part of the Level 2 evaluation, participants were involved in skill practices on issues involving administering policy. The instructors provided an assessment of the skills practice sessions using a brief checklist. In all, 84 percent of participants received a check for satisfactorily conducting a simulated investigation of an informal complaint.

On-the-Job Application

One of the initial actions required of participants was to conduct a meeting with their employees to discuss sexual harassment issues, review HI's policy on sexual harassment, and discuss what constitutes inappropriate and illegal behavior. Supervisors and managers received handouts and visual aids to assist with their meetings. As evidence that they conducted the meeting, supervisors and managers had to complete a meeting form and submit it to the Human Resources Department. The form had to indicate the time of the meeting, its duration, the names of the participants, and the specific topics covered. Within one month of the program, 82 percent of the participants had completed the meeting record. Ultimately, 96 percent completed it. Some managers did not conduct meetings because they did not have direct reports.

Six months after the program was conducted, an anonymous survey was conducted with a 25 percent sample of nonsupervisory employees. A total of 1,720 surveys were distributed and 1,100 were returned, for a response rate of 64 percent. The survey yielded an average score of 4.1 on a scale of 1 to 5. The rating represents the extent to which the behavior has changed in the six months since the program was conducted. Overall, the survey results indicated that significant behavior change had occurred, and the work environment was largely free of harassment.

A follow-up questionnaire was administered directly to all participants six months after the program was conducted. A total of 571 questionnaires were returned representing a response rate of 87 percent. The questionnaire probed the extent to which program materials were utilized and specific behavior changes had been realized. In addition, participants estimated the amount of improvement in sexual harassment complaints that was directly attributable to this program. Although the input from participants (managers and supervisors) may be biased, significant changes were reported. In regard to actions completed, 92 percent reported that some actions were completed, and 68 percent reported that all actions were completed.

Business Impact

Table 1 shows the complaint and turnover data for the year prior to the program and the year after the program. In the six-month follow-up questionnaire, participants were told the averages for the six months before and after the program, and they were asked to estimate the percent of improvement that the program caused. The right-hand column reflects the average percent improvement attributed to the program for each performance measure—internal complaints, external complaints, and litigated complaints—as estimated by the participants.

The exhibit also shows the turnover rate for the nonsupervisory employees for the 12 months preceding the program and the 12 months after the program. Participant estimates of the impact of this program on turnover were not collected because of the various factors influencing turnover.

Figure 3 shows a plot of the formal internal complaints of sexual harassment 12 months prior to the program and 12 months after the program. Prior to the program there was an upward trend of complaints, and management felt this would continue if it took no action to improve the situation. Also, no other initiatives were undertaken to focus attention on sexual harassment. The magnitude of the program, involving 17 training sessions with 655 managers and meetings with all employees, focused significant attention on the issue. Thus, it was felt that the trend-line analysis may be an effective tool for isolating the effects of training.

Table 1. Performance measures related to sexual harassment.

Business Performance Measure	One Year Prior to Program	One Year After Program	Factor for Isolating Program Effects (Percentage)
Internal complaints	55	35	74
External charges	24	14	62
Litigated complaints	10	6	51
Legal fees and expenses	$632,000	$481,000	
Settlement/losses	$450,000	$125,000	
Total cost of sexual harassment prevention, investigation, and defense*	$1,655,000	$852,000	
Turnover (nonsupervisory) annualized (percentage)	24.2	19.9	

*Includes legal fees, settlement/losses, portion of EEO/AA staff assigned to sexual harassment, management time for this activity, printed materials, and miscellaneous expenses.

The turnover rate showed improvement during this same time frame. However, other initiatives had been undertaken to help reduce the departure rate of employees because of the excessive levels of turnover. Recruiting processes had been enhanced, entry-level salaries increased, and more effective selection techniques employed during the same time period. These actions were initiated to develop a better match between the employees and the culture at HI. Thus, the trend-line forecast for the turnover rate would not be accurate because of the influence of these factors on the turnover rate.

To estimate the percent of turnover reduction directly related to this program, a version of the forecasting process was considered. During the needs assessment, exit interview data were reviewed for evidence of sexual harassment as a factor in the decision to leave. In these cases, 11 percent of the people in their exit interviews had mentioned sexual harassment. Employees are often reluctant to indicate the presence of sexual harassment, although the issue may be the reason for their departure. Thus, it was felt that this 11 percent figure was a conservative estimate of the number of terminations related to a hostile work environment of sexual harassment activity. A 12-month review of

Figure 3. Formal internal complaints of sexual harassment.

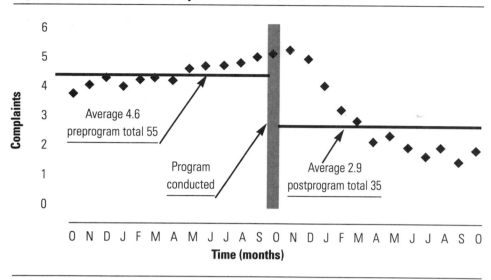

exit interviews, on a postprogram basis, revealed that only 3 percent of the interviewees mentioned sexual harassment or a hostile work environment among the reasons for their departure. Thus, the percent of employees leaving who listed sexual harassment as a reason dropped from 11 percent to 3 percent of terminations.

Monetary Benefits of Program

Figure 4 shows the calculation for the monetary benefits from the sexual harassment program. For the reduction of complaints, the value could be based on reducing internal complaints, external charges, or litigated complaints, but not all three. The value for each measure is shown in the exhibit. The values are developed by taking the total cost of sexual harassment prevention, investigation, and defense (from table 1), and dividing it by each of these three measures. Pre- and postprogram values are shown in the figure, and they are very similar.

The total value of the reduction for each measure was developed, leaving the decision of which measure to use. Because of the interest in tracking internal complaints, the evaluation team decided to use that value as the unit of improvement in the analysis. Thus, the value of one internal complaint was placed at $24,343 (that is, the amount HI would save if one complaint could be avoided). The lower value is used to be conservative. Another approach is to examine the total cost of sexual harassment, including prevention, investigation,

Figure 4. Monetary benefits from complaint reduction.

	Preprogram	Postprogram
Average cost of internal complaint	$30,090	$24,343
Average cost of external complaint	$68,958	$60,857
Average cost of litigated complaint	$165,500	$142,000

Unit of improvement = one internal complaint
Value of one internal complaint = $24,343
Total improvement: 55 − 35 = 20
Improvement related to program: 20 x 74% = 14.8
Value of improvement = 14.8 x $24,343 = $360,276

---

and defense and use a value equal to the reduction in cost. However, because there is a lag between measures of complaints and actual losses and legal expenses, the total costs from one year to the next may not reflect the actual cost savings.

Although the total improvement is 20 internal complaints, the improvement related directly to the program is 74 percent of that figure, or 14.8 complaints. The figure 74 percent represents the response supervisors and managers gave on their questionnaires about the extent to which the reduction in complaints is related directly to the program. The value of the improvement is $360,276. These calculations are as follows:

Unit of improvement = one turnover statistic (termination)
Turnover, preprogram = 6,651 x 24.2% = 1,610
Turnover, preprogram, related to hostile environment: 1,610 x 11% = 177
Turnover, postprogram: 6,844 x 19.9% = 1,362
Turnover, postprogram related to hostile environment: 1,362 x 3% = 41
Improvement related to program: 177 - 41 = 136
Cost of one turnover: 75% of annual salary = $27,850 x .75 = $20,887
Value of improvement: 136 x $20,887 = $2,840,632

The value for the turnover reduction was developed in a similar manner. The unit of improvement is one turnover statistic. The target group for the turnover reduction was nonsupervisory employees, which represented an average of 6,844 on a postprogram basis and 6,651 on a preprogram basis. For the 12-month period following the program, the employment levels at HI averaged 7,540 including 655 for the target group for training and 35 senior managers who did not participate directly in the training program. Prior to the program, the 24.2 percent turnover rate represented 1,610 employees who left voluntarily or were forced to leave because of performance. According to the exit interviews, 11 percent of those departures were related to sexual harassment. Thus, 177 terminations were related to sexual harassment. On a postprogram basis, the 19.9 percent turnover represents 1,362 employees. Postprogram exit interviews revealed that 3 percent were related to a hostile work environment. Thus, 41 employees left because of the hostile environment. The improvement related directly to the program is 136 terminations, a very significant number when the cost of turnover is included.

The average nonsupervisory salaries for the postprogram period were $27,850 and for the preprogram period, $26,541. Several industry studies on the cost of turnover were briefly discussed, which revealed ranges from 110 percent to 150 percent of annual salaries. Although there was sufficient evidence to use the annual salary as a cost of turnover, the team chose to be conservative and used 75 percent of the annual salaries, representing $20,887 as a cost of one turnover statistic. Consequently, the 136 yielded a staggering $2,840,632 as the savings generated because of the reduction in turnover due to sexual harassment.

Figure 5 shows the trend-line projections for the internal complaint data. The trend, established prior to the program, was projected for the evaluation period. As the projection shows, the impact of the program is even more dramatic than illustrated in the calculations because of the upward trend of the data. An estimated monthly value of 4.9 (from the vertical axis) yields an annual value of 59 complaints. Because the impact is more conservative using the participants' estimates, this figure was used in the analysis. Consequently, the actual calculations represent an understatement of actual performance. The trend-line results are very credible and could be used in the analysis. However, the ROI value is already larger than most people can comprehend. A conservative approach is needed to build credibility.

Figure 5. Trend-line projections for internal complaints of sexual harassment.

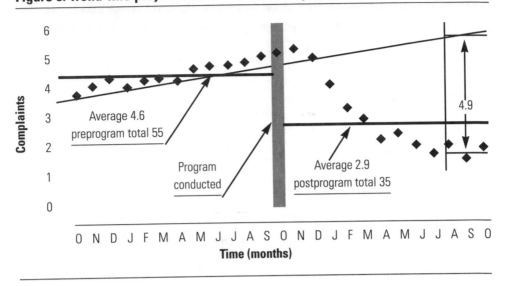

Program Costs

Participants' salaries and benefits were developed using midpoint values for the managers in each classification. Table 2 shows the midpoint values of participants.

Table 3 shows the program cost categories Most of the cost items were straightforward and taken from actual cost statements or estimates from those closely involved in the process. Program costs were fully loaded and included the cost of the needs assessment ($9,000), design and development ($15,000), and evaluation ($31,000). The needs assessment cost was an estimate based on the direct time and expenses involved in the process.

The development costs were low because of the use of purchased materials. Evaluation costs included an estimate of all internal and external costs associated with the follow-up evaluation including developing the ROI. Participants' salaries and benefits were included although it was not HI's policy to include them as a training expense for a one-day program for supervisors and managers. The time necessary for program coordination was estimated along with the time for facilitator preparation and delivery. When considering the average salaries plus benefits for these individuals, a value of $9,600 was estimated. Travel and lodging for coordination and facilitation was a minor factor, estimated to be $1,520. Program materials were $12 per participant and food and refreshments during the

Table 2. Salaries and benefits of participants.

Management Level	Number Participating in Program	Salary Midpoint Value
7	41	$32,500
8	435	43,600
9	121	54,300
10	58	66,700

Employee benefits costs as a percent of payroll = 39 percent.
Managers work an average of 47 weeks per year.

workshop were $30 per participant. The estimated value of the conference rooms used for the program was $150 per day, although the costs of internal facilities were not usually reported.

ROI calculation

The cost-benefit ratio and ROI calculations for these values are as follows:

$$CBR = \frac{Benefits}{Costs} = \frac{\$360,276 + \$2,840,632}{\$277,987} = \frac{\$3,200,908}{\$277,987} = 11.5:1$$

$$ROI = \frac{Net\ Benefits}{Costs} = \frac{\$3,200,908 - \$277,987}{\$277,987} = 1,052\%$$

Benefits based entirely on complaint reduction and turnover reduction are used in the cost-benefit ratio to yield 11.5:1. Thus, for each dollar spent on the program, $11.50 was returned. The ROI calculation, which uses net benefits, shows a return of 1,052 percent, an impressive and staggering amount. The results were much greater than the evaluation team and senior management expected.

Questions for Discussion

1. Was the needs assessment appropriate for this situation? Please explain.
2. Sort the objectives into different evaluation levels.
3. Critique the Level 2 and Level 3 evaluation results. Was the survey of nonsupervisory employees necessary? Explain.

Table 3. Program costs.

Cost Category	Total Cost
Assessment (estimated cost of time)................	$9,000
Program development/acquisition....................	15,000
Program coordination/facilitation time	9,600
Travel and lodging for facilitation and coordinators	1,520
Program materials (655 @ $12).....................	7,860
Food/refreshments (655 @ $30).....................	19,650
Facilities (17 @ $150).............................	2,550
Participant salaries and benefits ($130,797 x 1.39).......	181,807
Evaluation	31,000
	$277,987

4. Which Level 4 complaint measures are appropriate? Explain.

5. How would you critique the methods used to isolate the effects of the program on complaints and turnover?

6. How would you critique the methods used to convert complaints and turnover to monetary values?

7. Should this program be evaluated at Level 4 and Level 5? Explain.

8. Is the ROI lower or higher than you expected? Please comment.

9. Do you consider this estimate to be realistic?

10. How could this process be improved?

11. How would you present this data to management? To all employees?

The Authors

Dianne Hill consults in organization development with manufacturing, service, and aviation organizations in the United States, Canada, Mexico, Italy, Belgium, Croatia, El Salvador, and Saudi Arabia. Hill has served as a senior organization development consultant with an international company and a university business faculty member. Hill holds undergraduate and master's degrees in business and is pursuing a doctorate in human resource development leadership. Hill is currently writing a chapter on the future of aviation crew resource management to be published in Europe. Her article, "Pier Learning: People as Informal, Extended Resources" is published in the Ninth International Symposium on Aviation Psychology Conference Proceedings. Hill also conducted a Crew Resource Management workshop for the National Business Aviation Association's 49th Annual Convention. Hill may be contacted at Performance by Design, Box 27290, Austin, TX 78755-2290.

Jack J. Phillips has 27 years of corporate experience in five industries (aerospace, textiles, metals, construction materials, and banking). He has served as training and development manager at two Fortune 500 firms, senior human resource officer at two firms, and president of a regional federal savings bank. He has also served on the management faculty of a major state university. In 1992, he founded Performance Resources Organization, an international consulting firm that specializes in human resources accountability programs. He consults with clients in manufacturing, service, and government organizations in England, Belgium, South Africa, Mexico, Venezuela, Malaysia, Indonesia, South Korea, Australia, and Singapore as well as in the United States and Canada.

Phillips has been author or editor of *Accountability in Human Resource Management* (1996), *Handbook of Training Evaluation and Measurement Methods* (2d edition, 1991), *Measuring Return on Investment* (volume 1, 1994), *Conducting Needs Assessment* (1995), *The Development of a Human Resource Effectiveness Index* (1988), and *Improving Supervisors Effectiveness* (1985), which won an award from the Society for Human Resource Management. He has also written more than 75 articles for professional, business, and trade publications.

References

Phillips, Jack J. "ROI: The Search for Best Practices." *Training & Development,*, volume 50, number 2, February 1996, pp. 42-47.

Phillips, Jack J. "Was It the Training?" *Training & Development,* volume 50, number 3, March 1996, pp. 28-32.

Transforming Supervisors Into Innovative Team Leaders

A Consortium of Companies

Darlene Russ-Eft and Kathleen Hurson

This case involves calculating the return-on-investment (ROI) for training on innovation. Team leaders from several organizations tackled projects after the program was conducted and reported the results. Using a discounted cash flow technique, the rate of return was calculated and the results were impressive. The case illustrates the application of ROI for a unique type of training.

One Way to Get Bottom-Line Results From Training

American corporations face a new world order in terms of economic, social, and environmental circumstances. That order requires new organizations with new responses. Past activities and responses, such as downsizing, reengineering, and cost-cutting, have limited usefulness. Because market competition rewards the superior product, service, or process, organizations are now seeking ways to promote innovative thinking among their employees. Indeed, Kanter (1983) indicated that companies must identify and use effective methods for involving the entire workforce in innovative problem solving.

Later, Van de Ven (1986) reported that repeated meetings with chief executive officers of public and private organizations revealed managing innovation to be their central concern because it can lead to increased productivity and improved quality. Specifically, the attitude

This case was prepared to serve as a basis for discussion rather than to illustrate either effective or ineffective administrative and management practices. This paper was presented at the 1996 meeting of the American Evaluation Association.

toward innovation can make or break success. Indeed, Walton (1986) described the vision-led approach to management restructuring that emphasized increased effectiveness rather than greater efficiency. One of the factors leading to increased effectiveness valued outcomes, such as flexibility and innovation

One approach to investigating innovation involves examining structural and cultural factors. For example, Drazin and Schoonhoven (1996) reviewed and introduced a series of research articles examining community, population, and organization effects on innovation. Hemmasi, Graf, and Kellogg (1990) identified characteristics of industry structure, such as industry growth, that are related to executives' perceptions of competitors' rates of process innovation. Both structural characteristics and perceptions of competitors were, in turn, related to profitability. Feldman (1988) also examined organizational culture and broader social and historical processes that affected attitudes toward and the capacity for innovation.

A second approach to research on innovation and creativity focuses on the great idea generators like Thomas Edison and Albert Einstein. Indeed, Max Wertheimer's classic book *Productive Thinking* discusses Gauss, Galileo, and Einstein. Such case studies of geniuses have been written to help identify the key components of innovative thinking.

Current research recognizes that ordinary individuals can make important contributions. Though not as earthshaking in their consequences as those of the geniuses, their "ordinary" contributions improve societal and organizational life. In addition, many such contributions come from groups of people, rather than individuals working in isolation. So, recognizing the contributions of ordinary groups of people, we will adopt Van de Ven's (1986) definition of innovation as "the development and implementation of new ideas by people who over time engage in transactions with others within an institutional context." This definition appears compatible with those proposed by Thompson (1965) and Kanter (1983).

For example, Kanter (1983) depicted "corporate entrepreneurs," who work through participative teams to produce change. Within such environments, she suggested that three new sets of skills are required. First, "power skills" are needed to persuade others to invest needed resources. Second, "team skills" are needed given the increased use of teams and employee participation. Finally, "change management skills" prove essential, including an understanding of how small changes undertaken by teams contribute to strategic reorientation.

Such a definition of innovation enables us to apply the word to an organizational setting and to specific groups within those settings. We know, for example, that many innovative ideas come from first-line supervisors and their employees. These ideas, when articulated, developed, and implemented, lead organizations to success. Unfortunately, few studies identify the skills needed by first-line supervisors and their employees to make these innovations work.

The purpose of this study was to investigate the accomplishment of innovation in the workplace. We wanted to test a training process for helping first-line supervisors undertake innovative projects. We asked three major questions. First, what kinds of projects will these supervisors undertake? Second, what will be the results of these projects? Such results can be measured both in terms of project completion and in terms of dollar benefits to the organization. Finally, what factors affect the success of the projects?

Method

Subjects

We began by gaining the participation of five different types of organizations in this study. They included a restaurant, a newspaper, a university, an electronics manufacturer, and two community hospitals that were being merged. All organizations are located in the San Francisco Bay area. Four of the five organizations were able to provide facilities for the training sessions.

Training

The 42 supervisors who participated in the training held positions such as manager or department manager, or typesetting supervisor. Much of the training was drawn from an existing program and focused on interpersonal and planning skills required to encourage and oversee innovative projects,. The 10 three- to four-hour sessions trained participants in skills such as winning support from others, coaching for optimal performance, and resolving team conflicts. The program's format uses lectures, behavior modeling with realistic examples, discussion, practice, feedback, and planning.

The training included both specially developed and existing materials. Materials such as a Project Tracker were designed to assist participants in completing several critical steps in developing and implementing their projects. These steps involved activities such as planning meetings with managers and employees, logging project status, and determining the costs and benefits for the project at different stages.

Data Collection

Participants answered questionnaires and responded to questions at interviews both before and after training. Some of the posttraining interviews were videotaped. The data gathering focused on obtaining participants' description of their projects, their status-reports, estimates of benefits and costs, and ideas about factors affecting project status.

Training managers provided some oral feedback to members of the data collection team throughout the process. Finally, a discussion and focus-group session was conducted with the trainers. Both the training managers and the trainers focused on identifying factors leading to the project's success or failure.

Results

The types of projects selected by participants appear in table 1. They generally fell into three major types: developing new procedures, changing or improving the work flow, and providing new training.

The first type, developing new procedures, accounted for 38 percent of the projects. Examples of projects in this category included the following:
- fulfill a department goal of writing Monday closing procedures for financials
- update procedures manual for legal reasons
- improve distribution of audiovisual equipment.

The second major type of project, changing or improving work flow, accounted for 21 percent of the projects. Examples of these included the following:
- spread out work flow between advertising and production
- develop a cross-department activities calendar
- deal with a cutback in full-time employees without being threatened.

The third major type of project, providing new training, accounted for 12 percent of the projects. Some examples included
- design training for supervisors with low morale because of recent changes in job duties and stressful environment
- provide cross-training on complex medical equipment.

Other projects fell into providing new services, undertaking special planning, developing new systems, redesigning jobs, remodeling a reception area, reducing error rates, increasing sales, closing a line of business, and improving customer relations.

Table 1. Types of projects.

Project Type	Yes*	No*	Maybe*
Developing new procedures	9	5	2
Changing or improving work flow	5	2	1
Providing new training	2	2	1
New service	0	1	1
Planning	1	0	1
New system	2	0	0
Job redesign	1	0	0
Remodel		1	
Reduce error rate	1	1	
Increase sales	1		
Close business		1	
Improve customer relations	1		
Total	**23**	**13**	**6**

* **Table headings:**
    Yes   Completed or made significant progress on project
    No   Made little or no progress on project
    Maybe Made some progress on project

Bottom-Line Results From Innovative Projects

Fifty-five percent of supervisors worked successfully with their employees to implement their innovative projects within the 10-week period. An additional 14 percent reported progress but did not complete their projects during the 10-week training period. These projects appeared likely to be completed in the future. The remaining 31 percent stopped their projects prior to completion.

One example of a successful project involved the general manager of a restaurant who focused her project on raising sales volume. She set her goal to raise the average check by 50 cents per customer (using August averages as the base). She held employee meetings to stress the goal and present and practice sales techniques. Daily sales and check averages were posted for individuals to track their progress toward the goal. Within two months, the average check was up 77 cents.

To examine the results for the entire group, the authors used a discounted cash-flow technique to determine the rate of return. (See Brigham, 1985.) We determined the interest rate that equates the present value of future returns to the investment outlay (see table 2). Thus, we had to identify the present value and any future returns accruing as the result of training; and we had to determine the costs or the investment outlay. This procedure takes into account both the costs of training and the time value of money.

Costs for training included the following: costs for the program materials, costs for instructor training (including estimated salary and travel), and estimated trainer and participant salaries during the training sessions. Note that the costs for materials and instructor training were estimated using existing programs. The authors used estimates because new materials were developed for this research and the developers assumed the instructor role.

Dollar costs and benefits from the projects were provided by the participants at the conclusion of the training period. We received both fixed and variable estimates of the costs and benefits. For the variable estimates, we limited the payback period to be 10 weeks (the length of the training).

Under these conditions, we estimated the rate of return to be 35 percent when averaged over all 42 participants. This impressive rate of return continues to increase as we increase the payback period from 10 weeks to a year.

Table 2. Discounted internal rate of return (training + project costs) for selected trainees.

Project	Present Value Interest Factor (PVIF)	Future Value (FV)	Investment (I)	Net Present Value (NPV)	Internal Rate of Return (IRR)
MS	.125	60,000	7,354	146	700%
V	.7692	2,000	1,554	−15	30%
PS	2.8571	625	1,704	82	−65%
TW	.1667	8,400	1,444	−44	50%
BJ	.625	3,000	1,854	21	60%
PS	1.0526	16,500	17,354	14	−5%
BH	2.8571	580	1,524	133	−60%
SP	.1538	9,600	1,446	31	650%
DI	5	1,350	6,754	−4	−80%
AB	3.333	2,300	7,654	12	−70%
DD	4	350	1,584	−184	−75%

Factors Influencing Innovation

Analyses also identified factors both within and external to training that affected the outcome of innovative projects. Data from both the pre- and postquestionnaires suggested several factors relating to project completion. Table 3 presents the results of factors that may affect project completion. Chi square analyses revealed that the type of organization significantly affected project completion ($x^2 = 20.76$, df = 8, p <.05), but other factors such as the number of employees or type of obstacle involved in the project did not seem to affect project completion rates.

From interviews with participants, trainers, and training managers, we identified personal skills and traits critical to project completion. Two affects on success were the ability to influence others and confidence about one's ability to complete the project. An example of the kind of comment we heard is "My project was dropped in the very beginning. I discussed it with one person, and she said that it was a dumb idea."

Factors external to the training that affected project completion included degree of management support and timing vis-à-vis other organizational events. According to trainer reports, with strong management support, participants eagerly pursued their projects; without management support, participants seemed to find other, higher-

Table 3. Potential factors affecting project completion.

Location	Yes*	No*	Maybe*
Hospital	6	2	4
Restaurant	1	0	0
Newspaper	9	0	0
Electronic firm	2	3	2
University	5	8	0
Total	23	13	6
Project Definition	**Yes***	**No***	**Maybe***
Launch shows defined project	21	11	6
No defined project	2	2	0
Total	23	13	6
Number of Employees	**Yes***	**No***	**Maybe***
1-4	12	1	1
5-9	3	3	1
10-75	4	2	1
Total	19	6	3
Unknown	4	7	2
Obstacles	**Yes***	**No***	**Maybe***
Lack of management support	3	0	2
Lack of employee support	5	0	2
Personnel changes/absence	5	3	1
Lack of time for project	6	2	1
Poor timing-sessions/project	1	2	1
Total	20	7	7
No Information	**4**	**6**	**2**

* **Table headings:**
   Yes   Completed or made significant progress on project
   No   Made little or no progress on project
   Maybe Made some progress on project

priority activities that demanded their attention.

Independent of management support was the "good" timing factor within the organization. Groups that were in the midst of heavy-demand periods showed less progress on projects than did groups experiencing normal work loads. Furthermore, timing became even more critical when management support was lacking.

Discussion

This study obtained two important results. First, we were able to demonstrate a method for determining bottom-line impact of training through the calculation of internal rate of return (IRR). If we consider the development of people within the organization as an investment in human capital, then the use of IRR seems appropriate. Using the IRR method for this particular training, we obtained a 35 percent rate of return.

A second result focused on the training itself. The training effort provided one approach to helping supervisors lead innovators within their organizations. It led to improvements in the interpersonal and planning skills needed to encourage and oversee innovative projects. In addition to behavior modeling as the basic training method, the training included discussion, group practice with feedback, and planning. The study found that such training resulted in the initiation of innovative team projects among all trainees. These team projects involved such activities as developing new procedures, changing or improving work flow, and providing new training. Furthermore, most teams completed or made significant progress within the 10-week period designated for training.

The study also identified factors affecting project completion rates. These included the type of organization, management support, and good timing within the organization. It may be that these factors are related to a larger factor that can be called organizational support. Management support and good timing relate to the environment in which the organization operates. These organizational factors exist external to the training.

One factor related to the training was the personal skills and traits of the individual. Perhaps with additional training, individuals would become better able to influence others and become more confident of their own abilities and skills. To ensure success when undertaking project efforts, the training must

- provide strong assistance to participants in the identification and definition of potential projects
- train participants in how to quantify project benefits and costs
- provide participants with skills needed to influence others, including upper management and employees
- ensure management support throughout the projects.

Our study suggests a promising line of inquiry for identifying specific steps that organizations can take to increase first-line supervisors' success in implementing innovative projects.

Questions for Discussion

1. What personal skills or traits were critical to the completion of this project?
2. Do you think it is more difficult to measure personal skills and traits than it is to measure hard data such as sales figures?
3. What is the value of ROI in this process?
4. What factors affect the success of these projects? What improvements could be made?
5. How would the rate of return increase using a longer payback period than 10 weeks? What assumptions would one have to make?

The Authors

Darlene Russ-Eft, Ph.D., is director of research services at Zenger Miller. At the time of this study, she was division director of research services, with responsibilities for all corporate market and product research activities as well as consulting with clients about methods for measuring the effectiveness of consulting and training. Russ-Eft is also the author of many articles and is a frequent speaker at both regional and national psychology and training association meetings. She is Immediate past chair of the Research Committee of the American Society for Training & Development and has recently been elected to the board of the American Evaluation Association. Russ-Eft received a 1995 Editor of the Year Award from Times Mirror for her research. Darlene Russ-Eft can be contacted at Zenger Miller, 1735 Technology Drive, 6th Floor, San Jose, CA 95110-1313.

Kathleen Hurson is vice president of research and development at Zenger Miller. At the time of the study, she was senior vice president, research and development, at Zenger Miller, with overall responsibility for the research, development, launch, and maintenance of Zenger Miller products and services. In her 12-year career with Zenger Miller, she had been a key author and contributor to all of Zenger Miller's major products including FrontLine Leadership, TeamLeadership, Team-Effectiveness, Quest, Strategic Process Management, and Leadership 2000. Hurson is also an examiner for the California Golden State Quality Award (California equivalent of the Malcolm Baldrige National Quality Award).

References

Brigham, E. *Intermediate Financial Management.* Chicago: Dryden Press, 1985.

Drazin, R., and C.B. Schoonhoven. "Community, Population, and Organization Effects on Innovation: A Multilevel Perspective." *Academy of Management Journal,* volume 39, number 5, 1996, pp. 1065-1083.

Feldman, S. "How Organizational Culture Can Affect Innovation." *Organizational Dynamics,* volume 17, number 1, 1988, pp. 57-68.

Hemmasi, M., L.A. Graf, and C.E. Kellogg. (1990). "Industry Structure, Competitive Rivalry, and Firm Profitability." *Journal of Behavioral Economics,* volume 19, number 4, 1990, pp. 431-448.

Kanter, R.M. *The Change Masters: Innovation for Productivity in the American Corporation.* New York: Simon and Schuster, 1983.

Thompson, V. "Bureaucracy and Innovation." *Administrative Science Quarterly,* volume 10, 1965, pp. 1-20.

Van de Ven, A.H. "Central Problems in the Management of Innovation." *Management Science,* "volume 32, May 1986, pp. 590-607.

Walton, R. E. "A Vision-Led Approach to Management Restructuring." *Organizational Dynamics,* volume 14, number 4, 1986, pp. 5-16.

Wertheimer, M. *Productive Thinking.* New York: Harper & Row, 1959.

Measuring ROI in an Advanced Sales Skills Program

Apex Corporation

Wade A. Hannum

Results from sales skills programs are sometimes difficult to measure. When a learning solution is developed in direct response to corporate strategy and goals, it is subject to high levels of scrutiny from many levels of an organization. This case study follows a sales program from Level 0 analysis through a Level 5 return-on-investment (ROI). In programs with high visibility, an integrated evaluation strategy provides the fact-based information upon which results can be accurately and credibly calculated. The results are impressive, and the process was comprehensive.

Background

The business productivity industry has become extremely competitive since the early 1990s. Over time, customers have become educated about products and services provided by manufacturers in the area of office productivity. At the same time, businesses have restructured their organizations to be more efficient and market focused.

The traditional customer and vendor relationship is giving way to a new and radically different relationship. Today, business requires a vendor to become a consultant to a customer's business, especially in the area of office and business productivity. Successful vendor organizations in this market are characterized by a sales force that customers view as knowledgeable, credible, and reliable in terms of the product, business, the customer's business problems, and the way the vendor's

This case was prepared to serve as a basis for discussion rather than to illustrate either effective or ineffective administrative and management practices. All names, dates, places, and organizations have been disguised at the request of the author or organization.

product integrates with other products in the marketplace to enable customers to better meet their business goals.

Businesses today indicate they want to work with a company and people who understand their business, its goals, processes, and challenges, and who can make recommendations that support the customer in achieving their goals. Time is money, and businesses today will not invest their time with multiple vendors who only want to sell their product.

Organizational Profile

Apex Corporation is a manufacturer and distributor of high-tech, leading-edge solutions that enable improved business productivity and work-process improvements. It is a multinational corporation recognized as a leader in the field of business productivity improvement. Apex is a company that views quality as a business imperative. Its dedication to quality is pervasive throughout the company and has earned the company quality awards in the industry and high levels of customer satisfaction.

Apex sells its products and services in the United States through a sales force made up of more than 7,000 people. U.S. sales revenues across all products totaled more than $10 billion.

Bob Murphy, chief executive officer (CEO) of Apex, announced in his CEO's report, "For [Apex] to be the industry leader in business productivity solutions, our customers require us to be partners in the success of their business, not a vendor...."

Organizational Learning and Performance Requirement

The training organization was assigned the task of ensuring that the sales force was "consultative" in its sales relationship with customers, and it was asked to begin implementation four months later. The training requirements organization, a subset of the training organization, immediately conducted interviews with senior managers to assess the details behind the strategic direction, understand the business implications of the goal, and assess the plausibility of meeting the targeted time frame. Other areas analyzed included current and potential sales channels, sales performance, sales force competence, field and headquarters support resources, staffing, compensation, management practices, environment, learning trends, and current sales force work practices. The requirements group also identified people considered to be role model performers currently in Apex.

The analysis reported findings in terms of the desired state, current state, and the learning and performance profile of critical personnel. The data revealed seven critical gaps in the following desired-state skill, knowledge, performance, and work practices:

- Field personnel understand a customer's business requirements.
- Field personnel are solutions oriented, not product oriented (solve all the customer's needs).
- Field personnel understand how Apex solutions solve business problems.
- Field personnel consistently meet the account's, or customer's, total productivity need.
- Field personnel plan strategically with their customer.
- Field personnel effectively link technology to business solutions.
- Field personnel consistently raise the level of contact within an account.

The analysis identified the criticality of these performance elements against the goal and determined it would take nine months to construct an intervention to meet the learning need. With this information, senior management agreed to the revised plan and increased the budget for development and implementation of the intervention.

Solution

To meet the requirements of senior management and the field, the solution was identified as a customer-centered sales strategy that focuses on understanding the customer's business, its goals and requirements, and how Apex enables customers to meet their goals. The solution reflects regional fluctuations in the marketplace, is strategic rather than tactical, with focus on complex customer environments and technologies, providing for learning within natural communities of practice (current and desired), and open to the company-owned sales force and strategic selling partners.

The field indicated a dissatisfaction with traditional learning formats. They were considered too long, took too much time away from selling activities, and contained too much information to be absorbed in the allotted time frame.

Learning Intervention

The program is called Customer Centered Selling. It is an advanced sales training program; the intended audience includes all levels of sales representatives (sales reps), systems analysts, sales managers, and analyst managers. It consists of preschool activities, instructor-led modules, videos, case studies, action planning, and other small-group learning experiences.

The course is delivered in two sessions and is repeated as frequently as needed to train all the work teams in a business unit. The first session lasts three and a half days for managers, who attend a mandatory four-hour managers' orientation, and three days for others. The second session is three and a half days in length for managers, who attend a mandatory full-day workshop, and two and a half days for others.

Program Evaluation Strategy

In 1994, Level 1 evaluations were sent to all locations where training took place, and results were processed for each location. In 1995, Level 1 evaluations were sent to all trained locations. Based on the proposed 1995 strategy, a purposive sampling strategy was applied. Results were processed and reported for nine out of 28 region locations. The selection of the sampled locations was based on the following considerations:

- region locations that have completed session 1 in 1994 and were planning to complete its remaining deliveries in 1995
- instructors who are new to teaching Customer Centered Selling.
- fair representation of region locations from each area of the country.

To demonstrate that session 1 learning has occurred (Level 2), participants complete an interim feedback form describing how they used the tools and models in their application exercises (completed between sessions 1 and 2), the assumption being that if they can explain or justify the way they used it, then they understand and have learned.

A Level 3 evaluation measures the extent to which learning resulting from training is used on the job. The optimal time for conducting a Level 3 study is usually 3 to 6 months after participants have been trained. This period of time will enable participants to have the opportunity to try out the skills on the job and with their customers.

Level 4 and 5 evaluations measure the return-on-investment resulting from the learning intervention. This is a challenging undertaking given the nontraining factors that potentially also influence sales results. In this program, sales reps and analysts were asked to estimate the value of sales and revenue before and after training. They were also asked to estimate the contribution of training to the results.

Their input was then validated with their immediate manager.

To minimize the amount of time required of field participants, the same data-gathering methods were used for collecting Level 3 and some of the Level 4 and 5 data. To enhance the validity and quality of Level 3 and 4 evaluation findings, multiple methods were employed in gathering data. These included

- Surveys were sent to all participants who had completed Customer Centered Selling three to six months after training.
- Focus groups that lasted from one to one and a half hours were conducted in four regions.
- Follow-up phone interviews were conducted with survey and focus group participants to gather information for Levels 2 and 3.
- Sales revenue data of trained and untrained region locations were obtained electronically from the sales revenue database.

Although each of these methods has its merits in collecting either qualitative or quantitative data, or both, the combination of multiple methods helps to eliminate bias and ensure accuracy of findings. The combination Level 3 and Level 4 and 5 evaluation instruments address these key questions:

- background information questions
  — current and previous positions
  — length of time in positions
- level 3 questions
  — open-ended items on whether, when, and how Customer Centered Selling is applied
  — open-ended items on enablers and barriers of applying Customer Centered Selling to accounts
  — detailed account information to which Customer Centered Selling was applied
  — skill level (at end of training versus current)
  — frequency of using skills and worksheets
  — usefulness of tools and worksheets
  — benefits and changes, or both, as a result of applying the customer-centered selling approach
  — support and reinforcement received in applying these skills
  — confidence in the ability to use skills
  — motivating factors in applying the skills
  — satisfaction and adequacy of the training in preparing participants to apply Customer Centered Selling to accounts
- level 4 questions
  — forecasts of sales revenue and products or services sold

— actual sales revenue and products or services sold, with estimates of the percentage attributable to Customer Centered Selling.

Level 4 and 5 data were also obtained from the sales revenue database. To control the effects of extraneous variables (a major problem with Level 4 and 5 evaluations), three strategies were employed:

• Seasonality. All revenue data were compared before and after the two-session training event for each region location using the 1994 configuration (when the training for most of the current Level 4 sample occurred). Because training occurred almost every month in 1994 and in the early months of 1995, data from

Figure 1. Percent of plan pre- and posttraining analysis.

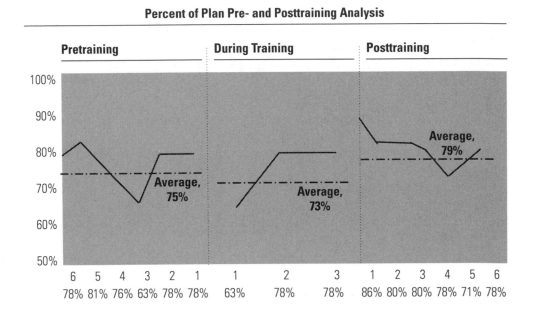

all seasons are included. Data for the six months preceding session 1, the months between sessions, and the six months after session 2 are compared across all trained region locations, thus minimizing the effects of seasonality, as figure 1 shows.

• Unique region-based factors (size, sales potential). All comparisons were normed as percentages of the region location's planned revenue for each month because the plans are built upon predictable sources of variability in sales potential.

- Other potential extraneous factors. The trained region locations are compared with an average of nontrained regions to control other potential sources of variability. Final results, shown month by month, can be interpreted as a ratio of each trained region location's percent of plan, divided by the average percent of plan for all region locations during the same month and year.

Results

Fourteen region locations completed training in 1994, and the results of all completed locations were processed. The next year 28 region locations had completed Customer Centered Selling training, and because of the sampling strategy in use then, evaluation forms received from nine region locations were processed.

Level 1 results of both 1994 and 1995 deliveries are positive and encouraging. The overall percent satisfaction rating is 96 percent for session 1 and 97 percent for session 2. Ratings with respect to instructor range from 83 percent to 100 percent. Between 75 percent and 100 percent of the participants agreed that they had achieved their learning objectives. The instructors were "excellent, knowledgeable and were able to relate their business experience to Customer Centered Selling concepts," to quote several participants.

A review of the write-in comments, as well as the interviews and focus groups, indicate that participants would have liked more time to practice and review exercises.

The response rates for the Level 2 forms were high. A total of 920 interim feedback forms from 39 region locations were received between 1994 and 1995.

The interim feedback form is evaluated based on the assumption that if participants are able to describe how they use the tools learned from Customer Centered Selling, then they have learned the concepts. This does not necessarily imply that those who did not describe how they used the tools did not learn.

A review of the Level 2 forms indicate that between 57 percent and 79 percent of the respondents were able to describe how they applied the tools to their accounts. The range indicates the respondents' ability with different tools because those who were able to describe how they used skills, used some more than others. This response supports the assumption that they have learned the concepts and skills from the training. Figure 2 lists the tools that were used and the percentage of respondents who were using them.

Figure 2. Percent of respondents using each tool.

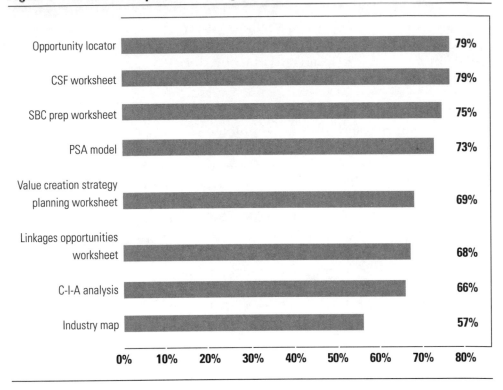

Demographics and Response Rates

Efforts were made to ensure the samples for our focus groups, surveys, and phone interviews were representative.

Thirty-one sales reps and analysts from four region locations participated in the focus groups.

A total of 465 surveys were sent to participants in 11 business locations. In spite of mailed and phone call reminders, only 57 surveys were returned, resulting in a far below-standard response rate of 12 percent. The low response rate calls into question the representativeness of the sample.

To test the quality of the sample, a nonresponse bias test was conducted. Results of this test showed that fewer than the expected number of statistically significant differences existed when the respondents and nonrespondents were compared; the sample can thus be considered representative, and our conclusions should be statistically sound. The number of respondents, 57, represents a reasonable number from which to draw conclusions. The sample consists of respondents with a fairly long tenure: Almost half of them (49 percent) have been in their current position for more than four years; slightly over a third (34 percent), for one to three years; 13 percent, between seven and 11 months; only 4 percent for less than six months.

Fifty follow-up phone calls were made to survey and focus group respondents, and 20 respondents participated in an in-depth phone interview. Demographics of phone interviewees are similar to those for the survey respondents, except for a higher percentage of analysts. Most of the interviewees are also fairly tenured, with an average of over four years of sales experience.

Application of Skills

Findings from focus groups, surveys, and follow-up interviews indicate that most of the respondents have applied some of the skills and concepts learned from Customer Centered Selling to their business accounts.

Although 88 percent of the survey respondents state that they have applied the concepts and skills learned in Customer Centered Selling to their business accounts, only 67 percent report having made more sales. Of those who made more document sales (56 percent of the total sample), 83 percent state that they used the skills learned in Customer Centered Selling in closing the sale.

Customer Centered Selling is used often during sales call preplanning and during account strategy sessions. Second-level data gathered from phone interview respondents suggested that although Customer Centered Selling is applied in most accounts, only some skills are used. Analysis of open-ended data indicates that the skills and processes reps and analysts use most often include the following:
- defining a customer as a relationship or transactional buyer using the account behavior spectrum
- defining a customer's buying style (how customers shop and buy)
- identifying the key business processes and operations of the company
- identifying or uncovering a customer's critical success factors
- understanding the decision-making process
- identifying the compelling event of a customer
- reaching a higher level of contact.

The skills and processes that are used less often are
- identifying the internal linkages within a customer's organization using a Production Systems Model

- identifying the relationship between a customer and a customer's customer via an industry map.

A review of the Level 2 and Level 3 data reveals a relationship between the tools that were learned most effectively during training (Level 2 data) and the tools that were reported to be used after training (Level 3 data). Of the seven skills and processes reported to be used most often, six were related to the top four tools indicated in the Level 2 findings, as figure 2 shows.

The respondents who did not apply all skills to all accounts used various criteria in determining which skills to use. Examples of criteria cited by phone interviewees include the following:
- type of buyer (transactional versus relationship)
- size of transaction, potential revenue, and types of solutions (copiers versus systems)
- possibility of partnering with print systems reps and gaining their support
- decision-making process of the company (for example, the more multilevel the decision-making process is, the more likely it is that respondents used Customer Centered Selling).

Application of Customer Centered Selling

Self-Assessment of Skill Ratings

Survey participants were asked to rate their skill level at the end of training and their current skill level on a five-point scale. Of the 17 skill areas, skill gains were reported in 11 (63 percent) of the skill areas. However, none of these changes is statistically significant. The greatest skill gains reported with the percentage of people who reported them follows:
- planning how to align with the most influential people in a sales opportunity (0.18)
- selection of the appropriate strategy for a given sales opportunity (0.16)
- uncovering the customer's critical success factors in order to understand the business priorities. (0.16)

In examining participants' average skill level at the end of training and their current skill level, no changes are perceived in two skill areas (12 percent):
- Describe an account or buyer in terms of the account behavior spectrum.
- Conduct an initial strategic business call.

Although the following skills were reported to be "moderate" with respect to both their frequency of use and criticality to the job, their average current skill level ratings are (also nonsignificantly) lower than the average skill level ratings at the end of training. Participants perceive three of the skills in this group, those labeled with an asterisk, to be used less often than the rest of the skill areas and to be less critical to their jobs. (The negatives before the number indicate that these are below what was expected.)

- Analyze opportunities to create external linkages. (-0.14)*
- Identify key customer business processes in a customer's organization using the Production Systems Analysis tool. (-0.12)*
- Develop appropriate value-creation strategies to align with the customer's buying style. (-0.09)*
- Analyze the relationship between my customer and my customer's customers and suppliers, using an industry map. (-0.04)

The following represent positive comments made by participants:

BETTER UNDERSTANDING OF CUSTOMER'S NEEDS AND BUSINESSES. Comments made by survey respondents, focus group participants, and phone interviewees support the ratings.

Many respondents stated that as a result of Customer Centered Selling, they have a better understanding of their customers' needs and businesses. Some of these sales reps said that they are "looking deeper into accounts," "providing meaningful solutions that better meet customers' requirements," and "reaching higher contacts within an account." Additional benefits that respondents cited included. "I become more global. I realize that in order for Apex to survive, I need to be a problem solver" and "Customer Centered Selling does not shorten or lengthen the sales process, but opens horizons that I do not see, so that there are benefits in the long term. I see more opportunities."

HEIGHTENED AWARENESS AND MODIFIED SALES APPROACH. Even respondents who had a lot of sales experience and stated that they have applied Customer Centered Selling concepts before the training were able to cite benefits of using Customer Centered Selling in their accounts. As a result of Customer Centered Selling, there is a change in how they use the skills and approach their accounts. Some typical comments follow:

- Customer Centered Selling heightened my awareness of the inner workings and relationships within accounts.
- Customer Centered Selling made me think of how Apex solutions can impact my customer's business.
- I look at things from a strategic point of view.

- Customer Centered Selling made me stop and think about principles as I approach the accounts.
- I was able to demonstrate to the customers how I could streamline their processes and improve productivity.
- I use it more frequently and it gave me a better understanding of its impact.
- I tend to ask more qualifying questions.

INCREASED NUMBER OF CUSTOMERS QUALIFIED. Of the survey respondents, 87 percent feel that their ability to qualify customers has improved since taking the Customer Centered Selling course. The 34 respondents have, on the average, qualified 4.5 additional customers.

- Twenty-four percent have qualified one to two more customers.
- Forty-seven percent have qualified three to five more customers.
- Twenty percent of the respondents state that they have qualified an additional six to eight customers.
- Nine percent have qualified nine or more customers.

LEVEL OF CONTACT. Over three-quarters (77 percent) of the survey respondents said that their levels of contact within their accounts have been raised. Twenty-six of their comments support these ratings. Of the survey respondents, 82 percent have been able to call on higher level customers in their accounts. Phone interviewees also said that their level of contact was raised. A small number of participants said they "have always called high" and are "already at the highest levels" and so were not able to call "higher" in their account.

APPLYING CUSTOMER CENTERED SELLING AS A DAILY PROCESS. Less than half (41 percent) of the survey participants stated that they have integrated the use of worksheets and tools into their work processes. A similar percentage of the 20 phone interviewees, 55 percent, said that they have incorporated Customer Centered Selling into their own processes.

IMPROVED EFFICIENCY AND EFFECTIVENESS. To many sales reps, Customer Centered Selling helped to refocus their efforts in their accounts and reassess the validity of the approach. Although Customer Centered Selling does not shorten the sales cycle, it helps reps to "avoid errors in sales cycles and improve close ratio," as stated by one sales rep. Some reps also said that they have become more organized in dealing with customers and making calls.

- For tenured reps, Customer Centered Selling had provided them with a "structured approach." One rep elaborated: "You learned the tools and knew the basics, but Customer Centered Selling does the fine-tuning."

- Thirteen phone interviewees who have generated revenue as a result of using Customer Centered Selling were asked if they would have gotten the transaction if they have not taken Customer Centered Selling or used the approach. Three respondents (23 percent) said no, three were not sure, and seven respondents (54 percent) said yes. Although seven indicated yes, most of them felt that if they had not taken Customer Centered Selling, they would have arrived at the transaction, but it would have taken longer. Examples of their comments include
- If I did not have Customer Centered Selling, I might not have got the account. I may not know where I am in the sales cycle.
- Yes, eventually, but it would have taken longer. We would have moved in circles. This allows me to continually move through the sales cycle. Customer Centered Selling saves time.
- Yes, maybe. This is because I have been a rep for a long time.
- Yes, but there may be a chance that I will lose the account.
- Applying Customer Centered Selling helps me to retain business.

INCREASED CONFIDENCE. Participants also reported increased "confidence in consultative selling." Some participants stated that as a result of using Customer Centered Selling, they have become more knowledgeable. One rep stated, "I am more confident making a call to senior executives. I do not feel intimidated, and I can talk in their language." Another rep said, "Before I was able to call high, but I would get nervous, now it becomes more natural."

CHANGE IN THE TYPES OF PRODUCTS SOLD. Over half (59 percent) of the survey respondents stated that they have changed the type of products they are currently selling since attending training. There is a consensus among the reps that they now focus less on selling single-use products and more on integrated products and consulting services.

ROI. Twenty-nine respondents were able to provide both forecasts and actual sales data to estimate the effects of Customer Centered Selling training on the bottom line, as table 1 shows. Because this is the Level 4 and 5 portion of the findings, these data are particularly important.

Calculating the ROI

The investment associated with Customer Centered Selling includes instructor fees and expenses; program analysis, development, and piloting costs, amortized over the total population targeted for training; costs associated with the time out of field for participants (salary and benefits), including a calculation for lost opportunity costs

Table 1. Respondents' forecasts of sales and actual sales.

	Forecasts of Sales Revenue	Actual Sales
Total	$13,629,000	$7,096,000
Average	$545,160	$443,500 (This figure is based on a different sample than the forecast and may not actually represent a smaller sale than was forecast.)
Average % attributable to Customer Centered Selling	38%	47%
Average $ attributable to Customer Centered Selling	$197,250	$215,719 (This figure is based on a different sample than the forecast. This sample does not include respondents who did not state how much of the actual sale is attributable to CCS.)
Number of respondents (N)	16	16

against their quotas; student travel, expenses, and support staff time. The investment per student attending the program totaled $7,000. The following ROI calculation uses the 16 respondents who provided completed data to the survey:

$$\text{ROI} = \frac{\text{benefits} - \text{cost}}{\text{cost}} = \frac{\$215{,}719 \times 16 - (16 \times 7{,}000)}{6 \times \$7{,}000} = \frac{3{,}339{,}504}{112{,}000} = 29.817, \text{ or } 2{,}981\%$$

Although the results are encouraging, they are based on incomplete data: A large number of respondents indicated that they were not able to provide evidence of the training's impact either because they were still working on their accounts or for other reasons.

Other than Customer Centered Selling, respondents attribute

their success in gaining a transaction to the following other factors:

- sales reps' and analysts' own experience and selling skills
- sales reps' and analysts' knowledge of account
- appropriate use of pricing
- sales reps' and analysts' technical and sales knowledge
- Apex product offering
- sales reps' and analysts' previously established relationship with customer
- availability of enterprisewide services.

ANALYSIS OF SALES REVENUE DATA. As table 2 shows, the effect of Customer Centered Selling is not as dramatic as we would have anticipated (nor are any of these differences statistically significant); however, the improvement in revenue in the three months immediately following training (from 75 percent of plan before training and 71 percent during training, to 82 percent of plan) is pronounced and translates into almost $25 million (if generalized to all region locations, rather than just the sample upon which these figures are based). The month after completion of training, in fact, shows the highest average percent of plan of all months included, with 86 percent.

Unfortunately, the gains made right after training are not sustained. This indicates a falling-off of the benefits of training, possibly because of an absence of ongoing support and feedback or because of a return to old habits.

When the percent of plan is compared to the average for each of the respective months represented in the sample, most of the figures are around 100 percent, indicating that the sample is representative of the population.

Barriers and Enablers to the Use of Customer Centered Selling

Factors Enabling Selling Skills

There is agreement among the respondents that they were satisfied with course content and delivery. Survey respondents indicated they were motivated to use the skills because they led to increased sales (86 percent said very motivating, and 12 percent, somewhat motivating), increased customer satisfaction (79 percent said very motivating, and 19 percent said somewhat motivating), and improved their ability to move the customer through the buying cycle (79 percent said very motivating, and 19 percent, somewhat motivating).

Respondents felt that Customer Centered Selling had prepared them to focus on productivity and the impact to their customer's busi-

Table 2. Sales revenue data obtained from the electronic database.

Before Training	Month 1 (N=19)	Month 2 (N=19)	Month 3 (N=19)	Month 4 (N=19)	Month 5 (N=15)	Month 6 (N=15)	All 6 (mean)
Revenue—actual	$1,811,465	$1,855,859	$1,285,829	$1,571,692	$1,741,198	$1,471,091	$1,573,261
Revenue—plan	$2,327,113	$2,362,760	$2,028,562	$2,029,368	$2,163,368	$1,755,946	$2,094,647
% plan	78%	78%	63%	76%	81%	78%	75%
% of plan/average	101%	101%	86%	100%	101%	100%	98%

During Training	Month 1 (N=19)	Month 2 (N=18)	Month 3 (N=11)	All 3 (mean)
Revenue—actual	$1,215,574	$1,562,595	$1,919,917	$1,566,029
Revenue—plan	$2,005,417	$2,158,123	$2,413,951	$2,192,497
% plan	63%	78%	78%	71%
% plan/average	89%	93%	100%	95%

After Training	Month 1 (N=19)	Month 2 (N=19)	Month 3 (N=19)	Month 4 (N=19)	Month 5 (N=18)	Month 6 (N=18)	All 6 (mean)
Revenue—actual	$2,102,861	$1,756,042	1,302,525	$1,650,183	$1,174,472	$1,168,372	$1,525,742
Revenue—plan	$2,445,187	$2,167,264	1,839,563	$2,118,265	$1,736,829	$1,542,807	$1,974,986
% plan	86%	80%	80%	78%	71%	78%	77%
% plan/average	105%	101%	103%	100%	96%	93%	100%

ness rather than on price.

They indicated that the ability to partner with other reps and analysts and the provision of training to all Apex sales populations demonstrated the corporation's commitment to Customer Centered Selling. This was cited as a motivating factor for using Customer Centered Selling.

The top three factors helping participants to apply the skill are on-the-job practice, classroom training, and job aids and tools. Rating relatively low as helpers is support from analysts, managers, and specialists. These results are surprising because of the inclusion of manager and peer coaching as integral portions of the training. It may be that managers do not always attend these coaching training sessions and, thus, are not prepared to offer active coaching and modeling.

Barriers

The structure of the course and timing of the delivery were a barrier to information retention. In spite of the design of the course to include practice exercises between sessions, some reps stated that they had trouble remembering what they had learned because of the structure of the course and the lack of follow-up. Some stated that they would have found it more beneficial had the training been spread out over several months and coupled with discussions with other reps or with their managers on different topics. One rep said about this type of follow-up: "This will allow me to practice on what I have learned, so that when we meet again after two months, we can share what we have learned with each other." This suggestion differs from the current status, whereby training is presented in a given period with no formal organized follow-up activities.

The timing of the delivery posed a problem for some reps. In some locations, training was delivered to the participants during the fourth quarter when they were busy trying to reach their goals. The failure to retain information demotivated some reps from applying all Customer Centered Selling skills to their accounts.

Insufficient Support Provided

Insufficient and inconsistent support was one of the main barriers in using skills taught in Customer Centered Selling. No work groups were formed to discuss what sales reps had learned. There was little evidence of any organized effort on a region level.

Only 51 percent of the survey respondents reported that their managers provided them with coaching in strategic business calls. And this was the highest percentage for the five factors. Only 37 percent of the respondents received help in developing a competitive account plan, and only 35 percent of the respondents received coaching on gathering critical success factors (CSFs) for sales calls, and only 5 percent received coaching or support in using the competitive and industry analysis model or in conducting a Production Systems Analysis.

Only 67 percent of the survey respondents said that they had the necessary support in their regions to make use of what they have learned in Customer Centered Selling. Examples of support included discussions of strategies, account reviews, and preparation for Strategic Business Calls. For those who did not receive the necessary support, many suggested the provision of refresher or review sessions, a resident expert within the region operation, and Customer Centered Selling success stories. One rep made a suggestion to "make Customer Centered Selling a part of the region process: have reps and managers discuss Customer Centered Selling during account strategy sessions." These results are surprising because the structure of the course is specifically designed to involve and empower managers to lead the Customer Centered Selling efforts locally.

Phone interview data supported this finding. Of the 15 phone interviewees who provided feedback, only five respondents stated that they have received support from their management in using Customer Centered Selling. The definition of support is expressed in the following comments:

- My manager makes sure that his whole team is constantly using this whole process.
- My managers understand Customer Centered Selling concepts.
- Managers use Customer Centered Selling terms more than before. They inspect us and ask questions to identify where we are in the account.
- My manager wants to know where I am in the account.

Ten phone interviewees did not feel that they had received adequate management support. Possible reasons for the lack of support stemmed from managers' lack of understanding of the importance of using the Customer Centered Selling approach, untrained managers, and inadequate follow-up. Following are examples of comments:

- Due to the region restructuring, there was a 100 percent turnover of managers. We now have managers who are not trained.
- Our managers do not understand the Customer Centered Selling approach. They still are concerned about how fast we close the deal. They do not know that Customer Centered Selling takes time.

- Managers are not consciously using Customer Centered Selling. I think they understand the Customer Centered Selling approach. But unless it is an issue, they are not aware of what we are doing. They do not get involved.
- Due to the region restructuring, Customer Centered Selling is not consistently used. We do not hear much of it. People forget about it. I do not feel that the people in my region bought into Customer Centered Selling.

Focus group findings indicated that restructuring and changes in reporting structure have had an impact on the management makeup in one region. Only one out of five managers remained in the region as a result of restructuring. Reps reported that before restructuring took place, the region manager was very supportive of Customer Centered Selling. A contest was implemented to encourage sales teams to apply Customer Centered Selling to their accounts.

Other comments from participants included the following:

TIME CONSUMING. There is a perception among some participants that the time required to review, learn, and use the information was too long. One rep said, "I need more time to do Customer Centered Selling. If we get more clerical support, we'll have more time. Then we will be able to spend more time face to face with our customer." Many of the sales reps do not feel that they can apply Customer Centered Selling to their accounts because of their workloads, especially those of the reps who sell copiers. This is especially true for reps who have more than 40 accounts.

NO IMMEDIATE RETURN. The sales cycle was perceived to be long. Some sales reps did not see any immediate return as a result of using Customer Centered Selling. Some reps reported that they had to spend an enormous amount of time building relationships with a customer, especially those who sell low-end products and have transactional accounts.

NOT APPLICABLE TO EVERY ACCOUNT. There is also the perception among some participants that Customer Centered Selling is applicable only to certain accounts. Comments provided by the participants included

- Not easy to fit to selling environment. Too academic an approach. Too complicated for problems simply solved.
- Most of my accounts are small owners.
- Climate of account, i.e., deeply negative due to lack of funding and downsizing.

Of the 20 phone interviewees, five stated that they did not apply

Customer Centered Selling to their business accounts. There was agreement among the analysts that they play a supportive role in the selling process. One rep explained: "I do not have the opportunity to apply these concepts in conjunction with the sales reps. Qualification and account strategy are determined by the rep. My involvement is in validating that the solution meets the customer's requirements (usually after the solution has already been defined and discussed with the customer) and implementing the solution in the customer's environment." Because this finding is based on the feedback provided by three analysts only, additional research is required before conclusions are made.

PRESSURE TO MAKE SALE. The pressure to make sales goals prevented some reps from trying out the concepts and skills learned in Customer Centered Selling. As one sales rep commented, "Reps continue to sell boxes because budgets force them to. Customer Centered Selling involves more time, something the rep doesn't have when it comes to their budgets and selling." Another rep stated, "How can we reinforce the use of Customer Centered Selling? There is no way we can reinforce it. We as reps get beat up in 30-day business."

PERCEPTION OF SALES REPS. A barrier identified by a sales rep was "our accounts/customers do not look at Apex as a consultant. Our customers still look at us as sales people." The fear of disrupting the already-established relationships between the customer and sales rep discouraged sales reps from reaching a higher level of contact.

Summary of Evaluation Findings and Conclusions

Evaluation of the Customer Centered Selling program provides consistent evidence that training participants were generally satisfied with the course content and delivery; that learning had occurred in the classroom; that respondents have applied at least some of the skills they learned to their accounts; and that respondents generated increases in sales revenue, even if these gains are not sustained over time.

Level 1 analyses indicate that reps and analysts are satisfied with the training they received. Results from the end-of-session evaluations indicate that on the whole, training participants reacted positively to the training. Ratings with respect to the perceived achievement of objectives, instructors, and course content were satisfactory.

Level 2 analyses indicate that reps and analysts have learned most of the concepts taught in Customer Centered Selling. Data received from the interim feedback forms provide evidence that many participants have learned the Customer Centered Selling concepts taught in session 1 and have tried to apply them between session 1 and session 2 training. There is insufficient evidence to conclude that all concepts or skills were learned because not all the tools were used due to a lack of opportunity or the rep's perception of their criticality. It is apparent that some tools are used more often than others.

Level 3 analyses indicate that reps and analysts have generally tried to use the skills learned in Customer Centered Selling. Data received from the focus groups, surveys, and follow-up interviews indicate mixed results. Although many respondents report having applied Customer Centered Selling to their accounts, it is important to note the following:

- Respondents do not experience much improvement in Customer Centered Selling skills and knowledge between the end of training and the survey period, indicating a general lack of usage, feedback, or results.
- Not all skills are applied to every account.
- Some skills are applied more than others, such as identifying critical success factors.
- There appears to be a parallel relationship between the skills that are learned (indicated in the Level 2 findings) and the skills that are most frequently used (indicated in the Level 3 findings)
- Although skill gains are reported in some areas, they are not significant. Findings indicated that in comparing respondents' average current skill level rating to the ratings taken at the end of training, skill gains tended to be lower for respondents who perceived the skills to be less critical and perhaps as a result, did not use the skills as frequently.

Analyses of Levels 4 and 5 indicate that although the short-term increase in revenue, projected at $25 million, would appear to justify the cost of the program, the increase is not long lasting. Data received from the focus groups, surveys, and follow-up interviews indicate that the bottom-line results are mixed, although many respondents report having applied Customer Centered Selling to their accounts. The application of Customer Centered Selling has appeared to yield benefits, but only a small percentage of respondents have provided evidence that they made more sales and generated revenue as a result of using Customer Centered Selling.

Although not every rep and analyst who applies Customer Centered Selling to their accounts generates revenue, many gain benefits as a result of using Customer Centered Selling. Respondents state that they have modified their sales approach and perception of customers to ensure that they were focusing on their customers' business and needs. As one rep stated, "Customer Centered Selling has made me think of how Apex can impact my customer's business." Participants report that they were more confident in approaching their customers and were able to qualify more customers and reach higher levels of contact. There was also evidence of selling other types of solutions than point solutions. Many respondents who successfully applied Customer Centered Selling to their accounts and generated revenue also were able to incorporate Customer Centered Selling into their daily processes.

Findings indicate that respondents who did not apply Customer Centered Selling consistently to their accounts have not incorporated Customer Centered Selling as part of their work processes. They do not feel that they have received sufficient support in using Customer Centered Selling. Some reps, especially those who sell copiers and have many accounts, find it time consuming to apply Customer Centered Selling and do not see the immediate return in applying Customer Centered Selling. Due to the pressures to make quota, some reps assess their accounts and determine which accounts they should apply Customer Centered Selling to, but others do not see the benefit in using Customer Centered Selling and do not make an effort to apply it. Some analysts stated that they did not have the opportunity to apply Customer Centered Selling because they were involved in a later stage of the selling process.

The motivation to apply the concepts and skills taught in Customer Centered Selling is contingent upon the participants' perception of the value of Customer Centered Selling. Although the key motivating factor for using Customer Centered Selling for some people is the belief that the application of Customer Centered Selling would lead to increased sales, the key factor for using Customer Centered Selling for others is the need to have adequate and consistent support. Although there is evidence that some managers used Customer Centered Selling terminology, understood Customer Centered Selling concepts, held account-strategy discussions, and ensured that they incorporated into their selling process, this finding is not consistent in all the trained regions. Furthermore, due to the region restructuring effort, there was a large turnover of managers in some region locations. The new managers might not have been trained or prepared to inspect or coach their reps or analysts. This finding indicates that different people are motivated by different factors and that it is important to provide the appropriate amount of support to participants so as to encourage them to apply what they have learned. Many reps suggested that there be periodic refresher or review sessions.

Implications

Today's business and market dynamics require learning organizations to become full partners in the business of business. Management looks for fact-based information as the basis of decisions in support of the organization. This case demonstrates how the ROI model can be implemented to provide fact-based information at each successive level of evaluation. Keeping in mind that Levels 1 to 3 evaluations represent internal (inward-looking) measures and represent in-process measures and help make the training better. Level 0 analysis provides the training community and Apex management with a fact-based view of their training requirements in training terms and provides for common understanding of the current and desired state. Level 4 demonstrated that training produced a return, but it does not quantify the return or tie the return to the desired behavior change or measure its value. Level 5 provides a model that reflects the common understanding (requirements identified) from Level 0 and ties them directly to the value of the results by isolating the effects of training, converting those desired results to monetary terms, and reporting those measures in business terms. Intangible benefits represent shifts in attitude, culture, thinking patterns, and even work practices. Where no value is currently placed on these elements, they represent benchmark data to be followed in the future.

The challenge of learning organizations is to be viewed as equal partners at the decision-making table in business. Level 5 provides a fundamental and credible measure, communicating business results in business terms to business decision makers about business issues. That's one giant step toward the table.

Questions for Discussion

1. How did the evaluation of the program highlight the effects of training?
2. How would you critique the evaluation strategy used?
3. How would you critique the conclusions based on the available data?
4. How credible was the ROI calculation?
5. Were all the costs included in the analysis?
6. The evaluation spoke of communities of practice. If it took four people (sales, analysts, support, and other specialists) to deliver the $215,719 average revenue level, what impact would it have on the

ROI level? Would it be credible?

7. How would you critique the process used to isolate the effects of training.

8. What would your recommendations be to recapture the ROI?

The Author

Wade A. Hannum is currently manager of requirements planning for Xerox Corporation's United States Customer Operations and is responsible for translating business strategy into learning and performance strategy to achieve workforce preparedness. Hannum has 15 years' experience in HRD. He has supported the development of new sales channels, developed the U.S. training strategy, implemented ROI as a training evaluation strategy, managed annual contracting processes, and provided consulting support to Xerox training organizations in Canada, Latin America, Rank Xerox, and Fuji Xerox. He holds a B.S. in marketing from the University of Maryland and is an M.A. candidate in human resource management, also at the University of Maryland. Hannum can be contacted at the following address: Xerox Corporation, 421 Haskell Drive, Arnold, MD 21012-1152.

Evaluation of Techniques for an Empowered Workforce

Eastman Chemical Company

Paul Bernthal and Bill Byham

Empowerment is an important issue in most organizations. This program involves the evaluation of an empowerment program for employees in a division of Eastman Chemical Company. The process captures the actual behavior change and converts the change to monetary values. The process uses utility analysis, which has been accepted by many organizations. The results were impressive, and the process uses a variety of techniques.

When this study was conducted in 1993, Eastman Chemical Company was the tenth largest chemical producer with over $20 billion in sales (20 percent of Eastman Kodak Company's sales). More than 12,000 employees produce more than 300 individual products (chemical, fibers, and plastics) at the 825-acre plant site of Tennessee Eastman in Kingsport, Tennessee. In 1993, Eastman Chemical Company demonstrated its commitment to extraordinary production standards by winning the Malcolm Baldrige National Quality Award. The TENITE® Division of Eastman, featured in this case study, produces a registered brand of plastic used in products such as toothbrushes, eyeglasses, and automobiles. TENITE is one of 12 divisions of Eastman Chemical Company.

Organizational Drive Toward High Involvement

Eastman is the leader in the application of a color-control technology to plastics. In recent years additional brands of plastics have

This case was prepared to serve as a basis for discussion rather than to illustrate either effective or ineffective administrative and management practices.

been introduced to the market, and competition has intensified. The challenge to improve Eastman's business performance, introduce new products more rapidly, and utilize assets in the most efficient manner have all increased. Part of the company's success and desire to maintain competitiveness led upper-level management to increase its focus on developing a high-involvement, empowered workforce. Talk of empowerment began in 1982 and eventually led to changes such as definition of a new work system, performance-pay changes, developmental coaching, division specific plans for empowerment, a human resource development study and plan, and an elaboration of strategic intent. A large part of the push for high involvement came from Bill Garwood, Eastman Chemical's president at the time this study was conducted. Published works such as David Hanna's *Designing Organizations for High Performance* influenced upper-level management's rationale and inspired its move toward high involvement. New or enhanced training programs included operator training (apprentice program), maintenance training, personal effectiveness (skills-based training for the individual), and training directed at how individuals and teams have an impact on the organization. In addition, an assessment program was introduced to help select team coaches and tailor training to individual needs. With the increased focus on high involvement and empowerment, many new systems were introduced to promote change during this growth period.

Training to Promote High Involvement

To meet the challenge of improving business performance, TENITE introduced training focused on interpersonal and meeting skills development. Improving business results by improving the use of TENITE's human resources was the driving force for changing from the traditional supervisor-worker model to a management style that recognizes the value of individuals working on a team with commonly understood and shared goals for the enterprise. The division believed that greater customer satisfaction, lower costs, and higher quality products would result from a training program designed to increase these interpersonal and meeting skills.

TENITE's team design required a high level of team skills: how to interact personally, how to plan and conduct effective team meetings that address business and personal needs, how to communicate, and how to solve problems. The firm Development Dimensions International (DDI) was chosen to supply the training materials because its training unit objectives closely matched the division's needs and because Eastman had prior experience using DDI products and knew them to be of high quality. The training plan that was developed took two years to complete and represented a sizable investment in improving and enhancing people's inherent abilities. With an investment of this scale, TENITE wanted to know if the training was effective.

In the past, Eastman had relied on the ubiquitous "smile sheet" (Level 1) as its primary form of evaluation, but it recognized the need for a better way to evaluate training and link it to business needs and outcomes. Specifically, the company wanted to ensure that on-the-job skills tied to business success could be linked to training objectives. By improving skills, upper-level management hoped to have a larger impact on the targeted business outcomes. Overall, a $3 million training investment was being proposed for the next three years. The champions for conducting the evaluation, Bill Henderson, training coordinator, and Nic Clemmer, senior mechanical engineer, were interested in thorough design, including multilevel and multimeasurement approaches. A pilot test was critical to ensure that the dollars would be well spent.

Needs Analysis

One of the most common mistakes in conducting an evaluation is attempting to detect the presence of training outcomes that have no link to individual or job-related needs. In other words, evaluation is only appropriate when selection of training has been based on a clear definition of needs. Eastman established a link between needs and training content in two ways. First, it examined its organizational strategy (for example, quality, cost reduction, safety, people-focus) and defined the behaviors associated with being able to meet its goals effectively. For example, to improve quality, Eastman felt that employees should be able to target problems before they occur and ensure equitable assignment of work and responsibility. The team training chosen to accomplish these objectives clearly addressed these skills. Second, DDI conducted a series of focus groups and discussions with various Eastman groups to assess training needs. The Organizational Effectiveness Team (leaders of the move toward team training) were involved in numerous conversations to determine team training objectives. Also, frontline workers and supervisors were involved in two focus group discussions to better understand the required on-the-job technical and interpersonal skills.

Study Design

Participants

The TENITE® Division trained 31 employees in five Techniques for an Empowered Workforce® training modules over a 16-week period. Almost all of the sample were male and ranged in age from the mid-20s to early 60s. Trainees could be classified as blue-collar workers responsible for operating machines, taking raw materials (powders), mixing plastics with dyes, heating and extruding plastic into strands, chopping the plastic into pellets, handling materials, moving, loading, and quality work in labs. Team leaders were trained along with frontline employees.

Training

The introductory module was Making the Difference, which introduces basic communication behaviors individuals can use in everyday interactions to build strong working relationships. The organization also used the modules titled Communicating With Others, Supporting Others, Handling Conflict, and Participating in Meetings. As a group, these five modules served to develop basic individual and group interaction skills and introduce concepts for forming empowered teams. A description of module objectives can be found in the "Measures" section below. All of the modules employed a heavy skill-building emphasis designed to demonstrate and practice team skills. The training sessions involved video instruction, lecture, skill-building exercises, and group activities. Training sessions lasted approximately four hours and involved six to 12 participants.

Design

One to two weeks before implementing the training program, a behavioral base-line was established by conducting paper-pencil assessments and group simulations for the 31 employees about to undergo training. Then, after the training implementation, all of the same assessments and simulations were readministered. To ensure that any changes in behavior noted after training were not a function of unmeasured variables, a comparable untrained control group of 32 individuals was also assessed before and after the training intervention. Descriptions of the measures are presented below.

Approximately one to two months after the completion of training, all groups underwent a second assessment period. In addition to readministration of paper-pencil assessment measures, trainees also re-

ceived reaction assessments and learning tests. Participants then engaged in a second assigned role group simulation with a different sce-
nario but identical task requirements. With very few exceptions, simulations were conducted using the same configuration of participants as
in the pretraining assessment.

Measures

Reactions

A 14-item reaction measure was designed to assess five outcomes:
affective reaction, applicability of skills, self-efficacy, behavioral intention to use the skills, and perceived learning.

Knowledge Test (Posttraining Only)

After the training intervention, both the trained and control
groups took an 11-item multiple choice test to assess changes in knowledge and awareness. Items appearing on the test were directly related
to the training content.

Group Simulations

Before training, all participants were engaged in assigned-role
group simulations composed of three to six participants and lasting up
to 50 minutes. Leaderless group discussions are commonly used in assessment centers and have been found reliable according to many commonly accepted standards (Gatewood, Thornton, and Hennessey,
1990). During the simulations, participants were asked to imagine that
they were part of a committee established to make decisions about
whether or not several imaginary employees should attend a leadership
training session. Each participant was assigned an imaginary employee
to champion before the group. Depending on the size of the group,
only one or two of the imaginary employees could be selected to attend
the training session. The simulation was designed to assess the following 11 meeting participation skills:
- opening the meeting
- clarifying information
- developing ideas
- agreeing on actions
- closing the meeting
- making procedural suggestions
- checking for understanding and agreement
- resolving conflict

- involving others
- maintaining and enhancing self-esteem
- listening and responding with empathy.

All simulations were videotaped and rated by professional DDI assessors using four-point, behaviorally based scales. These scales were designed to rate how well participants used their new skills in conducting meetings, resolving conflict, maintaining interpersonal communication, and reaching agreement in teams. Assessors were not aware of whether the videotaped simulations occurred before or after training, and they did not know about the participants' training experiences.

Self-Assessment

A 40-item survey was used to assess how frequently participants felt they used behaviors targeted by training. At the high end, a rating of seven indicated that the behavior was used to a "very great extent, always, or without fail." On the low end, a rating of one indicated a "very limited extent, never, or not at all." These 40 behaviorally based items were clustered (averaged) into 10 major areas for behavioral change, as shown below:
- maintaining or enhancing self-esteem
- listening and responding with empathy
- asking for help and encouraging involvement
- giving and receiving feedback
- understanding and avoiding conflict
- handling conflict
- resolving conflicts
- overcoming communication barriers
- providing coaching
- seeking support from others.

Assessment of Individual Participants by Team Members

In addition to the self-assessments, each participant received behavioral frequency ratings from three other participants in the study. This measurement provided an average rating of behavioral frequency as perceived by a group of observers. The same 40 behaviors used in the self-assessment were used in this assessment.

Assessment of the Team by Team Members

Participant were asked to rate how frequently they observed 16 behaviors that might be displayed in a team meeting. These ratings were clustered into five main areas of meeting participation skills:

- generating, exploring, and clarifying ideas
- keeping meetings on track
- setting action plans and follow-up
- preventing difficult meetings
- intervening effectively during difficult meetings.

Organizational Results

Data regarding results were based on two sources of information. First, information about percent of class 1 (products acceptable for sale), conversion costs (cost of converting raw material to produce output), operator morale, and operator input were identified as key areas for change. Second, a utility analysis based on Cascio's (1991) guidelines was used to determine dollar value return-on-investment.

Findings

Reactions

Overall, reactions to the training were positive. On a seven-point scale, subscale scores tended to be in the five to six range. The average score for all 14 items was a 5.18. The highest ratings appeared for behavioral intention (5.67), and the lowest rating was for affective reaction (4.95).

Knowledge Test

On the multiple choice knowledge and awareness test, the trained group showed a significantly higher ($p < .05$) average score (71 percent correct) than the control group (58 percent correct). DDI's administration of this learning test in other organizations has shown similar outcomes (that is, percent correct) for control group ratings.

Group Simulations

All changes in ratings were assessed using an analysis of covariance (ANCOVA) design. In other words, differences in posttest scores were compared while controlling for differences in pretest scores. The analysis did show a significant difference between the pretraining control and trained group overall assessment scores ($F(1,53) = 8.25$, $p < 0.01$). When controlling for this difference, the average overall posttraining assessment rating for the trained group was higher than the control group rating at a statistically significant level ($F(2,53) = 4.29$ $p < 0.05$).

Although the control group showed some marginal improvements, none were statistically significant. The correlation between the overall pre- and postassessment ratings for the control group was 0.66 ($p < 0.0001$), indicating good reliability for the ratings over a four to five month period. Furthermore, the control group showed significantly reduced performance ratings in two areas (the module Closing Discussions and Making Procedural Suggestions). The overall pattern of results showed that the trained group performed better than the control group. The most notable differences were seen in the modules Opening Discussion, Clarifying Ideas, Maintaining and Enhancing Self-Esteem, and Checking for Understanding and Agreement. Table 1 presents a summary of all simulation-based pretest and posttest scores.

Table 1. Group simulation ratings.

Behavior Labels	Before Training		After Training		Change Scores	
	Trained	Control	Trained	Control	Trained	Control
Overall**	2.46	2.63	2.72	2.63	.28**	−.02
Opening+	2.04	2.31	2.43	2.55	.54	.20
Clarifying**	2.94	3.25	3.41	3.14	.54**	−.17
Developing	2.77	2.72	3.00	2.93	.25	.18
Agreeing**	2.48	2.72	3.00	2.68	.43**	−.07
Closing	2.26	2.31	2.15	2.08	−.08	−.17**
Making procedural suggestions*	2.68	2.94	2.76	2.68	.07	−.32**
Checking understanding and agreement**	2.48	2.66	2.86	2.57	.46**	−.18
Resolving conflict	2.96	3.13	3.17	3.04	.20	−.07
Involving others	2.48	2.50	2.45	2.57	.04	.04
Maintaining and enhancing self-esteem*	1.97	2.22	2.45	2.43	.50**	.18
Listening and responding with empathy	1.96	2.13	2.07	2.14	.12*	.04

Note. Asterisks beside labels (column one) indicate significant **between group** differences for change scores. Asterisks beside actual change score values indicate significant **within group** differences.

* $p < .10$

** $p < .05$

+ Due to technical problems with some of the assessment tapes, only 13 trained and 20 control group members were used to compute difference scores for the Opening Discussion ratings.

Self-Ratings

Within-group analyses (change scores) revealed an increase in frequency ratings for all 10 clusters of behaviors trained during the intervention. All paper-pencil measures involving behavioral ratings of performance (self, other, team ratings) showed high internal reliabilities in the 0.80 to 0.90 range. Four of these changes were statistically significant (see table 2). None of the changes for the control group was significant, and almost all changes were in a negative direction. Between-group analysis of change scores showed notable differences for the overall ratings ($t(28) = 1.76$, $p < .09$), listening and responding with

Table 2. Changes in self-ratings, ratings by co-workers, and team ratings.

	Self-Ratings		Co-Worker Ratings	
	Trained	Control	Trained	Control
Ratings of Individuals	**.23**	**-.11**	**xx**	**xx**
Maintaining and enhancing self-esteem	.37*	.07	.26	−.05
Listening and responding with empathy	.33**	−.20	.26	−.16
Asking for help and encouraging involvement	.17	.13	.27	−.15
Giving/receiving feedback	.39**	.21	.42	.05
Recognizing, understanding, and avoiding conflict	.17	−.01	.29	−.05
Using appropriate strategies for handling conflict	.13	−.20	.16	−.04
Using a structured process to resolve conflicts	.04	−.01	.31	−.15
Recognizing and overcoming communication barriers	.16	−.11	.35	.02
Providing appropriate coaching	.21	−.30	.28	.10
Seeking support from others	.38*	−.30	.17	−.03
Team Ratings			**.34**	**.03**
Generating, exploring, and clarifying ideas			.24	−.29
Keeping the meeting on track			.59**	−.08
Developing plans for action and follow-up			.67**	.41
Identifying and preventing difficult meeting situations			.33	.14
Intervening effectively during difficult meetings			−.13	−.05

Note. Due to insufficient sample size (N=8 for each group), t-tests were not conducted for the co-worker ratings. All asterisks in this table refer to **within group** differences. For clarity, **between group** differences are referenced in the text.

* $p < .10$

** $p < .05$

empathy ($t(28) = 2.26$, $p < .05$), giving and receiving feedback ($t(28) = 2.33$, $p < .05$), and seeking support from others ($t(28) = 2.37$, $p < .05$).

Co-worker Ratings

Because of an error in the data collection procedure, we were limited in our analysis of the co-worker assessment data. To compute difference scores, we were forced to use the group simulation divisions as the unit of analysis. Because group simulations were run with the same groupings of participants for pretests and posttests, we were able to compute a co-worker rating average score for the members of the group. In other words, although the performance ratings were collected in reference to individuals, the analysis focused on the aggregate ratings for a group of individuals. Following this procedure resulted in an N of 16 (eight trained groups and eight control groups).

Ratings by co-workers showed the same pattern of improvement as the self-assessments showed. Changes in the trained group were universally positive and larger than those observed in the control group. Once again, the control group showed negative changes in almost all areas. Because of the limited sample size, we did not conduct within and between group statistical comparisons.

Team Ratings by Team Members

Ratings of team performance showed an overall within-group improvement for the trained group in four of the five areas. Two of these were statistically significant ($p < .05$): keeping the meeting on track and developing plans for action and follow-up. None of the changes observed for the control group were significant. Between-group comparisons showed notable differences for two ratings: generating, exploring, and clarifying ideas ($t(28) = 1.93$, $p < .06$) and keeping the meeting on track ($t(28) = 1.83$, $p < .07$). In general, the pattern of results showed a greater average improvement for the trained group than for the control group.

Relationships Between Measures

Some controversy exists over the implied causal relationship among reactions, learning, and behavior change (Alliger and Janak, 1989). In an attempt to examine the interrelationships between the variables in our study, we present a correlation matrix in table 3. Where appropriate, we controlled for differences in pretest assessments in the control and experimental groups (all correlations not involving reactions or perceived learning).

Table 3. Correlation of measures.

	Overall Reactions	Perceived Learning	Knowledge Test	Simulation Posttest	Self-Ratings of Behavior-Posttest
Overall reactions					
Perceived learning	0.85**				
Knowledge test	0.08	0.15			
Simulation posttest	-0.03	-0.14	0.20		
Self-ratings of behavior posttest	0.69**	0.55**	0.31**	0.23	
Ratings of group behavior posttest	0.67**	0.64**	0.26*	0.19	0.79**

* $p < .10$
** $p < .05$

Reactions and measures of perceived learning (for example, "I learned a lot from the training") were highly intercorrelated. Neither correlated significantly with scores on the knowledge test or ratings from the assessment (a measure of learning). Significant relationships were observed between reactions, perceived learning, self-ratings of behavior, and ratings of group behavior. These correlations imply that a halo effect might be influencing participants' ratings. More objective ratings of learning did not correlate with ratings provided by the participants. Few other significant correlations were observed. In general, our findings did not provide convincing support for the implied causal relationship between reactions, learning, and behavior change.

Utility Analysis

A utility analysis was conducted according to the procedure presented by Cascio (1991). For reasons of organizational confidentiality, some of the information used in the analysis (for example, salaries and discount rates) cannot be presented in this paper. Following is an annotated summary of the variables used in our utility analysis. A complete description of the procedures appears in Cascio's (1991) book chapter. (Note that many of the computations described in this section involve statistical techniques that cannot be adequately described within the confines of this chapter.)

Costs

For training of 31 employees, the costs were

- Per person of the training (costs were not tax deductible): salaries, instructor time, administration, supplies, facilities, materials, and the like = $821.
- Program expense: $25,451.
- Minimum annual benefits required: This value determines the required payoff a program must demonstrate to justify the investment. Given Eastman's required return-on-investment (ROI) and level of risk, we can determine the minimum annual benefits it must receive to justify the investment in the training program. Given Eastman's other investment options over the next four years, the training would have to generate more than $8,898.95 per year to justify the investment. Because the effects of training often dissipate or become obsolete after a period of years, we proposed a four-year benefit for our training (commonly used in these types of analyses).
- Standard deviation of salary required to break even (dt): 0.022. Several methods exist for estimating the productivity levels of individual employees. Schmidt and Hunter (1983) use employee salary as a basis for estimating the variability of employee productivity (SDy). Their findings show that the standard deviation of employee productivity varied from about 40 percent to 60 percent of average salary. We used the more conservative estimate of 40 percent in our analysis. Our findings show that an employee's annual job performance would have to improve .022 standard deviation units (.75 of 1 percent) to justify the training.

Benefits

We determined benefits as follows:

- Corrected d score (effect size) for assessment performance: Effect sizes (d) can be used to show the amount of change expected from a particular intervention (when comparing control and trained groups). Guzzo, Jette, and Katzell (1985) show an expected effect size of .78 for general training interventions, such as the one described in this case study. The effect size observed in the current case study was .80. When corrected for unreliability of measures (using test-retest correlations for control group performance), this value rises to .99.

Using the values calculated for sample size, SDy, and d score, we can calculate the expected payoffs for the training program:

- unadjusted estimated payoff per year $ 400,885.06
- total present value (TPV) over four years $1,144,518.16
- adjusted total payoff per year (includes $ 205,654.03
  corporate tax, variable costs, discount rate)
- adjusted total net benefit over all four years $ 587,137.82

In the end, our calculations produced a total ROI of 2,307 percent This value is quite large, and some people would probably question its validity. However, we are more strongly encouraged by the positive changes in behavior and learning specifically targeted by this intervention. As striking as this utility analysis might be, Eastman personnel were much more interested in the effects of training on behavior. In fact, the utility analysis was treated more as an additional check on impact than as a primary measure of training value. We strongly recommend that any utility analysis be conducted in conjunction with additional measures of training impact. At the time this analysis was conducted, Eastman had already observed several positive changes in outputs and behaviors and attributed them in large part to the new focus on teams (see table 3).

Conclusions

Most well-planned research efforts involve a range of measurement techniques that add perspective and depth to conclusions. The overall trend in our findings reveals that individuals who were trained began using behaviors associated with effective teamwork and interaction more frequently than people who were not trained. Depending on the measurement perspective, improvement was noted in several areas.

From the Level 2, or skill acquisition perspective, training participants showed improvement based on two different measurements. The knowledge test revealed that they were more aware of the concepts taught in training and were better able to select an appropriate behavioral response to hypothetical interaction scenarios. Similarly, in actual meeting situations, trainees were able to demonstrate an enhanced ability to understand different ideas, make sure that everyone had a good read on the information, and set up plans for taking action.

Level 3, or behavior change measures, showed that the trainees improved on a number of interaction skills. Most notably, both self-assessments and assessments by others produced notable changes in frequency of giving and receiving feedback. Other findings revealed an enhanced communication ability and a willingness to interact and work through problems.

Level 4, or results measures, showed sizable effects in terms of

ROI and casual observation of related changes. Although ROI was not the primary focus of this investigation, this final component of our measurement strategy lends further support to our other findings.

Although our findings were almost universally positive, we acknowledge that no research study is without flaws or limitations. For example, the leaderless group discussion was not specifically designed to measure all the training content. Rather, it was a task designed to illustrate participation in meetings. Therefore, parts of the simulation content might not have been directly related to what was taught in the training. This finding could have attenuated changes. Behavior change assessments were made one to two months after training. By conducting an assessment so soon after training, we may not have allowed enough time to demonstrate changes. Finally, the presence of a response shift bias is quite possible. Knowledge of training may have introduced a demand characteristic when rating co-workers or oneself. Many other small flaws or assumptions in our approach or design may bring our results into question. Fortunately, many other DDI studies of Techniques® training have shown similar positive changes using a variety of research methods and designs. The current evaluation achieved its purpose and supports the customer-driven approach important for an effective training evaluation (Bernthal, 1995).

This research shows that by using Techniques for an Empowered Workforce® training, Eastman Chemical Company is moving closer to achieving its objectives of cultural change. Implementing new training concepts takes a long time, and the results from this initial intervention show strong promise for this training program. By conducting this evaluation, Eastman Chemical Company has made a commitment to quality training for high involvement.

Questions for Discussion

1. How appropriate were the authors' attitudes about linking team skills to the bottom line? Can you think of a better way?
2. The percent return-on–investment in this study was very large. What was the value of the utility analysis in this evaluation plan?
3. What was the examination of the implied link among reactions, learning, and behavior change?
4. How would you assess the comprehensiveness and combination of methods and measures used in this study?
5. How appropriate was the needs analysis approach? To what degree did this study address the organization's goals and needs?

The Authors

Paul R. Bernthal is a senior research consultant and leader of the DDI Center for Applied Behavioral Research (DDI-CABER). Currently, he conducts research in areas such as alternative learning strategies, cross-cultural studies, and organizational culture change. Bernthal manages all of DDI's research activities and is an expert in evaluation, validation, and survey methods. He regularly speaks at conferences, and his work has been published in books and journals such as *Advances in International Comparative Management, Training & Development,* and *Group and Organizational Behavior.* He holds a Ph.D. in social psychology from The University of North Carolina at Chapel Hill. Bernthal can be contacted at Development Dimensions International, 1225 Washington Pike, Bridgeville, PA 15017.

William C. Byham, Ph.D., is president and co-founder of Development Dimensions International. DDI is in the business of helping clients make the best use of their people to implement organization-wide business strategies. An internationally known educator, consultant, and trainer, Byham is author of more than 160 articles, papers, book chapters, and monographs. He is widely regarded as a thought leader in selection, training, and human resource development. He has received numerous awards for his innovative training technologies and his commitment to research on the effectiveness of DDI programs. Recent book titles include *Zapp! The Lightening of Empowerment, Empowered Teams, Shogun Management, The Selection Solution,* and *How to Land the Job You Want.*

References

Alliger, G.M., and E.A. Janak. "Kirkpatrick's Levels of Training Criteria: Thirty Years Later." *Personnel Psychology,* volume 42, 1989, pp. 331-342.

Bernthal, P.R. "Evaluation That Goes the Distance." *Training & Development,* volume 49, number 9, 1995, pp. 41-45.

Cascio, W.F. "Using Utility Analysis to Assess Training Outcomes." *Training and Development in Organizations,* I.L. Goldstein, editor. San Francisco: Jossey-Bass, 1991, pp. 63-88.

Gatewood, R., G.C. Thornton III, and H.W. Hennessey Jr. "Reliability of Exercise Ratings in the Leaderless Group Discussion." *Journal of Occupational Psychology,* volume 63, 1990, pp. 331-342.

Guzzo, R.A., R.D. Jette, and R.A. Katzell. "The Effects of Psychologically Based Intervention Programs on Worker Productivity: A Meta-analysis." *Personnel Psychology,* volume 38, 1985, pp. 275-291.

Schmidt, F.L., and J.E. Hunter. "Individual Differences in Productivity: An Empirical Test of Estimates Derived From Studies of Selection Procedure Utility." *Journal of Applied Psychology*, volume 68, 1983, pp. 407-414.

Measuring the Impact of Sales Training

Big Apple Bank

Neil Rackham

Measuring the impact of any training program is a difficult and challenging process. This case illustrates some of the key issues and barriers to successful implementation of evaluation and presents the process used to measure the impact of sales training in a major bank. The program produced impressive results, but more important, the study highlights some difficulties of the complex evaluation process and solutions.

Introduction

At one time or another, most major corporations have decided to measure the effect of their sales training programs. Most of them have found that it's not easy to do.

Several months ago, a major New York bank came to our organization for help with designing and implementing an effective way to measure the results from its sales training. Previous measurement methodologies had not produced the kind of level managers were looking for.

"On the face of it," one manager said, "it seemed a no-brainer. We planned to run the training, then check and see what kind of improved results we were getting. A few telephone calls, a couple of printouts...maybe a half day's work in all. What could be simpler?"

The approach seems simple enough. If sales are up, the training was successful; if sales are down, the program was a failure. Yet, as human resource (HR) professionals are aware, an improvement in sales performance is usually the outcome of efforts from several functions,

This case was prepared to serve as a basis for discussion rather than to illustrate either effective or ineffective administrative and management practices. All names, dates, places, and organizations have been disguised at the request of the author or organization.

dozens of people, and a variety of competitive and market forces—of which training is just one part.

Background

The bank's trainers had each gone through their share of bad experiences trying to measure training results. As a result, when senior management asked them to evaluate the impact of their sales training, they knew they had to do a convincing job.

In the three months following the bank's last training program, there had been an 18.6 percent increase in sales productivity. During the same three-month period, however, the bank had launched a new product that filled an important gap in existing offerings; there were prime rate changes that made the bank's products more attractive to customers; the bank's sales force was reorganized, with changes in senior management and in sales policies; and a major competitor withdrew from the market while another lost ground due to a merger.

At first, the trainers thought it might be possible to account for the individual impact of these other variables and to give each a weight. Before long, however, they realized that accounting for the influence of each variable was a practical impossibility. They had come up against one of the great truths of evaluation studies: Any model that can measure all the variables that have an influence on results is likely to be impossibly costly and complex.

Using a Control Group

Originally, the best solution seemed to be to set up a matched control group. This group would consist of salespeople who had not been through the training but who had a sales record, tenure, and other characteristics that exactly matched those of the trained group.

Because control groups have wide use in science and medicine, they were the most obvious and respectable way to measure change when there are a range of intervening variables that could have an impact on the end results. However, anyone who has tried to use matched control groups knows that they have two crippling disadvantages.

First, for control groups to be effective, the members of both the matched and the experimental groups must remain stable for the life of the study. That kind of stability is unrealistic for our study. Assume that you need about six months of sales results to establish a performance database for choosing the groups in the first place. Then you need a period of, say, one or two months to cover the training period, followed by a three- to six-month evaluation period. That's a whole year of stability. Between promotions and job changes, most sales forces have a turnover rate well in excess of 25 percent. Many training studies that have tried to use control groups have abandoned the effort as changes in group composition have wiped out the validity of their research.

Second, the success of a study may be a failure. Ironically, in the rare cases where control and experimental groups are stable enough to allow a convincing study, researchers may still run into problems. For example, our organization once studied two groups. There were 46 people in the control group, 47 people in the group we trained, and during the entire period, only three people changed jobs. From a researcher's point of view, we had an almost ideal study. Even better, when the results came in, the trained group had outsold the control group by several million dollars. When the vice president of sales heard the results, however, he hit the roof. "Why didn't you train the control group, too?" he demanded. "That way, we could have had even higher revenues."

From an evaluator's point of view, control groups are a losing proposition. If the trained group shows no improvement, then your training is perceived to have failed. But, if you show a big improvement, you've demonstrated that your test has cost the company dearly. Either way, you won't be thanked.

In the bank's case, the more the people involved thought about control groups, the less practical and less attractive they seemed. Ultimately, they decided to try another method to link their training with bottom-line results.

Perception/Action/Results Approach

After the bank decided against control groups, our team suggested an approach known as Perception/Action/ Results (PAR), as shown in figure 1.

This approach classifies measurement into the following three categories:

- Perception measures assess what participants say about the impact of the training. The methods can range from a simple smiles test, in which participants rate how useful they found the training, to more elaborate ratings in which participants put a monetary value on how much the training has helped their sales. Perception ratings can be sophisticated evaluation tools and can provide trainers and training designers with useful information. Perception measures may have limited credibility in demonstrating bottom-line impact because they are based on individual judgments rather than hard facts.

Figure 1. The PAR approach.

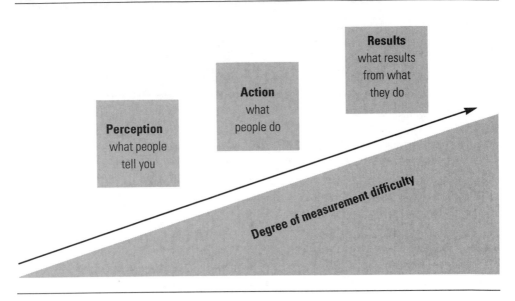

- Action measures evaluate what participants do differently follow-ing the training. These are typically observation measures of be-havior change and skill gain or tests of performance on knowl-edge and fluency instruments. Because action measures are based on behavior, they are generally more credible than measures based solely on perception. However, they are more difficult to design and can be time consuming and costly to administer.
- Results measures examine what bottom-line changes occurred as a result of the training and the skill, knowledge, and behavior that the training brought about. Measuring change in results is by far the most difficult evaluation challenge. Done well, howev-er, results measures provide the most convincing data of all.

The bank's trainers decided to use several measures from each PAR category. They reasoned that if they found a positive change through five different measures that were to determine the impact of sales training, they would have compelling cumulative evidence even if each individual test of the five was imperfect.

Measuring Perceptions

Their first test in measuring perceptions was to ask program par-ticipants to use a seven-point scale to rate the relevance of each session of the program (see figure 2). Previous research had shown that mater-

Figure 2. Perception rating scale.

Relevance

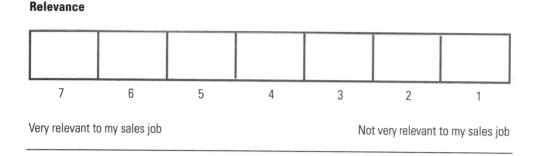

Very relevant to my sales job   Not very relevant to my sales job

ial from sessions that achieved an average rating of six or higher was more than four times as likely to be remembered afterward than material from sessions ranked three or lower (Warr, Bird, and Rackham, 1970). The bank's program achieved an average rating of 6.3, so there was a good chance that participants would retain the messages. (Notice that the scale goes from very relevant to not very relevant. Participants are usually reluctant to say negative things about training, so evaluators soften the negative end of the scale in their design instruments to get a more realistic response.)

The perception measure the bank's trainers used is just one of the many that are available. Other measures include the following:

- Quantified improvements. Participants are asked to identify specific accounts with which they intend to use the lessons learned during the program and to put a dollar value on the increased sales they expect will result. At a predetermined period following the program—generally three months—the evaluator follows up with participants to determine whether sales actually increased. Although this method can be challenged because the data are partially perceptual, it makes a more convincing story to senior management than the typical "89 percent of participants said they thought the training was useful" reports.

- Changes in constructs. In recent years, research psychologists such as Valerie Stewart have used repertory grid, one of these techniques, to test whether salespeople see the world differently after training. The grid technique explores peoples' "constructs," or the dimensions they use to make judgments. This kind of instrument can be very useful when the objective of sales training is to change salespeople from a product focus to a customer focus or when it is to move them from a transactional orientation to selling to a relationship orientation.

- Customer surveys. Collecting perception data from customers can be a valuable measure of the impact of training. The best customer studies, from a technical point of view, are those in which customers rate sales personnel both before and after training using a variety of rating scales that measure such things as helpfulness, attention to customer needs, or applications knowledge.

Measuring Actions

Measuring actions, the trainers next step, involved collecting data on behavior or what people actually do or know. This step can be more difficult than measuring perceptions, but it has the potential for being more powerful. The simpler action measures of behavior are those that measure knowledge gain or fluency. These knowledge tests are fairly easy to construct. If your sales training program has knowledge objectives (if you are teaching product knowledge, for example), then a simple questionnaire test of key facts is a useful tool. Many trainers know that a postprogram test is a good way to reinforce knowledge and to help it carry over to the job. But few know that using a test before the program also increases learning during the program itself. Pretests alert learners to the key knowledge items included in the test and make them more attentive to other knowledge items that might be important.

A harder aspect of measuring actions in sales training is to test whether or not selling skills have improved. Most sales trainers can recognize good selling when they see it, but have no idea about how to measure selling skills. Fortunately, research psychologists have developed a technique called behavior analysis that allows for precise measurement of selling skills. The behavior-analysis methodology involves two steps: First, select an observable behavior or action that is associated with sales success, such as addressing customers by name. This is done by measuring which specific behaviors occur more often in successful calls or by observing which behaviors top performers use more often than average performers. Second, determine if trainees emulate top performers' behavior after training.

The bank's sales training program taught salespeople to describe products as benefits and avoid overloading customers with product features. Using behavior analysis techniques, the trainers were able to count the frequency with which features and benefits were mentioned in sales calls before and after the training. Because they wanted to produce results that would be credible to line managers, they involved line managers in collecting the data using observation techniques during live sale calls.

Prior to training, line managers observed 46 actual sales calls, one by each person who was to be trained in the initial implementation. They discovered that features were mentioned four times more often than benefits and that their salespeople described less than one benefit to customers in the average sales call.

At the end of the training process, line managers again went into the field, and this time observed that the mention of benefits had more than doubled and those of features had fallen by half. This observation provided a convincing piece of evidence of the impact of the bank's sales training. Even better, because the action data had been collected by the line managers, it had a high credibility with the field staff.

Measuring Results

Finally, the bank trainers focused on measuring results. Results measurement can be both realistic and convincing if it uses a stepping-stones approach to develop additional evidence that training is linked directly to results, as shown in figure 3. The stepping-stones are two intermediate tests, each of which constitutes a step in the process of building a credible link between sales training and results:

Test 1 focuses on whether the models work in a particular market. Every sales program is based on one or more models of effectiveness. Whether your program teaches questioning skills, strategies for getting to decision makers, objection handling techniques, or responses to requests for proposals, you are giving people advice on how to behave differently to become more successful. In linking your training to bottom-line results, it's important to show that the models in your program work with your people and in their own marketplace. The bank's program was teaching that it's more effective to offer benefits than features during sales calls. They analyzed the number of benefits in suc-

Figure 3. The stepping-stones test.

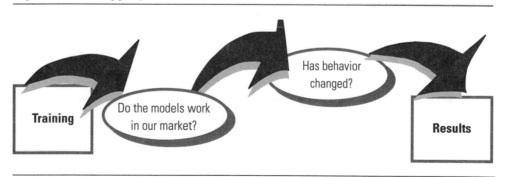

cessful and unsuccessful calls made by salespeople who would be attending the training. They discovered that there were more than twice as many benefits in their successful calls, thus validating their model that indicated it was good to offer benefits during sales calls. Their ability to show that the model they were teaching actually worked was an important stepping-stone in the process of linking training to business results.

Test 2 focuses on whether or not behavior has changed. This test answers the question, "Now that we know it works, what's the evidence that people are doing it?" The logic for this test is simple. Even if you can show that you're teaching the right things, you can't claim credit for the results unless you can also show that people are putting these things into practice. The bank had evidence that benefits more than doubled after the training. Coupled with evidence from the first stepping-stone test that benefits were linked to success in the marketplace, it had plausible evidence linking the bank's training with the 18.6 percent increase in sales that followed it.

When the bank's trainers presented their results to top management, they were in a strong position to show that their training had resulted in a positive impact on sales. The trainers had used the first stepping-stone test to measure if their models were valid. They had data on the effectiveness of nine different sales behaviors that they were teaching to their salespeople. They could show that their models worked for their people and in their marketplace. They could also confidently demonstrate to their management that that were teaching the right things. Through the second stepping-stone test, they knew how much of each of these key behaviors their salespeople were using before and after the training. Putting the two tests together, they could demonstrate that benefits were linked to success in their market and that their level had more than doubled after training. Senior management was prepared to give a good deal of credit to the training because it had seen evidence that the training had increased success-related behaviors and reduced unsuccessful behaviors.

These stepping-stones tests have been used successfully by many companies to measure the effectiveness of their sales training. However, it's an expensive and time-consuming undertaking. The bank's trainers had to study 236 calls to gather the data needed for their evaluation. Their effort required them to spend an average of half a day to gather the data from each call and with travel and waiting time, well over 100 days in the field. It's easy to see why solid evaluation studies like these are such an expensive proposition.

Continuous Quality Improvement

On the face of it, the high cost of evaluation seems an impossible problem: Worthwhile measurement isn't feasible and feasible measurement isn't worthwhile. But there is a solution, and it's a very effective one, too. If you think of measurement primarily as a means of proof, then it's only cost-effective for sales training in exceptional circumstances. If you look at it as part of an ongoing process in continuous improvement, however, it will start to earn its keep.

Put in today's terms, it's like a guided missile. We fire off our sales training in the general direction of the target. Long before it gets there, we take some measurements and use them to make a course correction if needed. A little later we take more measurements to see if we are still on target and, again, make corrections if we are not on course. In this way, instead of using measurement to find out too late that we missed the target, we can home in on where we want to be and make a direct hit. In other words, we've measured to continuously improve our performance and as a result of the measurement, we've hit a target we might otherwise have missed.

That's exactly what happened with the bank. In conjunction with the PAR process, the bank followed a number of continuous improvement steps for its training programs (see figure 4):

1. They looked closely at their success model—the skills and behaviors that they were teaching their people to use—and broke the model down into observable behaviors that could be measured in sales calls.

2. They next trained 16 sales managers to understand the model behaviors and to be able to observe them accurately during real sales calls.

3. Then each manager went out with three salespeople to watch them sell and to count the level of each behavior. The data from their observations were collected and processed to provide a baseline to show how their people were selling before any training took place. Managers had been expecting to find their people were offering four or five benefits per call. They were alarmed to discover that there was actually less than one benefit per call offered on average. Even worse, for every benefit their people offered to customers, they were offering more than four features.

4. Once a benchmark had been established, so managers saw for themselves how far their people were from hitting the target, the trainers ran a coaching workshop to provide managers with coaching skills and training tools to help their people learn to use the behaviors in the success model. The benchmark data were also used to give the first stepping-stones test. By classifying the calls that had been observed into

Figure 4. Continuous improvement.

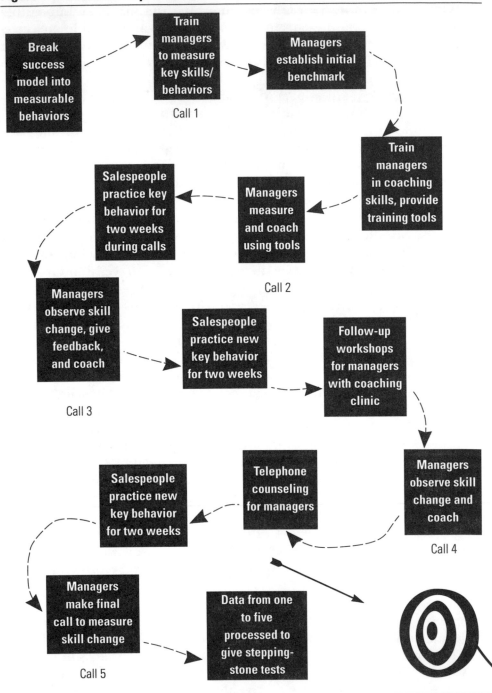

Break success model into measurable behaviors

Train managers to measure key skills/ behaviors

Call 1

Managers establish initial benchmark

Train managers in coaching skills, provide training tools

Managers measure and coach using tools

Call 2

Salespeople practice key behavior for two weeks during calls

Managers observe skill change, give feedback, and coach

Call 3

Salespeople practice new key behavior for two weeks

Follow-up workshops for managers with coaching clinic

Managers observe skill change and coach

Call 4

Telephone counseling for managers

Salespeople practice new key behavior for two weeks

Managers make final call to measure skill change

Call 5

Data from one to five processed to give stepping-stone tests

those that led to a sale and those that didn't, the trainers were able to get an idea of whether they were teaching the right things. Even at this early state, they found more than twice as many benefits in the calls that led to a sale, showing that—for this behavior at least—the model worked and one of the behaviors they were trying to develop was linked to success.

5. The managers next went out on another call with their salespeople. Before this call, they shared training materials to help their people understand and plan how to use more of the success behaviors. As before, they measured the use of key behaviors, but this time they also coached their people to help them improve their skills. An output of the coaching was that the managers selected, for each of their people, one behavior to focus on during their selling.

6. During the next two weeks, their salespeople practiced the key behavior that they had agreed upon with their managers. Some of the less experienced salespeople were practicing a simple behavior, such as asking questions to uncover basic data about the customer. More experienced people practiced harder behaviors, such as asking questions that explored the consequences of customer problems.

7. Managers then went out on another call with each of their people to observe improvements in how they were using the key behavior and, if necessary, to give them further coaching and training materials to help in its use. Salespeople who were still missing the target received a course correction in the form of training and coaching. For those who were on target, managers selected a different behavior that their measurements indicated needed attention.

8. During the next two weeks, salespeople practiced the key behavior that they had chosen with their manager. About 80 percent of the salespeople were able to move on to a new behavior, and the remainder continued with remedial practice of the behavior they were working on in step 6. Again, managers used a variety of training tools to help their people plan and practice these behaviors.

9. The trainers conducted a coaching clinic for the mangers, helping them with coaching problems and working together to devise additional help for areas where people were having difficulty. Again, this is an example of the kind of midcourse correction typical of continuous improvement in action.

10. Managers now went into the field for a fourth visit with each of their salespeople. Again, they measured and coached, choosing a new key behavior if appropriate.

11. Trainers arranged a series of telephone conference calls with managers to help them with last-minute training issues and to provide coaching advice.

12. Meanwhile, their people continued to practice the new key behavior, supplemented with one-on-one training and coaching sessions with their managers.

13. Managers made a final coaching call with each of their people to measure the level of key behaviors. Although this was the final call in this measurement study, in the spirit of continuous improvement, most mangers decided to continue with the process after the training period had ended.

14. Finally, all the data were analyzed. Sixteen managers participated in the continuous improvement process. Each had worked with three of their salespeople, making a total of 48 salespeople for whom data had been collected during five field visits, for a theoretical maximum of 240 calls for analysis. Illnesses and other unforeseen events resulted in the loss of four calls, so the final total for analysis was 236 calls. This database allowed the bank's trainers to carry out the two stepping-stone measurement tests.

Conclusion

During the process, the trainers learned several things. They learned that continuous quality improvement is not easy to implement but is much more powerful than conventional training approaches both in terms of results and measurement. Building the measurement in as a "guidance system" allows evaluation to earn its keep and to become a cost-effective change agent rather than a costly extra. Finally, involving managers in the measurement increases the overall effectiveness of the continuous improvement process and the credibility of the results.

Although measuring the impact of the sales program was not an easy process, it was worthwhile. By using continuous quality improvement together with a variety of measurement techniques the results were well worth the trainers' efforts and the bank's investment.

Questions for Discussion

1. In addition to the sales training program, several factors—including a new product, prime rate changes, a sales department reorganization, and loss of a major competitor—may have contributed to the bank's increase in sales productivity. What nontraining factors could have an impact on sales productivity in your work environment?

2. The bank's sales trainers decided against using a control group to measure results. Have you ever used a control group to assess results from training? Do you agree with the author's conclusion that control groups can have serious disadvantages?

3. The bank's trainers used a rating scale to measure employee perceptions about the company's training. In addition to this test and a "smiles test," what are some other ways that you could measure perception of training effectiveness in your company?

4. The bank's sales trainers used behavior analysis techniques (measuring actions) to count the number of features and benefits mentioned during sales calls. What other types of behavior could you measure in this way?

5. The bank's trainers employed a stepping-stones approach that used changes in benefits and features to build a bridge between training and results. If you were conducting such a test in your company, what stepping-stones would you use to link training to results?

6. As the case mentions, the PAR approach—combined with a detailed continuous improvement process—was the key to measurement success for the bank's sales trainers. Do you think this approach would work for your company? What would you do differently?

7. Throughout the entire measurement process, the bank's sales trainers worked hand in hand with its sales managers. What are the advantages of working this closely with line management? Are there any disadvantages? Would this approach work in your environment? If not, what other approaches would you suggest?

The Author

Neil Rackham is chairman of Huthwaite, an international research and consulting company. He has worked in over 30 countries and with more than 20 of the Fortune 100 companies. Rackham is author of over 50 research and technical papers. He has written several books including *SPIN® Selling,* a best-selling book that was published by McGraw-Hill in 1988. His newest books, *Getting Partnering Right* and *The SPIN® Selling Fieldbook,* were published by McGraw-Hill in 1996. Neil Rackham may be contacted at Huthwaite, Inc., Wheatland Manor, 15164 Berlin Turnpike, Purcellville, VA 20132.

References

Warr, P.B., M.W. Bird, and N. Rackham. *Evaluation of Management Training: A Practical Framework With Cases for Evaluating Training Needs and Results.* London: Gower Press, 1970.

Measuring the ROI for a Finance Course: An Evolution of Methods

Nortel Learning Institute

James A. Hite Jr. and Linda Trask

In most organizations, evaluation processes have evolved over time to reach a current level of sophistication that makes it possible to measure the return-on-investment (ROI). This case describes the evolutionary process at Nortel Learning Institute and illustrates how the ROI was developed for a finance course in the finance organization, or department, at Nortel. The case provides excellent documentation of this evolutionary path concluding with an example of an ROI-focused project that illustrates the progress in evaluation at Nortel.

Industry Profile

The global telecommunications industry has undergone major changes in recent years that can be summarized as a move away from centralization and government regulation. The industry has expanded and is in the process of exploring new waves of technology. Based originally on voice communications and the ability to transmit and switch calls, the industry is now involved in data and video transmissions and wireless transmission methods. Whether they are service providers or equipment providers, telecommunications companies are changing rapidly. Their missions have changed drastically, driven by a need to meet new communications demands and the growing use of the telecommunications networks by their customers. Changes in the marketplace are driving organizational,

This case was prepared to serve as a basis for discussion rather than to illustrate either effective or ineffective administrative and management practices.

technological, and product changes that are transforming the entire industry.

Organizational Profile

Nortel (Northern Telecom), with headquarters in Toronto, Canada, is a major global provider of telecommunications networks. The company has more than 57,000 employees worldwide. Its corporate mission is to deliver market leadership through customer satisfaction, superior value, and product excellence. To support this mission Nortel is organized into four units: a corporate staff function, a North American function, a world trade function, and a research and development organization called BNR.

Within the corporate structure, the Nortel Learning Institute (LI) serves chiefly the North American corporate population. In addition, it provides services on an as-needed basis to Nortel's world trade organization. LI's mission is to "partner with our customers to provide valued learning solutions to develop the knowledge, skills, and attitudes required to move Nortel to market leadership." The institute offers core management and leadership courses, special forums for managers at various levels, special strategic courses for managers and professionals keyed to widely recognized organization needs, and consulting services in human resources development.

Evolution of Evaluation of Formal Learning—Awareness Phase

In 1992, course evaluation was considered important enough to make it a special assignment. A manager in the institute was given the responsibility of implementing evaluation processes for the courses. Following that, a number of events occurred that served to emphasize the need for and value of evaluation data up to and including business-related measurements of effectiveness of formal learning. Evaluation in Nortel's Learning Institute has been and continues to be driven by practical business needs. For this reason, there is no straight-line process of implementation, and significant events in the process are scattered and sometimes obscured. But since its initiation, the evaluation effort has conformed to the institute's strategic plan, which continues to set the vision and goal.

Even before there was a document called a strategic plan, management's intention to evaluate had been established. Managers and professionals in the Learning Institute, in 1992, had seen that more rigorous methods for linking learning to the business would be necessary. The corporation itself was in a mood to encourage measurement, as it launched total quality management (TQM) initiatives, and began to focus more and more on customer value and customer satisfaction. It was a time that was well suited to the introduction of methods for the valuation of training.

Improved methods to collect evaluative data would help demonstrate the value of course work to the everyday operations of Nortel's business. In this way, the institute could accomplish two things. First, it could establish itself as a role model for the implementation of TQM in the corporation. Measurement of work and the valuation of various processes were high on the list of means through which quality would be improved throughout the corporation. Second, the institute would be able to demonstrate in ways other than the popularity of its course offerings that the learning it provided was of direct value to the productivity of the organization.

When the institute's strategic plan was put in writing, evaluation was a prominent objective. Without this level of focus and continuing emphasis, evaluation would not have come into the regular routine of the work of the Learning Institute. The supportive environment has been as important to evaluation as the processes themselves.

Trial Phase

Evaluation began moving into what could be called its trial phase because the process was still being tested when a letter was sent from the Learning Institute to the vendors that provided many of the courses it offered. The letter requested vendors to begin providing Level 2 instruments for courses and to begin considering evaluation plans for Level 3 data collection.

An advisory group of course managers was formed within the Learning Institute, and this group began a dialogue about evaluation, its benefits, and its processes. This group brought to the surface differences in opinion among LI staff, and it served as the focal point for development of evaluation policy.

During this same time frame (1992-1993), the institute settled on a standard format for a Level 1 instrument, which provides input on content, instructor, methods, and environment. In conjunction with the agreement on a format, a database was established that is now accessible by all LI employees and enables them to review Level 1 results and item analysis data.

Soon after the Level 1 instrument was standardized, a database was constructed to handle data from the emerging Level 2 evaluation tools. As the instruments for these two levels began to settle into place, toward the end of 1993, efforts to implement Levels 3 and 4 had begun to take shape.

Implementation Phase

There is no sharp dividing line marking the onset of implementation. The change from trial to implementation came as course managers and vendors became more comfortable with evaluation tools and methods and more certain that the results were of interest and use to management. The implementation phase is marked by continued experimentation with Levels 2, 3, and 4, and with a focus on including more and better evaluation data in management reporting. There is increased emphasis on documenting business results and accompanying interest in Level 4 methods, including ROI data collection and calculations. The initial implementation of Level 4 evaluation came in the early period of the implementation phase, when an opportunity presented itself in finance organization.

Definition of Results: The Finance Course

The Business Problem

A number of process and procedural improvements were identified during a total quality improvement initiative within Nortel's finance function. As the identified processes and procedures were reengineered, it was determined that a training initiative was necessary to implement some of the changes. One goal of the changes was to replace local business coding with global standard coding processes. In addition, the finance function wanted to support the change with training necessary to facilitate implementation of the new processes.

In partnership with finance, LI helped develop the profile for the learners: two major groups, approximately 400 results analysts and 300 business analysts and planners, required training. Locations were global, sometimes with a few people in each site. The need was high to transfer skills quickly, as the systems were revised to meet implementation schedules. As a part of the analysis phase, the function considered five questions designed to elicit evaluation criteria:

1. What do you want as an outcome, on a continuum, from those things you could live with to the ideal state of affairs?
2. What are the drivers, that is, what are the quantifiable business needs for the training intervention?
3. What performance outcomes do you expect from the training inter-

vention, and how will you measure (evaluate) the outcomes?

4. What on-the-job behaviors do you want to impact or change?

5. Who are the end users of the proposed training?

There emerged an intent to capture baseline quantitative data around cycle time, errors and rework, in order to demonstrate the overall efficiency of the reengineered systems. These data were collected by the finance organization and used later in calculating the percent change and percent savings to the organization of the entire reengineering effort, including training. The finance organization has requested that dollar figures not be published, so they have not been included in the data for this case, but percentage change data for these categories are included.

There also emerged a decision, from the initial planning for the training, that evaluation would include all four of Kirkpatrick's levels: reaction, learning, transfer, and results. The finance organization was especially interested in developing ROI data because the scope of systems changes would have high costs in both expense and capital dollars. Any contribution that could be demonstrated from training would help offset the overall project investment.

Collecting Postprogram Data

As of July 31, 1994, all training had been completed with the initial audiences. Approximately 641 people attended sessions, in the United States, Canada, Europe, Central and South America, and the Asia and Pacific areas. The sessions met the delivery criteria of the client, which included

- fast turnaround, with lowest possible costs
- ownership and operation of the training within the finance function
- facilitation by subject matter experts within the function
- evaluation data from four levels.

The evaluation data were first collected prior to implementation of the training, and that information served as baseline data. Data were developed in the following four areas:

- cycle time in the closing process
- number of users capable of inputting data and reporting on them
- posting and translation activity in the general ledger
- user confidence in the system, in finance, and in end-user line organizations.

During the training process, Level 1 (reaction) data were collected using the standard Learning Institute form. They were input into the LI database and analyzed by the finance and LI training implementation team. Level 2 data were also collected, based on the specific objectives for the course. Level 3 data were collected from a sample population of participants through informal telephone surveys one month after they had completed training. A customer satisfaction survey was also developed to ensure that end users were satisfied with the reengineered processes and the results obtained from them.

ROI data were developed from three of the four areas in which baseline data had been developed:

- Cycle time in the closing process. Target time for completion of the close process had been eight days. This was the desired time for completing close. After implementation of the new process and system and after the training, this was moved to five days, an improvement of three days, or a percent change of 28.6.
- Number of users capable of inputting data and reporting on them. The number of users on the system is a measure of increase in productivity, because only trained and capable users can access the ledger and do the necessary work to input or produce reports. The number of users increased after reengineering and training from 75 to 120, an increase of 45 users for a 60 percent change.
- Posting and translation activity in the general ledger. This is the measure of the speed of transactions. Posting transactions went from a premeasurement of five to a postmeasure of 20, indicating higher productivity and throughput, attributable to the hardware, software, and network changes and to the training. This increase represents a 300 percent improvement. Translation activity also rose, from one to five transactions per second, again attributed to system and process improvements supplemented by training. Translation activity showed a 400 percent improvement.

Isolating the Effects of Training

The effects of training were isolated by finance management and supervisors who had been involved in the entire systems reengineering project. In part, their decision was influenced by the evaluation results from Levels 1 to 3, which are summarized below:

- Level 1: Participants rated the course 3.8 on a four-point scale. Ratings covered instructor, instructional methods, environment, and content.

- Level 2: A presurvey and a postsurvey (also called pretest, posttest) were used. Because this was a new finance system, the presurvey served as a content organizer for the course, and it also picked up any knowledge of the system that had been acquired before the training session. The postsurvey indicated that participants were able to answer 95 percent of the questions correctly. The surveys checked knowledge acquisition only and did not use checklists or observations to determine relative skill levels. The course development team had decided that time was not available in the session to test skills, and that there would be high probability of significant skill improvement if knowledge gains were high.
- Level 3: Because skills had not been tested at Level 2, a high percentage of the population was included in a telephone survey conducted approximately one month after they had attended the training session (following a close cycle). From a 65 percent sample, 75 percent of the respondents were able to apply the new system and databases without problems. In addition to participant data, input was collected from managers and supervisors of participants to verify the results. Input was also collected from Nortel's internal customers. Although no predata existed, because this was a new system introduction with new products and services, the postresponse showed 93 percent satisfaction with the new system and the finance employees who operated it.

Based on these inputs and decisions regarding the preparation of the entire ROI package for the project, 25 percent of the effect of the project was attributed to training. When translated to the three key measurement areas, training was credited with the following improvements:

- cycle time in the closing process: 5 percent improvement in cycle time in the closing process (This represents 25 percent of a total measured improvement of 20 percent.)
- number of users: 15 percent improvement in the number of users. (This represents 25 percent of a total measured 60 percent improvement.)
- general ledger posting improvements: 75 percent improvement in general ledger postings (This represents 25 percent of total measured improvement of 300 percent.)
- general ledger translation activity: 100 percent improvement in general ledger translation activity. (This represents 25 percent of the total measured improvement of 400 percent.)

Tabulating Program Costs

The costs of training were divided into two categories:

course development, implementation, and maintenance	$60,000
course delivery costs	<u>$15,000</u>
	$75,000

Converting Data to Monetary Value and Calculating the ROI

The finance organization included all efforts associated with the project and all costs associated with the project in an overall calculation of ROI, including a calculation of capital investments.

Identifying Intangible Benefits

Intangible benefits were collected from two instruments and from informal feedback to instructors and finance management. Comments came from all of the regions represented in the training, and they were included as a part of the Level 1 evaluation data. Most of these comments were positive, as this selection demonstrates:

Tokyo: "The course will help me do my work more efficiently."

Hong Kong: "Definitely worth attending...(relevant to my work."

Dallas: "An important course for all finance personnel."

Ottawa: "Excellent class, would recommend to all finance people."

The second instrument that brought intangible data was the customer satisfaction survey. These customers' comments were also largely positive and indicated that the customers were satisfied with the products resulting from the new system.

Among the intangible benefits of the program were two with immeasurable but long-lasting impact. First, the development process through which the Learning Institute partnered with the finance organization resulted in the development of a course design process that was systematic, thorough, and reproducible. That process has since been used in several other finance training projects and has brought savings in time and effort in the project preparation stages and in the project development and production stages. Although these savings have not been measured, they have been recognized.

Second, the people responsible for the entire system development and introduction effort, including those who developed and implemented the training, were recognized with Nortel's 1993 CFO [Chief Financial Officer] Award of Excellence for Teamwork. This recognition of the effort had a positive impact on employee satisfaction, but no attempt has been made to quantify that impact.

Conclusion

Since 1994, when training was effectively completed in this course for the finance organization, the return-on-investment in training courses has become of increased interest in the Learning Institute and with its business partners. There are continuing activities within the institute to examine key courses for their effectiveness at Levels 1 and 2, for their impact in the workplace at Level 3, and the calculated ROI at Level 4. The trend is to examine courses selectively and to identify, especially for Levels 3 and 4, sample populations with which to work. The development of evaluation plans is increasingly a part of project design efforts.

There is every indication that more and more clients within Nortel will look to data from the Learning Institute evaluation processes to help them justify the expenditures necessary to develop their employees. With the continuing changes in products, services, and organizations, the need will continue to develop new capabilities and to add to an existing skills base within an organization. As performance development moves away from a concentration on formal training courses and toward an emphasis on a wide variety of learning support and performance support systems, so Nortel management will look for performance improvement data that will measure informal and nontraditional learning activity as well as traditional learning events. The evaluation processes exist to do this, and they will be applied as a management tool to support organizational change and performance improvement.

Questions for Discussion

1. If total benefits from the training course had been estimated at $950,000, and 25 percent of that was attributable to training, what would be the cost-benefit ratio of this training course?
2. What would be the ROI for this course if benefits attributed to the training course had been estimated at the following:

reduction in cycle time = $86,200
increase in number of users = $31,925
increase in general ledger performance = $67,875

3. Is it important to have a supportive management team when doing an ROI, and why?
4. How important was a customer satisfaction survey and why?
5. Why are intangible benefits worth measuring in the ROI process?

The Authors

James A. Hite Jr. is a senior advisor for human resource development with Nortel's Learning Institute. He currently serves on curriculum advisory committees for Nashville State Technical Institute's Telecommunications/Computer Technology Department, for the University of Georgia's Human Resources Development program, and for the University of Alabama, College of Continuing Studies' Training and Development Certificate Program. Hite holds a master's degree in English from Georgia State University and is engaged in doctoral studies in human resource development in Vanderbilt University's Peabody College. He can be contacted at Nortel, 200 Athens Way, Nashville, TN 37228.

Linda Trask is a performance consultant with Performance Consulting Associates in Nashville. Prior to this, she was an internal consultant in human resource development for the Nortel Training Institute, where she worked closely with the finance organization in the design, development, implementation, and evaluation of a number of training courses. She is a frequent presenter at professional sessions and has published in the areas of curriculum, course design, facilitation of subject matter experts through instructional design, and effective on-the-job training. Trask holds a master's degree and an Ed.D. degree in human resource development from Peabody College at Vanderbilt University.

Using ROI Forecasting to Develop a High-Impact, High-Value Training Curriculum

Commonwealth Edison

Jim Graber, Gerry Post, and Rick Erwin

Sometimes it is important to forecast the return-on-investment before pursuing a program or series of programs. In these situations, management requests that an estimate of the return be developed before allocating the funds. Although there are a variety of approaches to use for forecasting, this case describes the process used at Commonwealth Edison to allocate the funds for a variety of training initiatives and projects. The process builds on the principles of forecasting financial benefits and provides an important tool for the training or human resource development (HRD) manager.

Overview

Training evaluations based on return-on-investment (ROI) are rapidly gaining acceptance as an essential element of training. By contrast, few organizations seem to forecast ROI prior to training. When the benefits of ROI forecasting are understood, forecasting will become a staple in practitioners' tool boxes. We hope that our experiences at Commonwealth Edison will stimulate others to take a closer look.

Forecasting ROI before training is not proposed as a substitute for a training evaluation. ROI forecasts and ROI evaluations have a synergy. ROI forecasts rely on accurate evaluations of training costs and training impact. Similarly, ROI evaluations benefit from baseline data that ROI forecasts can provide. Ideally, both forecasts and evaluations

This case was prepared to serve as a basis for discussion rather than to illustrate either effective or ineffective administrative and management practices.

should be combined in a program that will have more impact than either by itself.

Introduction to ROI Forecasting

The purpose of ROI forecasting is to identify the training that will provide the highest possible payback and, generally, to make wise training and development decisions.

Training itself has no inherent value; its worth is dependent on the performance gains it catalyzes, the performance gaps it addresses, and the opportunities it can create in a given environment. We need the right training for the right people at the right time with the right costs. ROI forecasting does not affect the cost of training. However, it maximizes the payback from limited training resources, and it helps to avoid wasting training dollars.

Richard Swanson and Deane Gradous (1988) wrote in the preface of their pioneering book titled *Forecasting Financial Benefits of Human Resource Development:* "What HRD decision makers have needed for a long time is a tool to reduce the complexities of choosing among alternative investments in HRD." They continued, "Post analysis comes far too late in the HRD process to be useful for most decision-making purposes. We believe that what the HRD profession needs is a method for forecasting the costs and benefits *before* choosing to implement a program."

Wasteful Training Allocation

If an organization has done a competent job of assessing training needs, then selecting from among the available alternatives is straightforward, right? Wrong! Actually, there are a large number of factors to consider in choosing the optimal training mix. Consider the following:

- Is a course that addresses one critical need a better deal than one that is more expensive but addresses two?
- If only 10 persons need to learn a specific skill, is it better to offer them the course in-house or send them to an external training course?
- Should we first address the largest skill gap or the gap in the most critical skill?
- Which is more important, the skill gap that affects the most employees or the skill gap that affects the most critical employees?

If a person has 10 developmental needs, the ones that should be addressed first will depend not only on criticality for the job or organization but also on the size of the employee's skill gap, the program costs, the needs of other employees that could bring down the per capita costs of training, and the like. Optimal selection of training is complex and benefits greatly from an ROI perspective and analysis.

Many different approaches are utilized to allocate training. In some cases, the employer plays a major role in matching individuals and training, but other approaches give employees a lot of control over the training they receive. Some of the more common and wasteful approaches to training allocation include the following:

- Tidal wave approach: Employers flood the same training over an entire organization, as is common with quality training. Never mind that this training may be wasted on persons who don't need it for their jobs, won't need it for several years, or already have a firm grasp of the material.
- Forced march approach: Everyone in a particular job takes a certain sequence of courses. Salespersons might have to complete 10 courses in two years, for example. Wasted dollars stem from the differing needs and backgrounds of the employees.
- Grocery store approach: Employees choose courses from the company training catalog. Unfortunately, instead of basing their decisions on sound business reasons, employees may choose training courses because of time, location, participation of their friends, convenience, the need to spend dollars in the training budget, or the like. Again, far less than optimal benefit is achieved.

When uniform training decisions are made about any intact group of persons, the potential for wasted training dollars is significant. Individual differences should be considered in training decisions. However, an employer will not be able to arrive at the most profitable training allocation by concentrating just on individuals. For example, it is often impractical or too expensive to run a training program for two to three people. Also, there is often a need to prioritize training and provide more of it to individuals with a significant or critical proficiency gap because sufficient resources are not available to address all training needs. ROI forecasting offers us a way to choose from the wide array of alternatives.

Forecasting ROI or Evaluating ROI

We feel that doing an ROI analysis prior to training has some significant benefits over performing the analysis following training. These advantages follow:

- An ROI analysis before training enables identification of the highest ROI alternatives. We can compare the expected value of a wide range of training options and then choose the one that gives the highest ROI. We might use an analysis to choose from alternative training topics, training methods, training vendors, and even training participants. ROI evaluations after training provide an estimate of program ROI, but they don't reveal if another option would have been better.

- An ROI analysis helps avoid costly, poor decisions. Wouldn't it be better to know the value of training before we spend money on it? Determining ROI after a training investment is at best a justification, particularly if there is no intent to repeat the training. The most useful information is that which helps form the investment decision, and to do that, it must be available before the investment commitment is made.

- An ROI analysis before training is consistent with common business practices. An analysis prior to making a decision is the most accepted approach in business environments. Putting time and money into analyzing training that is already completed is much less appealing to business. Evaluations may be better suited to academic research.

- A pretraining ROI analysis matches the speed at which businesses operate. In our fast-paced organizations, training needs arise very rapidly. There is a need to assess the value of one or many training alternatives promptly, to select trainees quickly, and the like. Most often a pilot program and lengthy evaluation are not possible. ROI forecasting is a viable alternative.

- An ROI analysis that takes place before training makes it possible to apply ROI results flexibly and accurately. Unless future conditions are very similar, we may not get the same ROI from subsequent training. Training can have entirely different results with a different group of employees. Forecasting factors in some of these variables and projects will likely result in necessary alterations, even if a training program was successful in the past.

- A pretraining ROI analysis benefits communication. Sometimes projections from ROI forecasting are needed to sell training and justify its value. Management may be less willing to risk a pilot study and a potentially neutral or negative evaluation. ROI forecasting is a relatively low-cost, low-risk approach that is available when it may be needed most—at the beginning of a project.

Forecasting of ROI requires making some assumptions, which can lead to some uneasiness. However, many assumptions must be made when doing ROI evaluations, for example how much of a gain in sales is due to training, marketing, management practices, or the economy?

In fact, as Phillips (1995) has noted, many assumptions are required for most financial calculations, even those calculations that we typically assume to be very objective. These are three examples. A change in an accounting rule or convention can have a major effect on a company's reported profit and loss. Inventories are often estimates. Short-term gains don't reflect possible long-term damage.

To increase comfort with the assumptions, seek input and gain agreement from the people who will review the study. Be conservative in estimating training benefits, while being very complete in costing out training, including the impact of time away from work. That way, there will be confidence when you project training that will have a positive ROI. In fact, the true ROI will probably be much higher than forecast.

Background on the Study

Commonwealth Edison (ComEd) is a large, Midwestern Electrical Utility. Its training groups are reengineering themselves to be better attuned to the strategic direction of the company. Increasingly, HRD professionals are expected to demonstrate the value they provide and to help the company leverage the return for each training dollar expended. These dual needs to demonstrate value and gain the most possible from training and development programs inspired ComEd to test ROI forecasting.

Three pilot studies were conducted—two in operating divisions and one with a central training group called Personnel Development (PD), which was utilized by all divisions. Based on the early positive results, ROI forecasting is currently being rolled out for over 500 managers, with expectations of continuing to expand its use. This case study describes the PD pilot study.

Goals of the Personnel Development ROI Study

ROI analysis is a tool that PD can use to show the value of the training it provides to the corporation. It is also a tool that PD can provide as a service to the training groups in the operating divisions, each of which has its own significant training budgets and curriculums. The anticipated benefits and goals of the ROI student included the following:
- analysis of critical skill requirements for each job
- assessment of current skill levels of employees
- identification of critical employee development needs
- advice on highest impact cost-effective training

- determination of who would benefit from specific training
- high-impact individual feedback reports on current developmental priorities.

Outline of Steps and Deliverables

The general sequence and deliverables for the ComEd PD Study were

Steps	Deliverables
1. *Identify required knowledge and skills:* Group similar job tasks, assign weights, select critical skills for the instructor, designer, and the like.	*Job profiles* for positions. This includes key accountabilities, weights, and critical skills, both technical and interpersonal.
2. *Assess employees:* Assess the current levels of competency of the PD staff members on the skills required for their positions.	*Customized skill questionnaires* for each position to assess knowledge and skills of individuals on the critical skills for their position. Ratings completed by job incumbents and their manager.
3. *Calculate gaps and costs:* Perform a gap analysis between required skills and current skill levels.	*Group skills development report* showing a listing of skill gaps for the PD staff as a group, ranked by annual cost of lost performance. *Individual skill development priority report* showing skill gaps ranked by annual cost of lost performance. *Individual skill performance ratings* showing ratings on a one to five scale for each skill and the breakdown for self versus manager ratings.
4. *Evaluate training programs:* Determine what knowledge and skills are taught by each program and at what level. Evaluate costs of training programs.	*Catalog of training programs* showing courses, descriptions, maximum and minimum number of participants, skills addressed, expected proficiency level after course, and detailed breakdown of costs.
5. *Calculate ROI/select optimum training:* Identify existing training programs and approaches that meet current training needs and suggest developmental areas where training should be obtained.	*Group curriculum* showing suggested courses and forecasted ROI of each. *Course rosters* showing suggested course participants and forecasted ROI for each. *Recommended course* reports for each staff member.

Step 1: Identify Required Knowledge and Skills

The ROI forecasting process began by selecting employees or supervisors, or both, who are familiar with a job (for example, instructor or designer). These subject matter experts (SMEs) met typically from one to two hours.

SMEs agreed on the key accountabilities of the job, which they obtained largely from job descriptions. Next, the key accountabilities were given a weight based on their importance and the typical time spent doing them during the year. These weights added up to 100 percent, as each of these accountabilities for an instructor show:

- accountability A, 44 percent
  — instructs and facilitates training programs
  — facilitates meetings or processes
  — provides recommendations to self-directed work teams.
- accountability B, 32 percent
  — serves as liaison for various training groups
  — provides consultation to line management.
- accountability C, 24 percent
  — serves as project manager for various activities
  — serves on committees, prepares brief presentations, and the like.

We had SMEs use an estimation procedure (called the Casio-Ramos estimation procedure) to get more accurate weights. Employees picked the highest weighted accountability and gave it 100 points. Every other accountability was then compared and given a lesser number of points. For example, an accountability that is only half as important was given 50 points.

Finally, the SMEs identified the critical skills for each key accountability. We suggested that the SMEs limit themselves to the most critical skills and try not to exceed seven to 10 skills for each accountability. They selected the skills from a list of both soft and technical skills that had been modified before the meeting to include technical skills that are important for ComEd and for the Personnel Development Training Organization specifically. SMEs suggested additional skills that were added to the list. Following were the critical skills on the list for accountability A:

- managing time
- listening
- knowing how to learn
- training needs analysis
- adult learning theory

- formal presentations
- speaking with others one on one
- motivating others
- decision making.

Accountability A had a weight of 44 percent for the nine skills, for a 4.88 percent weight per skill.

Step 2: Assess Employees

Step 2 is employee assessment. We could have used a variety of assessment approaches such as written tests to assess reading and math and other basic skills and exercises to assess the interpersonal skills required for the jobs covered in this study. The most viable choices for this and most similar studies, however, are ratings by self and others—we used self and manager ratings—that cover a broad range of skills. There is good evidence that these ratings are quite accurate if raters have adequate orientation or training, or both.

We used a five-point rating scale—beginner, novice, skilled, advanced, and expert—with a generic definition next to each term. The definition for "novice," for example, was, "I am able to perform simple job tasks requiring this skill without assistance. I require assistance to perform moderate or complex tasks requiring this skill."

Skill assessment questionnaires were completed separately by employees and managers, and both perspectives were weighted equally. There are other good approaches. In a different pilot study we conducted in a division, the manager and employee first gave their own ratings and then were brought together to discuss them and come to agreement on ratings.

Step 3: Calculate Gaps and Costs

We identified employee skill gaps and then estimated the cost of the gaps in terms of lost performance. Although we used special software designed for this purpose, these calculations can be performed by a wide variety of software programs readily available in most organizations.

We began by estimating the value (annual contribution) of employees in the study. That is, if Chris Smith was 100 percent proficient at his job, what would his worth be? We made an assumption that at a minimum, the value is the cost of his wages and benefits, a value that is set by the free market. No company will be profitable if employees do not produce value that is at least equal to salary and benefits. Therefore, the value of an employee making $21,500 a year and receiving a typical benefits package (about 40 percent of salary, or $8,600 in this case) could very conservatively be estimated at about $30,000 per year.

Other organizations may want to follow a less conservative approach. For example, value could be estimated as sales per employee. In this case, a company that grosses $10 million per year and has 100 employees would have an average employee value of $100,000. There are a lot of ways to estimate employee values; we chose an approach that makes sense to the customers of our study.

Rather than calculate the value of each employee, we simplified the process by using the median of employees' pay range to establish their value. Therefore, we set three levels, one for each group of employees in the study: professional, supervisory, and middle management. The value of the middle-management job was set at almost double that of the professional level, which means that a deficiency in an employee in middle management is going to receive considerably more weight than a deficiency of an employee two levels below.

To increase its value as a good measure of training need, we calculate "skill gap" differently than is typically done. Traditionally, a skill gap has been calculated as "2" if a person is rated 3 out of a potential 5. However, two skill gaps of 2 have very different significance if one skill is highly critical and the other is not. Therefore, we calculate a percentage skill gap that reflects the traditional rating scale gap plus the importance of the skill to the job. Then, we use the dollar value of the job to calculate the dollar impact of a skill gap.

The first step for calculating a skill gap, identifying the importance of a skill, appeared in step 1 where each of the skills supporting this accountability had been given an initial weight of 4.88 percent. If a skill, say managing time, is also critical for other accountabilities, it will receive additional weight. Although this approach gives us a good first approximation of skill weight, we ask the SMEs to look at the estimates and to identify those weights that need to be raised or lowered.

Our second step for calculating a skill gap is the traditional one: calculating the difference between an employee's skill level and the optimum skill level (a "3" on a 5-point scale leaves a gap of 2). Because we had two raters (self and manager) and because we value the ratings equally, we averaged them to arrive at the appropriate employee rating. However, is a skill gap of 2 twice as important as a skill gap of 1? Based on our rating scale and training objectives, we didn't think so. We used the following scale that gives greater weight to skill gaps of employees at the lower end of the scale:

1 = beginner = 5 percent proficiency   4 = advanced = 85 percent proficiency

2 = novice   = 25 percent proficiency   5 = expert   = 100 percent proficiency

3 = skilled   = 50 percent proficiency

Therefore, a rating of "3" translates into a 50 percent skill gap, but a rating of "4" is only a 15 percent gap.

At this point, we can calculate the cost (significance) of a skill gap, as the following equation shows. First a value is determined for the contribution of the skill to the job. Then, the skill gap (for example, 50 percent) is multiplied by the skill value to determine the cost of the skill gap. Assume the following:

- Salary and benefits = $100,000
- Formal presentations have a 4.8 percent weight.
- Chris Smith is rated a "3" on formal presentations, equal to 50 percent proficiency.

The calculations follow:

$$\$100,000 \times 4.8\% = \$4,800 \text{ (the skill value for a fully qualified employee)}$$
$$\$4,800 \times 50\% \text{ rating} = \$2,400 \text{ (the size of the gap from the optimum)}$$

Step 4: Evaluate Training Programs

We evaluated training programs by skills taught and cost of training. Training programs can teach one or several skills from our skills list. The budgeting course, for example, was rated as teaching two skills on our skills list: developing budgets (4) and profit and loss statement use (2). The "4" reflects that most participants leave the course with an advanced skill to develop budgets, and the "2" reflects that the course will only bring participants to a novice level on using profit and loss statements. These are the same levels used to assess employees in step 2.

For this study, we relied on instructors and course designers to tell us the skills and levels of training programs. Feedback we received from some program participants suggested that we should also collect training program ratings from them, preferably within a few months after they completed the training. At that time, they would be in a good position to accurately evaluate how much a particular training program really helped them do their job.

We also estimated the costs of each course. From that, a per-head cost could be easily determined. To arrive at a cost, we considered the following:

- program length
- maximum and minimum number of participants
- design cost (for new program)
- instructor costs per program
- facility costs per program

- material costs per student
- variable costs per day (meals, hotel, travel, and the like)
- lost productivity costs.

Program length multiplied by daily employee value allowed us to estimate lost productivity due to employees being in training instead of at work. In most cases, this is likely to be the largest cost.

Step 5: Calculate ROI and Select Optimum Training

With training program benefits and costs, we had all the information we needed to calculate an ROI forecast and select a curriculum that would optimize ROI of training.

To arrive at a total benefit and a total cost for a group of employees, we added individual data. Costs and benefits may vary for each individual. For example, program costs will vary per person if the cost of lost productivity during training is considered. Costs also vary with the number of people in the class because there are certain fixed costs regardless of how many people attend. Benefits vary based on the size of an employee's gap as well as the importance of the skill to his job and his job to the organization.

Using Chris Smith again, here is how we forecasted the costs of a problem-solving and decision-making course for him:

development	$ 1,000
facilities cost	$ 200
sets of course materials	$ 200
instructor costs	$ 600
food costs	$ 200
cost of time away from work	$12,000
total costs for 15 participants	$14,200
per person costs	$ 950

The proficiency at the end of the course was expected to be advanced, or 80 percent proficient. Because we had 15 persons who would be good candidates for the course, we divided the total costs by 15 to arrive at an average course cost of $950.

We also forecasted the benefits of a decision-making program for Chris. Before training, Chris was rated at a "3" (fully competent) or 50 percent of optimum. Based on our experience with this course, it was estimated that Chris would be at a "4" (advanced) or 80 percent level, for a 30 percent improvement after taking Decision Making 101. We had already estimated the value of decision making for Chris's job in step 3, so it was easy to calculate that the estimated value of a 30 percent improvement was about $1,500: (If Chris were 100 percent proficient, the value would be $5,000.) We calculated the following:

Benefit = gain in proficiency

Proficiency after training = 80% x $5,000 = $4,000

Proficiency before training = 50% x $5,000 = $2,500

Benefit = $4,000 - $2,500 = $1,500

An ROI calculation for Chris Smith follows:

$$\text{ROI} = \frac{[(80\% \times \$5,000) - (50\% \times \$5,000)] \times 100}{\$950}$$

Benefit = $1,500 Cost = $ 950

This is the standard ROI calculation. The numerator is benefits minus costs. The denominator is costs. The numerator is divided by the denominator, and this result is multiplied by 100. To calculate ROI for our group of 22 employees, we added the individual benefits.

The return on the $950 investment is $1,500. The net gain is $550, and the return-on-investment is 57 percent. Is this a good training investment?

Although the 57 percent ROI that we project Chris Smith would get from taking Decision Making 101 appears to be a good return, that doesn't mean that we should make this investment. Once we have investigated the other possibilities, we might find that there are some 100 percent or 200 percent ROI investments available. We may have many employees that would get twice as big a benefit as Chris. And, we may have other courses for Chris that would provide a higher return. One of the key advantages of ROI forecasting is that it helps us find the best training investments, not just the good ones.

Our next step was to find the best courses for our available training dollars. For the purposes of this study, we set a hypothetical budget of $25,000 for the 22 professional positions in PD. We wanted to know how we could best spend that money and what the benefits would be. We also decided for this pilot that when calculating training program costs, we would not consider lost productivity due to being in training rather than on one's job.

Based on one of the skill gaps we had identified in step 3, we chose 11 training programs from the PD curriculum that we felt might be useful. Then we calculated the expected ROI for each and received these results:

total budget	$25,000
total cost of curriculum	$11,883
performance benefit	$50,720
ROI	326.8%
number of courses with positive ROI	6
average cost per trainee	$ 304
average benefit per trainee	$ 1,299
average cost per program	$ 1,697
average benefit per program	$ 7,245

These results show that only six of the 11 courses we had considered showed a positive ROI. Therefore, we would only be able to spend about $11,800 wisely, using the remainder from the $25,000 some other way. The ROI we calculated was about 327 percent. We selected the following courses, shown with the cost, benefit, and number trained. As the figures show, training for even one person may have a positive return-on-investment:

Course	Cost	Benefit	No. trained
Problem Solving and Decision Making	$4,800	$27,023	16
Situational Leadership	$ 173	$ 744	1
Interpersonal Management Skills	$3,200	$11,975	8
Successful Presentations	$2,780	$ 8,470	8
Managing Conflict	$ 420	$ 1,140	5
Budgeting	$ 510	$ 1,368	1

We could have achieved a higher forecasted ROI and used more of the available budget if we considered more training programs, including some from external vendors.

Linking ROI Forecasts to ROI Evaluations

The ROI forecasting approach we have described easily lends itself to Level 3 and Level 4 evaluations because employee assessment data that are collected initially to help make a forecast serve as a pretest. Presuming that employee assessments are repeated on a regular basis, each assessment after the first becomes a posttest for the previous assessment. Also, persons that took training can be compared to a matched group of those that didn't.

If Level 3 evaluations are the focus, then employee assessments should be worded to ensure that employees are evaluated on whether they demonstrate a skill rather than on whether they have the skill. This perspective is consistent with the notion of performance consulting whereby HRD professionals concern themselves with performance gaps whether they are due to skill deficiencies or other factors.

To facilitate rigorous Level 4 evaluations, a few more changes may be desirable. The focus of the job analysis, as shown in step 1, changes from job tasks to job outcomes. Also, some practitioners may wish to define training benefits as a performance change on an outcome such as sales and time expended. However, with the current emphasis on competency development, other practitioners may be quite comfortable with our approach of using changes in employee value as the benefit gained.

Conclusion

With several pilot studies successfully completed, a project has been initiated in one of ComEd's divisions for more than 500 management personnel. The job analysis approach is being used to validate a competency model for the division and to identify the most critical competencies for each management job. A competency-based pay system is being implemented, and the demand for training is expected to soar well beyond the current high levels. ROI forecasting will help us identify the highest priority training with the most value for ComEd and individuals.

We believe that ROI forecasting holds great promise. The data provided are a great aid for complex training decisions. Certainly the demand for wise use of training resources will continue to increase. ROI forecasting allows training professionals to give top value to their clients, and that is truly our mission.

Questions for Discussion

1. What is ROI forecasting? What are the benefits?
2. The ROI forecasting approach described here relies primarily on three sets of data: critical skills and their weights for each position, employee assessments on critical skills, and evaluation of training that has an impact on critical skills. Why is it important to use all three? What would be lost without identification of critical skills? The employee assessment? Training evaluations?
3. What is the basis of the authors' argument that allocating training resources wisely is a much more difficult task than is initially apparent?
4. What is the method used to convert the potential benefit to monetary value? Is the estimate of benefits "conservative"? Why or why not?
5. How might this ROI forecasting approach be used as a basis for a competency-based pay system?
6. As a consultant on this project, how might you go about strengthening this forecasting methodology?

The Authors

Jim Graber, Ph.D., is an industrial/organizational psychologist. He consults, teaches, and writes in the following specialties: training needs analysis; training evaluation, performance management/performance appraisal; compensation; and employee selection and testing. He has completed work for private- and public-sector organizations such as Digital Equipment, United Airlines, AT&T, Commonwealth Edison, Rand McNally, the City of Chicago, and the various federal agencies including the Department of Defense, Office of Personnel Management, the Federal Aviation Administration, and the Environmental Protection Agency. Jim Graber has taught most recently at the University of Illinois at Chicago, and formerly at Northwestern and Roosevelt universities. He writes articles for a variety of publications and speaks frequently to local and national groups. Graber's work is currently focused on improving ROI forecasting techniques and the development of software to assist with ROI forecasts and evaluations. Jim Graber can be contacted at 5807 North Whipple Street, Chicago, IL 60659.

Gerry Post is supervisor of training and development with Commonwealth Edison (ComEd) with responsibility for a broad range of management development opportunities for all its divisions. Post specializes in accelerated learning and presentation techniques and is a sought-after frequent speaker at training conferences. Post recently completed several trips to Poland to train Polish utility officials in leadership and management techniques. Post is currently completing work on an Ed.D. degree in education from Northern Illinois University.

Rick Erwin is a development leader with ComEd, Fossil Division, with responsibility for executive and management education, training needs analysis and assessment, and evaluation. Erwin has taken the lead role in spearheading the development of world-class ROI forecasting and evaluation for ComEd and is currently involved in the development of ROI evaluation software.

References

Phillips, Jack, "Measuring the Return on Investment in Training and Development," two-day seminar in Nashville, TN, October 1995.

Swanson, R.A., and D.B. Gradous. *Forecasting Financial Benefits of Human Resource Development*. San Francisco: Jossey-Bass, 1988.

A Preprogram ROI for Machine Operator Training

Canadian Valve Company

Tim Renaud and Jack J. Phillips

Before funds can be allocated for major training programs, management sometimes needs information on the forecasted return-on-investment (ROI). In this case, which involves the training of machine operators, the proposed program included significant capital expenditures and the creation of a training facility. Prior to pursuing the project, an ROI was developed using a small-scale pilot effort. The ROI was developed using methods typically reserved for postprogram evaluation. The results of the process can apply to almost any type of setting in which a major training expenditure is under consideration.

Background

Canadian Valve Company (CVC) has enjoyed a long and profitable history as a family-owned business, serving the international industrial valve market. CVC machines, polishes, and assembles valves to be shipped to the worldwide market from several strategically located plants. The company has enjoyed tremendous growth in recent years, much of it in foreign markets.

The company's growth and persistent employee turnover have always left a critical need for new machine operators. Unfortunately, the skilled labor market was unable to adequately supply trained machine operators, and CVC had to develop its own training program. Machine operators work various equipment including lathes, drill presses, and

This case was prepared to serve as a basis for discussion rather than to illustrate either effective or ineffective administrative and management practices. All names, dates, places, and organizations have been disguised at the request of the author or organization.

milling machines. New employees recruited for the machining area were usually untrained, inexperienced operators who received on-the-job training by their supervisors using the regular production equipment. This approach had created problems because new trainees were not productive during initial employment, and production machines were virtually out of service during training. Production management considered the traditional on-the-job training methods not very effective, and the training time to prepare new operators appeared excessive. In addition, the problems of high scrap and excessive machine downtime were often by-products of ineffective initial training provided to new employees. Too often a new machine operator, in the midst of frustration, left the company and became a turnover statistic.

The production division, led by Bob Merkle, was concerned about the approach to training and wanted some changes. The human resources manager, Jim Gates, thought that a separate area for training was needed along with a comprehensive training program. In an initial conversation, Merkle concluded that a structured training program taught by an experienced instructor away from the pressures of production should reduce costs, increase productivity, and improve the training process. Jim Gates saw an excellent opportunity to make a significant impact with training, and he wanted to use the resources of the Ontario Training and Adjustment Board (OTAB).

Jim Gates and the Opportunity

A 10-year employee with Canadian Valve, Jim Gates had worked in production before taking on the job of human resource development manager. He understood the company's business and was anxious to help the company solve problems. He had earned an excellent reputation for producing effective programs and saw the comprehensive program to train new machine operators as an excellent opportunity to show the benefits of training and boost his own career opportunities at CVC. He was becoming convinced that if there was any area of training and development in which a cost-benefit analysis could be forecasted, it would be with the machine operator training and he was very interested in pursuing this project.

Bob Merkle and the Challenge

A task-oriented production manager with an engineering degree, Bob Merkle joined CVC as a management trainee 20 years earlier and progressed to vice president of production. Most of his job assignments were in the production area. He was very concerned about the bottom line and took great pride in his cost-control methods and strategies to improve efficiency.

In all his years in production, Merkle was never completely convinced that training was worth the time and effort. He had supported it primarily because the president had a strong commitment to training and development. Although his employees had always participated in programs, both on and off the job, he was skeptical of the results they produced. He felt training was best accomplished on the job by the immediate supervisor.

In recent months, however, his own production supervisors had complained about the approach to training new machine operators and the problems that new recruits created for the various departments. The production supervisors wanted to hire experienced operators and often could not understand why they were not available. The employment office had tried unsuccessfully to find experienced machine operators, using a variety of recruiting strategies. The production departments had to settle with unstructured on-the-job training with inexperienced operators.

Gates had initially approached Bob Merkle about the idea of a separate training area utilizing off-the-job training. On a pilot basis, they borrowed a production machine from one department and prepared it for training. A relief supervisor was assigned the task of training new recruits. Gates and the supervisors were pleased with the experimental effort and the reaction from the union was positive. Consequently, they took the proposal to Merkle to consider establishing a comprehensive training program.

The Project

After listening to the initial proposal from Gates, Merkle seemed to be interested in pursuing the process. Finally he said to Gates, "Jim, prepare a detailed analysis of the savings that this new approach to training would generate. Contact the Ontario Training and Adjustment Board to see if funding assistance is available to help with this type of program. Be sure to include a labor representative on your team. Calculate the benefits of this approach in terms of an expected return-on-investment. Based on the analysis we will go forward with it." Merkle knew the president would support the project if the payback were sufficient.

Gates was pleased with the assignment and added, "This is an excellent project. We know we can deliver a top-notch training program that we all can be proud of, and one that will bring significant improvements. With the help OTAB, we will complete the task and have the full proposal in two weeks." Gates assembled a task force to work on the project.

A major issue in developing the program was the question of where the training should take place. The task force concluded that training should take place out of the production environment where the trainee could learn under the close supervision of a professional instructor who was experienced with all the machines. As a result, Gates explored the possibility of locating a separate area in a remote section of the main production area. In his view, this assignment had three major tasks:

1. Develop a complete training plan detailing the type of training, program duration, training outlines, training structure, and training organization.
2. Design a preliminary layout of the area planned for training and determine how to procure machines for training.
3. Estimate the expected benefits and costs for the proposed program.

Although challenging, the tasks were feasible and could be completed in about two weeks. Gates was very excited about this opportunity.

John McIntosh

Gates contacted John McIntosh, a consultant for the Ontario Skills Development Office (OSDO), who was assigned to a local college near Canadian Valve's main location. McIntosh provides training and development consulting services to local clients from this location. Having worked in a variety of training and manufacturing companies before joining the OSDO program, he is always eager to help his clients with training plans. Because of the sheer number of clients, however, he was limited with the amount of time he could spend with them to develop a cost-benefit analysis (CBA).

Program Benefits

Although small in scale, the experimental pilot project revealed surprising results. Trainees were able to reach target levels of productivity much faster than expected, and their error rates were much lower than anticipated. In addition, the trainees seemed to be more satisfied with their jobs. In a brief meeting with McIntosh, Gates and his staff identified several areas for potential cost savings. Most of these were developed after an analysis of the performance of the employees in the pilot training program when compared to the performance of the employees who had not participated in the training. Gates and McIntosh decided that they would drive the project evaluation with several important performance improvement measures. Other benefits could be identified as additional reasons for moving forward with the project. They expected improvements in productivity, scrap rates, safety, and maintenance expense. Other benefits were not so obvious. Previously, trainees had become frustrated when supervisors did not have time to work with them on a one-on-one basis to develop skills. The frustration led to a turnover statistic. The following performance measurements were isolated:

- reduction in time to reach a standard proficiency level (training time)
- improvement in the scrap rate for new employees
- improvement in the employee safety record (first-aid injuries)
- reduction in equipment maintenance expense
- reduction in turnover of new employees.

These tangible benefits were to be used in the analysis. Gates and McIntosh could see other benefits. Low tolerance production could be performed in the training area as practice work for the trainees. Limited small-scale research and development projects could also be performed there. Although these benefits would be monitored, there would be no attempt to place a monetary value on them. They would be listed as intangible benefits.

Employees in training make mistakes and sometimes do not meet with friendly responses from their supervisors, so they were always frustrated during their initial stages of employment. This training program, if implemented properly, should improve employee attitudes and morale. Another benefit was improved absenteeism. When employees are frustrated and having difficulty on a job, they sometimes remove themselves from the frustration and take a day off. The anxiety or frustration may cause problems, leaving employees thinking they are actually sick when they are not. Finally, another advantage is a reduction in training responsibility for supervisors. With an influx of new employees in the shop, many supervisors have complained that they do not have time to train them. Consequently, they neglect other duties. This new approach to training should free supervisors to perform what they do best—plan and coordinate the work of machine operators and keep them motivated. Because of the difficulty of measuring these additional intangible benefits, Gates decided not to use them in calculations of cost savings. Instead, he would rely on the improvements in the five tangible measurement factors listed earlier.

Converting Data to Values

One of the most difficult tasks in completing an ROI evaluation is estimating the expected benefits from the program. This calculation is more difficult to do than a postprogram evaluation where the results can be compared to a before-and-after situation. With this assignment, Gates had to estimate the benefits, relying on two sources of information. First, the pilot program, which was conducted earlier, presented some measurable improvements, and this information was used in each of the five tangible benefit areas. As part of the analysis of the pilot results, Gates asked the relief supervisor, who was responsible for the training, and his department manager if there had been other actors that contributed to the results. The answer was negative.

Next, Gates and McIntosh consulted with production supervisors who were involved in early discussions of the concept of the program. In a focus group format, they discussed the benefits of the new approach to training and provided estimates of the extent of improvements that could be achieved. When combined, these two approaches formed the basis for estimating the potential improvements that would be relayed directly to the new approach to training.

Training Time

As a standard practice, supervisors recorded the production shortfall with new employees until they reached the standard rate for a machine. These losses were essentially lost production as a result of trainees taking time allowed to learn to operate a machine at a standard rate. Company records indicated that more than $65,000 was charged to trainee losses in the machining areas during the previous years. The pilot program showed a 64 percent reduction, and the supervisors estimated that trainee losses could be reduced by 50 percent with a structured training program in a separate area. The lower value was used, resulting in a projected savings of $33,000. (Note that all dollars are in Canadian funds.)

Machining Scrap

Although many factors contribute to machining scrap, one of the biggest factors is lack of training with new and inexperienced operators. The supervisors estimated that there could be at least a 10 percent reduction in total scrap costs with the new training program. To be conservative, the lower value was used. In machining areas the annual cost of scrap was $450,000 for all product lines. A 10 percent reduction results in a $45,000 savings. This figure was significant because the potential for scrap reduction was high. Management felt that the estimate was conservative.

Turnover

The turnover rate in the machining area was eight employees per month. Because of the smaller numbers of employees involved in the pilot program, turnover reduction data were inconclusive. The supervisors felt that a significant percentage of this turnover was directly related to ineffective or insufficient training, or both, and they estimated that a new approach to training could reduce this turnover rate by at least 30 percent. This value was used in the analysis. The turnover of eight employees per month translates into 96 employees per year. The estimated cost to recruit and train a new employee was $4,000, representing a total annual cost of $384,000. A 30 percent savings is $115,200.

This estimate was considered conservative. The $4,000 cost to recruit, employ, and train a new employee includes unproductive time in the first week of employment. On the average, new employees who left the company during the training program worked longer than one week. Therefore, the cost to the company was probably greater than $4,000 because some lost production occurred after the first week.

Safety

Most of the accidents in the machining area were not lost-time injuries, but were first aid injuries that were treated in the company's medical facility. First-aid injuries were used in the analysis. The pilot program reflected a 25 percent reduction. The supervisors estimated that accidents could be reduced by 30 percent with an effective training program that emphasized safety practices. The number of first-aid injuries in the machining area was averaging 86 per year with the majority of them involving new employees. The total cost in a year for these accidents (including outside medical costs, workers' compensation, and first aid) was $57,000. The 25 percent value was used, resulting in an annual cost savings of $14,250.

Maintenance Expense

Effective training of new employees should result in less maintenance required on production machines. A part of the current, unscheduled machine downtime is caused by new employees improperly operating equipment during their training period. The pilot program showed a dramatic reduction of 45 percent. However, the supervisors estimated that the unscheduled maintenance expense could be reduced by 10 percent each year with the implementation of the training program. The lower value was used. The annual unscheduled maintenance costs for the machining areas were $975,000. The annual savings would be $97,500. This estimate was considered to be very conservative.

Savings Summary

The total projected annual savings are as follows:

		Pilot Results ($)	Supervisor Estimate ($)
Training time		41,600	33,000 ✓
Machining scrap		76,500	45,000 ✓
Turnover		N/A	115,200 ✓
Accidents		14,290	14,250 ✓
Maintenance expense		438,750	97,500 ✓
	Total	571,100	304,950

The values with the check (✓) were used in the benefits calculation, resulting in a total of $304,950. To ensure that top management bought into the process, Gates and McIntosh reviewed the benefits analysis and the assumptions, including the logic, with all the supervisors and the managers in the machining area. Collectively, they felt the estimates were conservative and supported the projected cost savings.

Program Costs

The cost for the proposed program involved the acquisition of the necessary equipment, the salaries and expenses of two instructors, and the additional administrative overhead expenses connected with the training program. The most efficient approach was to utilize space in a remote, currently unused part of the plant. A nominal rent of $10,000 per year was to be charged to the project. The initial program development cost was estimated to be $15,000. This amount was spread over two years. The equipment cost was less than expected. Most of the equipment planned for the new facility was surplus equipment from the production line that was modified and reconditioned for use in training. The total equipment cost was estimated to be $95,000. This figure included $7,000 initial installation expenses. The cost included the equipment for staffing two cubicles for the instructors and providing them with various training aids, including overhead projectors. This investment was prorated over a five-year period.

The salaries of two instructors plus benefits and expenses were estimated to be $80,000 per year. The overhead costs, which include normal maintenance, were estimated to be $15,000 each year. The total annualized costs are as follows:

equipment (prorated)	$19,000
space (rental)	10,000
program development (prorated)	7,500
instructors	80,000
maintenance	15,000
	$131,500

Although there may be other costs, Gates and McIntosh thought that these were the most significant costs and covered what would be necessary in the proposal. As with the benefits, cost figures were reviewed with production managers as well as the finance and accounting staff to ensure that there was complete support for the numbers. With minor adjustments, they were ready to move forward and calculate the return.

As part of the funding assistance available from OTAB, a reimbursement of one-third of the development costs and instructor costs was available. However, to ensure that the costs are fully loaded, this reimbursement was not considered in the analysis.

Calculating the Expected Return

A comparison of the costs with the savings yields the following calculations. The benefit-cost ratio (BCR) is

$$BCR = \frac{304,950}{131,500} = 2.3\%$$

The first-year net savings are as follows:

annual gross savings	$304,950
less program costs	131,950
net savings	173,450

The expected ROI for the first year is

$$\text{ROI (\%)} = \frac{173{,}450}{131{,}500} \times 100 = 132\%$$

The investment in the equipment and the program development spread over several years (five years and two years, respectively). This approach assumes a useful life of five years for the building, equipment, and program development.

This estimate of BCR and ROI seemed to be a little high but was expected in this case. Gates attributed high value of this ratio to the following reasons:

- The equipment costs were low, using the salvage value plus costs for reconditioning. New equipment would cost much more but have a longer useful life.
- There was no additional investment in a new facility, which would have added significantly to the start-up costs.
- However, several items make a case for the BCR and the ROI to be undervalued: The cost savings were probably understated because the lower value was used when two values were available. Pilot program results were usually greater.
- The reimbursement of a portion of the costs from OTAB was not considered in the analysis. Thus, the actual project costs are overstated.
- The potential monetary benefits from the intangible measures could add to the cost savings.

Presentation

With calculations developed, the project was ready for presentation. The training program details had been designed with input from production supervisors and the training staff. Both Gates and McIntosh contributed to the final arrangement for the proposal. The engineering department assisted in the layout and work flow. Gates set up a meeting with Merkle and the production managers and presented the proposal in the following order:

- program design

- equipment procurement and layout
- program benefits
- costs
- expected return-on-investment and cost-benefit analysis
- intangible benefits.

Although there were a few questions, the methodology, assumptions, and calculation were fully supported. The managers were particularly impressed with the conservative approach used in the analysis and the involvement of the supervisors. The project was approved in the meeting.

As Gates left the meeting, he felt a great sense of accomplishment in demonstrating the potential benefits of training on a forecasted basis. He knew that now the challenge was up to his group to show that the project would realize the benefits forecasted. He would use a comprehensive measurement system to track the performance measures used to estimate cost savings and would report on results in six months.

Questions for Discussion

1. How credible is the process? Explain.
2. Without the information from the pilot program, could the ROI be forecasted? Explain.
3. How would you critique the methods used in converting data to monetary values?
4. An important part of any ROI calculation is to account for other factors. Which may influence output measures? How is this issue addressed in this case?
5. Are the projected costs for the program reasonable? Explain.
6. How realistic are the values for BCR and ROI. Explain.
7. How helpful is the role of OTAB in this process?
8. How important are the intangible benefits? Could other intangible benefits be identified? Should they be converted to monetary benefits?

The Authors

Timothy P. Renaud, P.Eng., B.A.Sc., is the principal consultant at Training & Education Strategies. He received his engineering undergraduate degree from the University of Waterloo in 1981.

Specific areas of expertise include training and consulting on how to build and implement quality management systems that meet the ISO 9000 series of standards. In addition, his work has involved numerous customer improvement efforts to reduce error rates and cycle times. Building and installing training management systems is also a service offered to clients. Renaud is also a consulting associate with Performance Resources Organization.

Association memberships include the American Society for Quality Control (ASQC) and the Professional Engineers Ontario. Tim Renaud may be contacted at Training & Education Strategies, 5 Darby Road, Guelph, Ontario, Canada N1K 1R4, or by e-mail at trenaud@qualityservice.com.

Jack J. Phillips has had 27 years of corporate experience in five industries (aerospace, textiles, metals, construction materials, and banking). He has served as training and development manager at two Fortune 500 firms, senior human resource officer at two firms, and president of a regional federal savings bank. He has also served on the management faculty of a major state university. In 1992, he founded Performance Resources Organization, an international consulting firm that specializes in human resources accountability programs. He consults with clients in manufacturing, service, and government organizations in England, Belgium, South Africa, Mexico, Venezuela, Malaysia, Indonesia, South Korea, Australia, and Singapore as well as in the United States and Canada.

Phillips has been author or editor of *Accountability in Human Resource Management* (1996), *Handbook of Training Evaluation and Measurement Methods* (2d edition, 1991), *Measuring Return on Investment* (volume 1, 1994), *Conducting Needs Assessment* (1995), *The Development of a Human Resource Effectiveness Index* (1988), and *Improving Supervisors Effectiveness* (1985), which won an award from the Society for Human Resource Management. He has also written more than 75 articles for professional, business, and trade publications.

An Information Technology Program Evaluation

NYNEX Corporation

Janet F. Chernick

*This case study describes the evaluation of ALPHA IV, a 62-day informa-
tion technology program for NYNEX telecommunications managers who
support, manage, or market products and services in the information technology arena. Demonstrating the value of any program, especially one that
represents this level of financial commitment, is important to ensure continued funding and support. The results of this evaluation were used in
that effort. The return-on-investment depicted in this case reflects actual
evaluation results; however, the associated numerical calculations cannot
be shown due to the proprietary nature of the information.*

Organizational Profile

NYNEX is a global communications and media corporation that
provides a full range of services in the northeastern United States
and in high-growth markets around the world. The corporation is a
leader in telecommunications, wireless communications, directory
publishing, and video entertainment and information services, according to Nynex's 1995 annual report. Its telecommunications sector employs approximately 60,000 people, of whom 14,000 are in
management.

*This case was prepared to serve as a basis for discussion rather than to illustrate either effective or in-
effective administrative and management practices.*

Background

NYNEX's training and education department has implemented a uniform, systematically applied training evaluation process to provide the organization with information about the quality of the training programs, the level to which they satisfy their customers' needs, and the benefits received from training. Kirkpatrick's (1994) four levels of evaluation are an integral part of the process. Level 1 information is obtained through questionnaires administered at the conclusion of all training programs. Level 2 evaluation is accomplished through learning tests or exercises designed into the training programs. Levels 3 and 4 data are collected on selected programs. Decisions about which programs will be evaluated at these levels are made jointly by the staff members responsible for training evaluation and their clients and stakeholders. The decision to evaluate the ALPHA IV program was part of this systematic evaluation process.

Program Description

The ALPHA IV program is an intensive study in information technology developed for NYNEX managers who are involved in the sale, design, implementation, or support of data communications services or information systems. The program has a marketing focus, highlighting NYNEX customers, costs, and competition. It consists of five 10- or 14-day training modules, spread over a six-month period. The program combines lecture presentations, laboratory exercises, and case studies to emphasize customer applications of the various technologies.

In addition to learning how computers and communications technologies operate and interrelate, participants can expect to graduate from the program knowing how to do the following:
- position NYNEX products/services in the competitive marketplace
- apply the technologies to solve customer problems
- discuss various issues that need to be resolved in data communications.

Success in the program is measured by participants' ability to converse with technical specialists. Oral examinations are given to evaluate each participant's performance in attaining the desired proficiency level.

NYNEX partnered with Hill Associates of Colchester, Vermont, for the design and delivery of the program. Corporate expectations for the program are
- increased data sales

- enhanced sales and customer relationships
- strategic positioning of NYNEX products and services in the marketplace
- application of appropriate technologies to cost-effectively meet customer needs
- improved levels of interdepartmental cooperation.

Evaluation Plan

In April 1995, Charles Sullivan, staff director of NYNEX Training and Education and project manager for the ALPHA IV program, contacted Jan Chernick, associate director responsible for training evaluation, about the possibility of conducting a follow-up evaluation on the ALPHA IV program. Although Level 1 program feedback was consistently very positive, no formal follow-up evaluation had been conducted to determine the program's impact on sales or other results. Cost-control measures, including budget reductions and downsizing, were being experienced in the business and were negatively affecting program enrollment. Sullivan hoped that evaluation results would show significant bottom-line benefits to NYNEX beyond the qualitative, positive comments received from the end-of-program evaluations, and that these benefits could be used to promote enrollment.

Chernick and Sullivan met to develop the evaluation plan, and they developed a series of questions that helped participants identify observable behavior outcomes that could be attributed to attending ALPHA IV.

Another evaluation issue that needed to be addressed was what measurement would be used to calculate return-on-investment (ROI). Because one of the program's goals was to increase data sales, Chernick and Sullivan decided to use data sales as a source of information. However, not all participants were salespeople, so other measures had to be developed to quantify benefits for nonsales job functions. No formal measurements existed to track behavior changes for these functional areas, and it was highly unlikely that any would be initiated. Consequently, Chernick and Sullivan decided to attempt to quantify these behavior changes by identifying time savings attributable to increased work efficiency or quality. Participant estimates of their time savings appeared to be a viable source for this measurement.

The training and education department's standard follow-up evaluation process is survey-driven. Chernick and Sullivan agreed that written surveys would be the best way to collect most of the data. Sullivan also enlisted the aid of the NYNEX marketing staff to obtain sales revenues from corporate reports. Care was taken to ensure the confidentiality so that sales could be tracked without identifying individuals.

Scope of the Evaluation

The newly designed evaluation was administered to the 128 ALPHA IV graduates who had completed the program within the past year. Surveying participants' managers were also considered, but internal reorganization had significantly changed reporting relationships. Consequently, it was highly unlikely that enough participants would have reported to the same manager long enough to collect the data required. NYNEX contracted with Stats & Surveys of Honeoye Falls, New York, to administer the survey, compile the data, analyze the results, and produce the evaluation report.

The evaluation plan called for two measurement components: an impact evaluation of the program's contribution to NYNEX business results and an ROI component.

Impact Component

The survey measured the impact of the program. Impact information obtained included the following:
- satisfaction with the program and its impact on graduates' job performance
- value of the program
- opportunities to apply learning back on the job
- perceptions about the impact of ALPHA IV on career development.

ROI Component

The marketing staff provided sales data to the evaluation staff, who compared the sales revenue before and after ALPHA IV. In addition, the survey asked graduates to indicate changes in work efficiency they had implemented since attending the program. Given that multiple factors influence changes in results (for example, personal sales techniques, incentives, business conditions, and new systems), it was necessary to isolate the effects of ALPHA IV from the other factors that influence results. To isolate the effects of ALPHA IV on these variables, participants estimated the percent of sales or work efficiency changes, if any, that they attributed to their attendance in the program.

Analysis of the Data

Of the 128 surveys distributed, 67 were returned for a 52 percent response rate. Overall evaluation results were very positive. Return-on-investment was calculated to be 1,022 percent, which means that ALPHA IV returned $10.22 for each dollar invested after the program costs have been covered. Respondents whose job functions were sales or sales support gave significantly higher ratings than respondents with other functional responsibilities.

ALPHA IV was found to have a positive impact on job performance as measured by the percent increase in sales that respondents attributed to attending the program. In addition, more than 85 percent of respondents reported that the program improved the efficiency and quality of customer interactions and led to more focused discussions.

Impact Results

Participants used a scale of 1 to 5 (1 being Not Satisfied, Not Valuable, and 5 being Very Satisfied, Great Value, and the like) to rate their satisfaction with the program and its impact on job performance, program value, opportunities to apply learning, and other variables. Table 1 shows responses to these variables.

Almost all the participants surveyed had at least some opportunity to apply what they learned in ALPHA IV on the job; 31 percent said they applied "almost all" of what they learned, and 66 percent said they applied "some" of what they learned. Overall, 87 percent of the respondents said they would recommend the program to others.

ALPHA IV provides training that should facilitate the performance of major work activities. The survey listed these activities and asked respondents to rate how often and how well they performed each one. Frequency and performance ratings for each work activity are shown in table 2.

Cross-tabulation of the data by job function showed that all work activities were performed "occasionally" or "often" by at least 50 percent of the respondents and could be performed "with help" or "by themselves" by at least 60 percent of the respondents. Where there was a statistically significant difference in the results, it was always the sales or sales support job function group that had the higher percentage.

ROI Results

CALCULATING VALUE FOR INCREASED SALES. Forty-four percent of all graduates surveyed said sales was a function of their jobs. Of these, 72

Table 1. Program satisfaction ratings.

Variable	Rating	Percent Respondents
Satisfaction with impact of ALPHA IV on job performance	4,5 satisfied	81%
Value of the program	4,5 valuable	73%
Better prepared to do my job	4,5 agree	84%
Increased my confidence in discussing information technology applications with my customers	4,5 to a great extent	93%
Impact of ALPHA IV on my career development	4,5 positive	62%*

Scale:
1 Not satisfied   2 Fairly satisfied   3 Moderately satisfied   4 Satisfied   5 Very satisfied

* This percent, although considerably lower than the others, was viewed as positive because during the period covered by this evaluation, limited career movement was taking place throughout NYNEX due to workforce reductions resulting from corporate downsizing efforts.

percent said their sales had generally increased (32 percent of the total respondents sampled). These respondents were then asked to estimate the percent of increase in their sales results attributable to attending ALPHA IV. Table 3 shows those responses:

The marketing staff provided sales data for 18 of the program participants, and it consisted of annual sales revenues the year before and the year following their attendance at ALPHA IV. Their combined pre- and postsales gain was 263 percent. The dollar value of this gain was divided by 18 to obtain an average sales gain per graduate. An assumption was made to apply this gain to the number of graduates who said their sales increased (32 percent of the 128 respondents, or 41 graduates). Therefore, the average sales gain was multiplied by 41 to obtain a projected net gain for those who reported increased sales. To isolate the percentage of this gain that people attributed to attending ALPHA IV, the projected net gain was multiplied by 48 percent (the mean in-

Table 2. Frequency and performance ratings.

Frequency of Performance Since Training		Work Activity	Ability to Perform Since Training	
Occasionally	Often		Can Do With Help	Can Do by Myself
34%	63%	a. Actively discuss relevant information technologies	21%	78%
46%	48%	b. Converse comfortably with "technologically sophisticated" customers or internal/external clients	35%	63%
15%	56%	c. Strategically position appropriate NYNEX products and services in the marketplace	15%	64%
30%	49%	d. Apply appropriate technologies to cost effectively meet internal or external customer needs	17%	68%
51%	45%	e. Use information found in trade journals to supplement your knowledge	13%	82%
27%	40%	f. Identify sales opportunities	12%	61%
36%	23%	g. Identify internal opportunities to apply information technology to add value or reduce cost	20%	49%
45%	49%	h. Enhance internal/external customer relationships	17%	76%
22%	33%	i. Close sales	15%	45%

Table 3. Percent of increase in sales results attributable to attending ALPHA IV.

Less Than 25%	25%–49%	50%–74%	75% or More
5%	43%	33%	19%

Mean increase in sales = 48%

crease in sales attributable to attending ALPHA IV, as shown in table 3). This calculation produced a dollar amount that represented the increase in sales revenue people attributed to the program. Shown as a formula, these calculations become:

$$\begin{array}{ccc} \text{average sales gain} & \text{# of graduates who said} & \text{projected net gain in} \\ \text{per graduate} & \text{x} \quad \text{sales increased} & = \quad \text{sales} \end{array}$$

$$\begin{array}{ccc} \text{projected net gain in} & \text{% of gain attributed to} & \text{increase in sales} \\ \text{sales} & \text{x} \quad \text{program} & = \quad \text{revenue attributable} \\ & & \text{to program} \end{array}$$

CALCULATING VALUE FOR INCREASED WORK EFFICIENCY. Graduates were also asked what impact their attendance at ALPHA IV had on efficiency or quality that resulted in time savings, if it had any. Their responses produced a method for isolating the effects of ALPHA IV on work efficiency, as table 4 shows.

Table 4. Impact of ALPHA IV on efficiency or quality resulting in time savings.

Area	Negative Impact	No Impact	Positive Impact
a. More efficient internal/external customer interactions	0%	15%	85%
b. Improved quality of internal/external customer interactions	0%	12%	88%
c. More focused product/application discussions	0%	14%	86%

In each of the three areas, sales and sales support personnel were significantly more likely to report a positive impact than personnel in other job function groups. Respondents who specified a positive impact for any of the three areas involving efficiency or quality were asked to indicate the time savings, on average, that they could attribute to the increased efficiency or quality. When they thought about their response, they were asked to consider examples like amount of time saved on sales calls and amount of time saved on internal or external customer negotiations. Table 5 depicts their responses.

Components used to calculate a value for increased work efficiency were

- mean time savings per week reported by graduates (2.19 hours, as shown in table 5)
- a 45-week work year
- average hourly rate of the participants
- the number of program participants (128).

The formula to calculate net efficiency savings was

$$\text{Net efficiency savings} = P \times AW \times H \times 45$$

where

P = the number of program participants
AW = the average work hours saved per week (2.19)
H = average hourly rate of participants
45 = number of weeks worked per year.

Table 5. Average time savings attributable to increased efficiency or quality.

Time Saved	Percent Respondents
None	4%
30 minutes per week	4%
1 hour per week	16%
2 hours per week	23%
3 hours per week	9%
More than 3 hours per week	11%
I don't know	34%

Mean time savings = 2.19 hours per week

The formula used to calculate the ROI was

$$\text{ROI} = \frac{\text{value of changed performance - costs}}{\text{costs}}$$

Components of value of changed performance were the sales gain attributable to ALPHA plus the net efficiency savings. Cost components were Hill Associates' program costs, student travel expenses, student salary expense while in the program, and program evaluation costs.

Concerns and Lessons Learned

Overall evaluation findings on ALPHA IV were very positive, and therefore, no recommendations were made to change the program. Cross-tabulating the data across work function areas, such as sales versus no-sales positions, produced some interesting differences in the ROI, but most of it was realized by the gain in sales revenue. Work efficiency benefits for those not involved in sales actually produced a negative ROI. Because ALPHA requires 62 days to complete over the course of a year, it is an expensive program for NYNEX, both in tuition costs to Hill Associates in and time off the job for participants.
Evaluation recommendations suggested giving some thought to shortening the program for participants not directly involved in sales or sales-support functions; however, any decision to separate the population based on job function would need to be carefully weighed against the value of having people with mixed work functions in the program, which many respondents specified as a value in their written comments about the program.

A second area of concern was the method used to measure the value of improved work efficiency. The evaluation team felt that this value may have been understated because it reflected only participants' perceptions of their own work efficiencies, and the possibility existed that these efficiencies may also be beneficial to other people's work (for example, internal or external customers or suppliers). Although not specifically measured within the context of the quantifiable data, numerous written comments by participants suggested clear benefits, but neither the client organizations nor the evaluation team could identify a viable way to measure such benefits.

A third area of concern is the high ROI. Julian Puretz, research consultant from Stats & Surveys, suggested that the ROI percent was probably overly inflated because participants' high satisfaction with the ALPHA IV program caused them to overstate the percentages of sales and work efficiencies they attributed to attending it. These percentages were an integral part of the ROI calculation. Puretz referred to this phenomenon as an "attribution error." To control for it, he suggested the ROI percent be reduced when reporting results. He commented, "If you assume a 100 percent overestimate in their judgments, then your ROI is still 511 percent. The difference to your client is a *positive* return versus a *very positive* return!" Both ROI percents were subsequently reported.

Conclusion

This evaluation clearly demonstrates the importance of planning ROI evaluation early in a program's development cycle. Difficulties were encountered articulating behaviors to be measured and then tracking them. Had this been done while the program was being developed, a control group could have been formed to facilitate measurement. In addition, a system could have been developed for tracking costs and sales revenue to make it a more reliable, less cumbersome process.

Questions for Discussion

1. How would you critique the evaluation design and method of data collection?
2. What do you think about the way the effects of the program were isolated?
3. What other ways to obtain quantitative measures could you suggest?
4. What suggestions do you have for obtaining quantifiable measures from others, in particular, managers and customers?
5. What could be done to address the concerns about measuring the value of improved work efficiency?
6. What is your opinion about the credibility of the ROI?
7. Do you think participants' satisfaction with the program biased the results? Why or why not?
8. What would you do differently if you were conducting this evaluation?

The Author

Janet F. Chernick, project director of Black Consulting Associates in Shrewsbury, Massachusetts, is a consultant specializing in training evaluation and instructional design. Formerly with the NYNEX Corporation as an associate director responsible for training evaluation, she had significant training experience at NYNEX, with prior assignments in training development and delivery. She holds a Bachelor of Science degree in business administration from Clark University and a Master of Science degree in training and development from Lesley College. She has published an article on evaluating pilot programs which appeared in *Training & Development*. She can be contacted at Black Consulting Associates, Box 182, Shrewsbury, MA 01545.

Acknowledgments

Jan Chernick would like to thank Jane Perkins, a training evaluation specialist formerly with NYNEX; Charles Sullivan, staff director, NYNEX Training & Education; Julian Puretz, research consultant of Stats & Surveys; and Edward Seager, senior member of the technical staff of Hill Associates for their input and suggestions for this case.

References

Kirkpatrick, D.L. *Evaluating Training Programs*. San Francisco: Berret-Koehler, 1994, pp. 21-26.

Measuring ROI for Negotiation Sales Training

Texas Instruments Systems Group

Herb Graff and Rob Schriver

Negotiation skills is a difficult area to evaluate. This case shows how Texas Instruments has evaluated negotiation skills training. Gathering data with a unique participant survey provided a posttraining picture of return-on-investment based on estimates of money and time saved. The case shows what happens when a company asks for feedback with a one-time study for a 10-year history of three related courses.

Background

The Texas Instruments (TI) Systems Group (SG) is focused on utilizing technology that provides customers with new ways to accomplish their objectives. This group provides radar and navigational systems, missile guidance and suppression systems, avionics, and surveillance technologies. The division's advanced work in defense markets has led to important civilian applications—such as infrared night-vision cameras and wireless communications systems.

Organizational Profile

The networked society offers many opportunities for TI's technology. TI's core competencies are at the heart of the digital revolution. The company has an opportunity to grow rapidly in the next decade because of its good market positioning with products and technologies plus a sound global presence.

This case was prepared to serve as a basis for discussion rather than to illustrate either effective or ineffective administrative and management practices.

The Course Manager

The three negotiation training classes that Herb Graff was responsible for at Texas Instruments (Effective Negotiations I, Effective Negotiations II, and Communicating for Agreement) have received positive Level 1 feedback during his tenure as course manager. However, before Graff's efforts, there had never been any posttraining studies done to show the results or impact of the courses.

Impact Study

On August 9, 1989, Graff met with his manager, Leo Griffith to discuss the status of the three negotiation courses he was delivering and managing: Effective Negotiations I (ENI), Effective Negotiations II (ENII), and Communicating for Agreement (CFA).

They discussed everything from the course content to the average course evaluation scores. With high Level 1 evaluation scores and very positive written comments after each class, they concluded that things were generally going quite well. And yet a number of key issues were raised concerning the curriculum's ability to meet the needs of a myriad of diverse customers, including course participants, training coordinators, production managers, and line supervisors.

At the conclusion of this meeting, Graff decided that some kind of an "impact study" would be helpful to determine if these three courses were, in fact, meeting all of the different customers' needs and ultimately benefiting the corporation. After all, these negotiation courses had been part of the training curriculum for 10 years (since 1979), and to the best of his knowledge, nobody had ever done a follow-up study to determine their real value to past participants specifically or to TI in general.

Graff then developed his approach to this research based on the idea of an internal mail campaign. He reasoned that this would put him in direct contact with current TIers who had participated in any one of the three negotiation courses or in a combination of them. By the time this study was launched, 1,397 people had taken these courses since their introduction, but only 1,260 of them were still TIers; 137 of them had left the company. Graff also felt that this method would be fairly efficient and rather straightforward.

Since time was a critical factor because the bulk of Graff's time was spent delivering courses, he ruled out face-to-face interviews and elaborate telephone interviews. He wanted feedback from all the training coordinators, as well. He felt that their perspective would be unique in that they might be able to see the cumulative effect of all this negotiation training over such a long period of time.

Courses

The System's Group's (formerly Defense Systems and Electronics Group [DSEG]) human resource development (HRD) management and development training branch was responsible for the three courses. Each of these courses was normally offered every other month at TI. The course descriptions and objectives follow:

- Effective Negotiations I (ENI) is a three-day, basic theory and skills course designed for TIers who are directly or indirectly involved with TI's buying or selling functions (namely, sales, purchasing, contracts, marketing, and engineering). It is especially important for those who interface with TI suppliers.

The course objectives are
  — Define "effective" negotiation.
  — Identify and apply key strategies and tactics.
  — Learn how to efficiently and effectively plan for critical negotiations.
  — Identify the traits of successful negotiators.
  — Learn how to effectively negotiate agreements that lead to mutual satisfaction for all parties.

- Effective Negotiations II (ENII) is a three-day, skill-building course designed for TIers involved in buying or selling functions. Effective Negotiations I is a prerequisite. It is also recommended that TIers wait six months after taking ENI before taking ENII. ENII further develops and enhances negotiation skills based on techniques explored in ENI.

The course objectives are
  — Identify and apply the five negotiation stages used during negotiation planning.
  — Effectively negotiate changes to previously agreed upon contracts.
  — Identify and implement advanced tactics and strategies used by successful negotiators.

- Communicating for Agreement is a three-day, introductory course designed for TIers involved in buying and selling functions plus supervisors, managers, and buyers (buyers must have taken Basics of Supervision before attending this class). The course addresses knowledge, skills, and attitudes required for successful negotiations.

- The course objectives are
  — Define "negotiation" and describe its uses and abuses.

— Demonstrate the skills used to negotiate positively to enhance relationships.
— Explain and apply the situational influence model in the negotiation process.
— Identify and analyze influence styles.
— Explain the range of strategies and tactics applied in generating lasting agreements.

The Manager

An 11-year veteran with Texas Instruments, Leo Griffith was manager of the management development training branch of the HRD division. Griffith reported to the director of HRD, who in turn reported to the vice president of human resources in Dallas. Griffith agreed with Graff that he should look at all the negotiation courses. Thereafter, Griffith gave Graff his full support to conduct the study.

Project Tasks

There were 11 steps to follow for obtaining the data for the project:
1. Develop a comprehensive questionnaire and a cover letter explaining the study's purpose.
2. In tandem with the questionnaire, develop worksheets to help sort and organize all the incoming data.
3. Obtain the necessary database from which questionnaire mailing labels could be easily generated.
4. Field test the questionnaire by sending out a test mailing and evaluating the percentage and the quality of the returns.
5. Edit the questionnaire as required based on the results from the test mailing.
6. Once the questionnaire meets all the requirements, send out the remaining questionnaires.
7. After all the questionnaires have been returned (based on the expected percentage as determined by the test mailing), begin sorting and organizing the data using the worksheets.
8. If possible, analyze the data in terms of an actual return-on-investment (ROI) dollar amount for TI. Also, look for other nondollar values that occurred as a result of the training.
9. Consolidate all the data into easily understood tables, charts, and matrices.
10. Write a comprehensive report explaining the result in detail. Especially focus on the value of the training both to the individual participants as well as to TI as a whole.

11. Submit the final report along with recommendations for facing the challenges ahead.

Results

In September 1989, Graff had designed and developed a questionnaire with which he hoped to measure the impact of TI-DSEG's negotiation training on the overall functioning of the organization. Specifically, he wanted to focus on the dollar value of the training versus the total costs incurred. His objective was to determine as accurately as possible TI's actual ROI. As a side issue, Graff also wanted to determine the value of this training beyond the financial issues, by identifying some of the program's intangible benefits. The three negotiation courses continually emphasized the importance of long-term, professional business relationships as well as all the obvious economic variables. Graff felt that there should be some yardstick for that effort.

To test the effectiveness of the questionnaire, 30 questionnaires had been mailed out to active TIers who were past participants of one or more of the negotiation courses. Within three weeks, eight had been returned (26.7 percent). After determining that the questionnaire had, in fact, elicited the kind of data Graff was looking for, the full complement of 1,230 was sent out to active TI employees.

Graff received a total of 318 completed questionnaires (including the eight from the test mailing), representing an overall return rate of 25.9 percent.

Findings

The findings are listed below:
1. On a scale of 1-10 (low impact-high impact), all three courses were rated above the midpoint. The average scores were: ENI=7.13, ENII=7.38, and CFA=6.89.
2. As a result of the HRD negotiation training, 55 percent of the respondents said they saved TI time and money, and 60 percent felt the courses helped them avoid mistakes during negotiations.
3. Of the 318 respondents, 107 felt they could actually quantify their savings and reported saving TI a total of $68,707,050 over the 10-year period, 1979-1989. Subtracting the total costs of all the training over the 10-year period ($2,346,960) yields an additional savings or profit to TI of $66,360,090, for a $28.27 ROI for every dollar TI invested in the negotiation training after the initial investment had been recouped. (See "costs," which follows.)

4. By annualizing the reported amounts of time saved for TI, a total of 5.11 person-years in labor were saved (see "time savings," which follows). Although this would only add an additional $.24 to the $28.27 ROI figure, the greater benefits in overall improved performance and efficiency are still truly valuable (based on labor rates originally used to calculate course costs).

5. In the anecdotal data, respondents repeatedly discussed their improved abilities to avoid costly mistakes during the negotiating process. Although these results were not quantified in this study, they represent a substantial contribution to TI in helping to prevent the loss of proprietary information, unwarranted audits and investigations, and the loss of money that might otherwise have been left "on the table."

6. In the textual data, respondents repeatedly referred to their improved external and internal relationships as a result of the negotiation training. They also felt they were more professional and confident in negotiating on behalf of TI, especially when dealing with sole-source suppliers and international customers. Past participants also discussed their improved abilities to conduct positive, *true* win-win negotiations by having more empathy for the other party (see "participants' comments").

Costs
Following are the costs that TI incurred for the training:
- $1,380 per TIer is calculated for the labor costs
- 1,397 TIers have attend all three of the classes since 1979
- $1,927,860 total labor investment since 1979

plus
- $300 per TIer for course tuition
- 1,397 TIers have attended all three of the classes since 1979
- $419,100 total tuition investment since 1979

equals
- $2,346,960 total investment in the three courses.

Using these figures and the information from the respondents (see table 1), the ROI for the entire population is calculated as follows:

$68,707,050 total reported savings (107 respondents) - $2,346,960 total costs (since 1979)
= $66,360,090 savings or profits

$66,360,090 savings or profits/$2,346,960 total costs x 100 = 2,827 ROI

Table 1. Courses taken versus dollars saved.

Course	Amount	Percent of Total Savings	Average/ Response	Ratio
EN1 (55)	$17,594,350	25.6%	$319,897	1.0:1
EN1 + EN2 (26)	$35,299,000	54.3%	$1,434,577	4.5:1
EN1 + EN2 + CFA (10)	$8,035,000	11.7%	$803,500	2.5:1
EN1 + CFA (9)	$5,640,000	8.2%	$626,667	2.0:1
CFA (7)	$138,700	.2%	$19,814	0.1:1
Total for all courses (107)	**$68,707,050**	**100.0%**	**$642,122**	

This 2,827 percent ROI means that for every dollar TI invested in negotiation training, a $28.27 savings or profit was returned as estimated by the course participants (this, after returning the initial investment of $2,346,960, which was the total cost of all the negotiation training for all participants during the 10-year period, 1979-1989).

Time Savings

Participants indicated time savings in terms of planning, "at the table" negotiations, implementation, and debriefing. Out of a total of 318 respondents, 113 of them listed specific amounts of time saved, as follows:

- 4,383 hours, which translates to a savings of 2.26 person years, based on 1,936 business hours per year
- 46 days, which translates to a savings of .19 person years, based on 242 business days per year
- 14 weeks, which translates to a savings of .29 person years, based on 48.4 business weeks per year
- 26.5 months, which translates to a savings of 2.37 person years, based on 11.2 business months per year.

The total saved amounted to 5.11 person years.

Participants' Comments

In their surveys, many participants described how the courses helped them negotiate on behalf of TI. Following are some of their comments:

> At the time I helped conduct negotiations for material on a program as a manufacturing engineer, and collectively we negotiated a 22 percent decrement ($4.1 million profit) off quotes. Our training was with your Effective Negotiations I. Much of our success is attributed to our training.
>
> I am currently involved in multimillion dollar negotiations with a prime contractor. The [negotiation] training has enabled me to recognize tactics and negotiation behavior which would have escaped me before. I am a more capable representative of TI interests as a result. I feel much more confident in negotiations because I know what behaviors I may be faced with, and have some knowledge of how to deal with them.
>
> I have to do very little direct negotiation for TI. However, this course has been helpful in knowing what not to reveal to an outside supplier or customers which might hinder the negotiations of other TIers.
>
> As a buyer, I try to use what I learned everyday. I negotiate terms, freight, cost, price, delivery, etc., and I have passed along many tips from the course to my fellow buyers.

Some 124 respondents also described mistakes that they felt they had avoided as a result of the training.

Conclusion

These classes were mainly buying- and selling-oriented courses primarily designed for staffs in field sales, contracts, and purchasing as well as for others who deal directly with suppliers. There should be an introductory class coupled with an advanced, or follow-on course.

A relationship and communications-based course to help TIers deal more effectively with their teams and colleagues on a day-to-day basis may also be needed. By understanding the basics of everyday negotiations, TIers would improve their internal relationships as well as professional dealings with those outside the company.

Questions for Discussion

1. What suggestions do you have to improve the approach to this impact study?
2. Do you think that all of TI's costs were included in the cost-benefit analysis?
3. How credible do you think this ROI calculation is for TI management?
4. How accurate do you think the participant data are?
5. What do you see as the critical issues in this case study?

The Authors

Herb Graff is the negotiations training manager at the Texas Instruments Learning Institute in the Systems Group of Texas Instruments in Dallas, Texas. Graff has a master's degree from the University of California at Los Angeles (UCLA) in anthropology. He can be contacted at Texas Instruments, Defense Systems and Electronics Group, 7800 Banner Drive, Mail Station 3928, Dallas, TX 75265.

This case study was developed by Herb Graff. Rob Schriver assisted Graff in the final preparation of the study and the format of the publication. Rob Schriver is a program manager for the Center for Continuing Education at Lockheed Martin Energy Systems in Oak Ridge, Tennessee. Schriver is currently working on his Ph.D. in human resource development at the University of Tennessee.

Training's Contribution to a Major Change Initiative

First Union National Bank

Ronnie D. Stone, Douglas R. Steele,
Debra M. Wallace, and Wesley B. Spurrier

Many organizations are facing significant change that transforms the way in which employees are performing their work. The following case illustrates how the return-on-investment is calculated for an extensive training program for relationship bankers. The program evaluates the impact of training in the face of a variety of other change initiatives, including a reengineering effort implemented prior to the training. The case illustrates one approach to isolate the impact of the various factors contributing to improvement.

Industry Background

Mergers, acquisitions, and the financial demands of customers have continued to increase competitiveness in the banking industry. The commercial banking sector is a highly competitive business dealing in billions of dollars annually. The markets of commercial banks are typically segmented by market size. A commercial bank usually assigns one or more bankers to customers and prospects within each market segment. Commercial bankers are expected to anticipate the needs of their customers and grow relationships and business. They are also expected to prospect and develop new customers in each market segment. This case describes how one commercial bank launched a major change initiative to achieve its strategic objectives. The initiative in-

This case was prepared to serve as a basis for discussion rather than to illustrate either effective or ineffective administrative and management practices.

cluded a strategy to train its bankers to change their approach with customers and prospects and to introduce new investment banking products as solutions for issues facing the customer.

Organization Profile

First Union National Bank (FUNB) operates in 12 states from Connecticut to Key West, Florida. Headquartered in Charlotte, North Carolina, FUNB has 45,000 employees in all phases of banking and assets of $140 billion. The commercial bank, a major business line, has approximately 2,000 employees. The commercial bank serves three market segments—corporate, middle, and commercial. The vision of the commercial bank is to be the best in the financial services industry. Through its Vision 2000 program, the bank intends to be sought by customers and feared by competitors and to be a source of pride for employees.

Reengineering of the Commercial Bank

In July 1993, as part of the commercial bank's Vision 2000, John Georgius, vice chairman of First Union, initiated a reengineering effort. The reengineering was implemented to offer more commercial products and services and to place greater emphasis on partnering with customers to create business solutions. In addition, there was a need to decrease the turnaround time for loan requests. Processes were changed so that relationship managers, relationship sales managers, underwriters, and portfolio managers became members of relationship banking teams, known as deal teams. The incentive program was redesigned to provide incentives to all deal team members to become relationship bankers and financial consultants with everyone focused on meeting the needs of the customer. In 1994, to support the reengineering effort, process training was provided for the bankers. Additionally, Ben Maffitt was named executive vice president of commercial banking, responsible for managing support functions of the commercial bank and driving the desired change.

Reassessing the Organization Change Initiative

Throughout the reengineering effort, several things occurred to convince management that there were additional major issues to be addressed. During the process of reengineering, First Union entered into the capital markets line of business, and management wanted to become more aggressive in cash management sales. With these new services, Ben Maffitt and other members of senior management believed bankers would need to be able to look 24 months into the future to determine their customers' needs. Although the reengineering had changed bankers' positions, incentives, and support processes, it had not changed how they approached and served their customers. Management felt that bankers needed to be able to introduce products in a more consultative way and with a focus on solutions. Ben Maffitt put it best when he said, "We re-engineered their processes, but not their mindsets."

Management made the decision to pursue the possibility of a major training initiative with the expectation that it would result in significant change in how bankers approached their jobs and their customers. Management also realized the desired change in mindset would take 24 months. The time needed for change, combined with the need to anticipate customer needs 24 months into the future, was the genesis of the name Project XXIV. The goals of Project XXIV were to create a bank that is

- proactive, not reactive
- based on relationships, not transactions
- based on solutions, not products
- composed of financial consultants, not vendors
- committed to delivering the bank, not solely credit
- based on the team sale, not the solo sale.

Organization Needs Assessment

During the reengineering process, the commercial bank funded the Commercial College, a section of First University, the bank's training division within human resources. The Commercial College was generally charged with providing learning solutions to improve the performance of commercial bankers. Ben Maffitt charged Doug Steele, director of the Commercial College, with assessing the current situation and identifying the learning gap. The next step was to develop and deliver the necessary intervention to improve performance, or at least begin that process.

Steele initiated a needs assessment to determine the nature and scope of the training needed. The Commercial College staff interviewed members of senior management who served on the Project XXIV Steering Committee, members of the First University Advisory Board, and other bank employees to determine training design needs, barriers to implementation, and other considerations. The results of the needs assessment indicated that bankers did not understand the capital markets products or many of the concepts necessary to become trusted financial consultants and advisors to their customers. At the conclusion of the assessment, a report with recommendations was presented to senior management. To achieve the Project XXIV goals and to enhance the transformation, two training programs—financial consulting and relationship selling skills—were recommended. The aim was to help transform the First Union banker into a financial sales consultant with emphasis on the ability to apply skills and knowledge traditionally employed by investment bankers. Management approved the recommendations and significant resources were committed to developing and implementing the training program to help achieve the goals of the project.

Project XXIV Program Design

Design work on the training project began in January 1994. The management of First Union was confident that the training would pay off. Therefore, the training design included evaluation only at Level 1 (participant reaction) and Level 2 (learning). A return-on-investment (ROI) impact study was not in the initial evaluation plan. First University staff worked with two Boston-based consulting firms—Clarity Advantage Consultants and Brown Performance Group and their principals, Nick Miller and Pam Brown—to design the financial consulting portion of the program. Both of these firms were also primary contributors to the needs assessment process. The financial consulting portion of the program consisted of four courses: CEO [chief executive officer]/CFO [chief financial officer] Experience, Funding Decisions, Capital Investments, and Operating Efficiency.

The financial consulting course was designed to give bankers the "context" for sales calls and the corporate finance tools to support the analytical approach needed to uncover their customers' financial needs. The CEO/CFO Experience was designed to make the banker more aware of the issues CEOs and CFOs faced.

Relationship Selling Skills training was a highly successful sales training program developed by Huthwaite of Purcellville, Virginia. It was designed to provide skills in planning and making face-to-face sales calls and in questioning customers and prospects to obtain information, uncover business problems, and determine benefits and solutions.

Project XXIV Program Implementation

Project XXIV training began in May 1995 with a pilot and concluded in early 1996. About 750 employees were trained in seven states plus the District of Columbia. Area presidents, relationship managers, relationship sales managers, underwriters, and portfolio managers participated. Most of the four financial consulting courses were delivered by faculty from the University of Virginia who were experts in financial products and services. Bankers attended the four courses for six days' over a four-month period.

Relationship Selling Skills was delivered by Clarence Fisher, a Commercial College senior trainer and consultant, and human resource generalists Kevin Hagan and Howard Bush. Managers attended four days of training. During the last two days, they were joined by non-managers. All participants were taught the skills and techniques, but managers also learned a process for coaching their employees.

The ROI Impact Study

In early 1996, discussions Doug Steele held with senior management resulted in the decision to evaluate Project XXIV training. Although Level 1 participant reaction was positive and Level 2 learning satisfactory, management wanted to know how employees were applying what they had learned. Had the mindset reengineering worked? The high cost of the training in terms of dollars and resources and the significant change expected as a result of the training were the impetus behind the evaluation discussion. Senior management was more interested in the behavior change, but Steele persuaded management that an ROI evaluation could also be beneficial and could be determined during the same evaluation study. Because the bank was involved in acquisitions and would soon have to invest in training additional bankers, there was a need to complete the study as quickly as possible.

Joan Coggins, director of learning services for First University, contacted Performance Resources Organization (PRO) to pursue the feasibility of an ROI impact study. The impact study was planned, designed, and implemented with an August 12 deadline. PRO provided support to the staff of First University during the evaluation process.

ROI Planning Meetings

Several planning meetings were conducted around the schedules of the evaluation project team to accomplish the following:
- identify the purpose of the evaluation
- determine the process to be used for the evaluation
- gather appropriate information about the training program, its objectives, and expected on-the-job behavior changes

- identify business performance measures to be influenced by the training and the expected time frame of the influence
- identify the availability and internal sources for business performance data and the possible methods of converting data to a dollar value
- discuss strategies for data collection and isolating the effects of the training
- discuss other factors such as reengineering that could influence business performance improvements
- discuss potential intangible benefits, barriers to training transfer, program costs, and other relevant information
- discuss the target population and logistics of the evaluation.

ROI Process

Because the decision to determine the ROI for Project XXIV training was not made until after the program had been implemented, the process of calculating the ROI was much more difficult. Although the original objectives of the training did not reflect Level 4 business

Figure 1. ROI model.

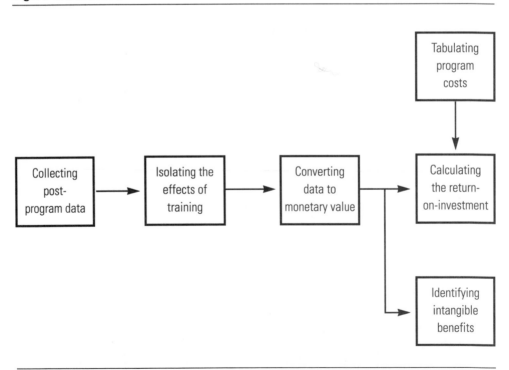

measures, the Commercial College evaluation team was able to identify them. Figure 1 illustrates the process used to evaluate the training.

The Data Collection Plan and ROI Analysis Plan

Before data collection plans could be developed and implemented, it was necessary to determine which group or groups would be used in the analysis. One group, the entire commercial banking group in Virginia, had completed both programs and approximately six months had elapsed since the training. Thus, the time variable became the primary determining factor for selecting the sample group to participate in the study. Fifty-nine Virginia bankers and 33 managers had attended both programs from June through December 1995. This group also had the advantage of being a cohesive unit because it covered one geographical area.

A data collection plan that focused on Level 3 (job application) and Level 4 (business results) measures was developed, as figure 2 shows.

The Level 3 measures were behavior changes and frequency of application linked to the Project XXIV training program objectives. After exploring performance data availability at First Union, the quality of the specific data, and the perceived linkage to Project XXIV training, the following Level 4 measures were targeted by the data collection plan:
- new relationships established
- new business from existing clients
- loan growth
- deposit growth
- increased sales of other products
- increased sales of capital markets products
- sales of cash management services
- improved customer satisfaction
- decreased employee turnover.

The first two data items, "new relationships established" and "new business from existing clients," were ultimately omitted from the analysis because a new process that was installed to collect new business relationships and new business from existing clients had been implemented inconsistently during the desired time frame. In addition, the item "increased sales of other products" was not significant. Thus, the evaluation focused on six Level 4 data items.

Four data collection methods were planned to collect the Level 3 and Level 4 data to determine the success of this program. First, performance monitoring was to gather performance data throughout the

Figure 2. Data collection plan.

Program: First Union National Bank; ROI for Project XXIV   Date: 06-05-96

Evaluation Strategy: Data Collection Plan

Level	Objective(s)	Measures	Data Collection Methods	Timing	Responsibilities
III Job Application	Apply prospecting, selling, and financial consulting skills from Project XXIV training	• Behavior changes • Prospect group utilization	1. Follow-up questionnaire, participant self-assessment	6-9 months	1. and 2. Project XXIV Team
	Customers' solutions	• Skill frequencies • Planning and calling activity	2. Follow-up questionnaire, manager assessment 3. Customer survey		3. Marketing and Project XXIV Team

Figure 2 (continued). Data collection plan.

Level	Objective(s)	Measures	Data Collection Methods	Timing	Responsibilities
IV Business results	Increase sales volume in all areas	• # New relationships • New business from existing clients • Total sales • Loan growth • Deposit growth • Cash management services • Capital market products • Other products and services • Customer performance impact	Performance monitoring of business measures Follow-up questionnaire Customer survey	6-9 months	Project XXIV Team (Looking at output and customer service)

commercial bank to determine business impact. This included routine reports and other performance records. Second, questionnaires were to be developed to obtain information directly from participants regarding the application of the skills and the impact of the program on business measures. The participants were considered to be knowledgeable about the processes and able to provide reliable estimates of their influence on business measures. The challenge was to provide enough questions and details to ensure the accuracy of the process. Third, questionnaires were also used to obtain information from managers concerning the success of the program and its application within the team. Interviews were conducted with a small group of team members and managers from North Carolina. The primary purpose of the interviews was to test the questionnaires and frame additional issues for the questionnaire for both managers and team members.

Finally, through a questionnaire, a sample of customers provided information about changes in the approach and role of the First Union banker. As part of the data collection effort an ROI analysis plan was also developed. The ROI analysis plan outlined

- the methods to be used to convert data to dollar values
- the strategies to be used to isolate the effects of training
- the program cost categories and the means to capture them
- the potential for intangible benefits of the program.

Isolating the Effects of Project XXIV Training

Several factors could contribute to performance improvement. In this case, possible factors were the reengineering effort that preceded Project XXIV training, support of the deal team, incentives, coaching by managers, capital markets liaison assistance, and other training initiatives. It was important, therefore, to determine strategies to isolate the effects of the training. Four strategies were considered: a control group arrangement, trend-line analysis, estimates taken directly from the participants, and estimates taken directly from the managers of participants. The considerations were the following:

- Control groups: Because of the various implementation schedules of Project XXIV training, a control group arrangement was considered. Each possible combination or potential arrangement was explored to see if the scheduling of the implementation could yield two groups with six months' posttraining experience in which one had received training and the other had not. Unfortunately, this approach turned out to be impossible, and the control group arrangement for analysis was abandoned.

- Trend-line analysis: Historical data for the business performance measures were plotted for the first six months of 1995 to see if a trend had developed. These data were then projected through the implementation period for Virginia bankers, June through December 1995, and then to the postprogram evaluation period, January through June 1996. Because of the multiple influences involved with this project, in addition to the Project XXIV training, trend-line analysis became a very difficult process. An attempt was made to isolate the effects of training using the trend-line analysis for loan growth, deposit growth, capital market sales, cash management services, and employee turnover. However, these variables were extremely erratic with no clearly defined trend. This left no choice but to abandon trend-line analysis as a strategy.
- Participants' and managers' estimates: In the case of the Project XXIV training, it was felt that the team members should be knowledgeable about the factors that influenced their performance and able to provide reliable estimates. This strategy was ultimately chosen using a section of the questionnaire as the tool. The same information was obtained directly from the managers in the manager questionnaire. Table 1 depicts a segment of the questionnaire that was used to obtain this estimate with actual estimates from team members and managers.

Administering the Questionnaires

Questionnaires were mailed internally to all 92 commercial bank participants (including 33 managers) in Virginia who attended both programs. Accompanying the questionnaire was an introductory letter from Virginia executives that explained the purpose of the study and asked for the questionnaire to be completed and returned within 10 days. The questionnaires were anonymous to encourage candor. Completed questionnaires were returned to Performance Resources Organization for independent analysis and reporting. Table 2 shows the response profile.

The team member questionnaire was used to collect significant on-the-job behavior change and business impact data. Questionnaires were nine pages long and addressed 32 skill and behavior areas linked to the training objectives. Data were gathered on the frequency with which skills were applied, the importance of each skill, and how much job effectiveness had improved as a result of the training. Figure 3 shows a synopsis of the results of one section of the questionnaire devoted to collecting business performance data.

Table 1. Isolating the effects of training.

Several factors often contribute to performance improvement. In addition to Project XXIV training, we have identified some of the other factors below. Look at the factors and indicate what percentage you tribute to each as appropriate. If you feel that some of the factors are not appropriate, then do not assign them a percentage.

Please select the items that you feel are appropriate by writing in your estimated percentages as they apply.	Team Input Percentage improvement attributed to:	Manager Input Percentage improvement attributed to:
Project XXIV Training	32.5%	22.7%
Commercial Bank reengineering—new focus on consulting, commercial products and services, and partnering with customers	23.6%	23.4%
Support of deal team	15.6%	15.2%
Incentives	7.8%	11.4%
Coaching by manager	8.8%	10.9%
Capital markets liaison assistance	8.3%	10.0%
Other training initiatives: *please specify*	0	0.9%
Other: *please specify*	3.3%	5.5%
Total of all selected items must = 100 percent	**Total 100 %**	**Total 100 %**

Table 2. Questionnaire response profile.

	Number Sent	Number Returned	Percentage
Team questionnaire	59	27	46%
Manager questionnaire	33	15	45%
Customer questionnaire	78	31	40%

The manager questionnaire paralleled the team questionnaire design. The same issues in the team questionnaire were covered in the manager questionnaire. Managers were asked to provide input on changes in skills based on their observation of their team.

Because of the importance of the customer input, a customer survey was sent to a sample of customers. The questionnaire explored the various skills and roles expected from First Union relationship bankers along with questions about the extent to which bankers helped customers achieve success in their business. By design, the questionnaire was brief, focusing quickly on changing the nature of the relationship between the First Union banker and the client. Each relationship sales manager was asked to provide 10 customers to use in the study. The questionnaires were mailed directly to the customers, who returned them directly to Performance Resources Organization in a self-addressed, stamped envelope.

Converting Data to Monetary Value

The data collection plan included several approaches to converting data to a monetary value. The specific benefit from each of the six business performance measures had to be converted to dollar values so they could be compared to Project XXIV program costs. First Union National Bank monthly reporting for loan growth, deposit growth, capital market product sales, and cash management services shows not only the revenue stream but also the actual margin from these performance measures. Historical turnover cost data were not readily available to indicate the actual cost of turnover in the commercial banking area. As a substitute, external data revealed that in financial institutions, an approximate cost of turnover is one to one and a half times annual base salary compensation. The value is based on several bank studies on the cost of turnover. To be conservative in the

Figure 3. Business performance results.

4. Please identify any specific job accomplishments or improvements you have achieved that you can link to the Project XXIV training. *Think about new behavior you have applied or the application of skills as a result of the training.*

(e.g., improved strategic assessment of customers needs; developing and presenting recommendations to customers that resulted in the sale of FUNB solutions; approached customer from an investor perspective that helped them solve a major financial problem; delivered expanded solutions to customers by acting as a financial consultant to them; applied strategies for team selling that paid off; had sales successes that resulted directly from more effectively planning for sales calls; etc.)

5. Please comment on the ways your accomplishments or improved performance have contributed to customer solutions and the profitability of First Union National Bank.

Think about how your improvements actually resulted in influencing a business measure such as those measures in question #3. Measures such as more output (e.g. increased sales, loan growth, increased cash management services, new business, etc.); or fewer errors; time savings; cost savings or improved customer service.

6. Estimate your contribution (from question #5) in annual dollars. *Think of specific ways that you can convert these accomplishments or improvements into dollars. Along with the monetary value, please indicate the basis of your calculations.* (e.g., team selling techniques saved you an average of three hours a week which resulted in you actually spending more time making additional sales calls, etc.)

Estimated annual $_____
OR
Estimated additional incremental annual revenue $_____

Your basis for the estimate. _____

7. What level of confidence do you place on the above estimates?
_____% (Confidence (0% = No Confidence, and 100% = Certainty)

conversion, a value of one times base salary was recommended for use in the analysis.

For the customer satisfaction measure, it was decided that no value would be placed on the actual rating. Instead, customers would be asked to indicate the specific added value they received.

Tabulating Program Costs

To calculate the ROI, the next step was to tabulate the costs for the training programs. All fully loaded costs related directly or indirectly were included. Cost reporting mechanisms, although appropriate for some cost items, were insufficient to capture the overall fully loaded costs. Consequently, estimates were used to determine costs for some items.

To collect values that could be used in subsequent analyses, cost per participant was developed so the value could easily be used with other groups if further analysis was required. Two major cost categories were used. The first involved the design and development costs of internal and external costs in the needs assessment and program development. A total of 151 offerings were planned for Project XXIV training over a two-year period. Because 20 Virginia offerings were being evaluated, assessment and development costs were prorated. The total prorated amount was $43,836.

Delivery costs were the second major category. The program included the following specific delivery costs:

- salaries and benefits of participants $323,943
- hotel, travel, meals, and facilities   122,620
- facilitation and instruction   93,499
- administrative and support costs   7,880
- participant materials   79,820
- coordination and overhead   27,127

Costs were obtained directly from various cost or responsibility centers charged to specific projects. Facilities costs included the cost of using external facilities and a similar charge for internal facilities. Average salaries with a 28.5 percent factor for benefits was used. This was multiplied by the number of days of training. Coordination and overhead expenses required assumptions and adjustments.

Another cost category was the cost for evaluation, which included the cost of the ROI impact study. The Commercial College evaluation team felt that the impact study was a separate project from the Project XXIV training and elected to omit evaluation costs from the analysis.

Identifying Intangible Benefits
A final step identifies the intangible benefits. These are program benefits that were considered important, but could not be translated into monetary values.

The Results of the ROI Study

Change in Behavior
The participant and manager questionnaires provided significant information on changes in behavior of the Virginia bankers. Although space limitations do not allow all details to be reported here, useful information was obtained that indicated the skills were being used on the job. The skills and behavior that received the highest application rating were as follows:
- Obtain information on prospects prior to contact.
- Maintain an active prospect file.
- Ask situation questions to obtain facts and information during the call.
- Use problem questions to identify customers' issues and concerns.
- Use benefit statements in response to customers' explicit needs.
- Identify the customers' sensitivity to various risks.
- Offer alternatives when addressing a client need.
- In a sales call, take a strategic approach.

    The top five positive comments about the training were as follows:
- Training improves strategic assessment of client needs and objectives.
- Training has made us view ourselves more as consultants.
- Relationship Selling Skills provides common terminology for discussing sales calls and planning.
- Training has brought us up to speed with competitors.
- Our group is thinking "out of the box" on requests from customers.

    The most frequently mentioned barriers to performance were the following:
- There is a lack of time.
- It's too easy to drift back into old habits.
- The incentive plan is not consistent with Project XXIV goals.
- There is tension on some teams.
- The training is too basic.

Linkage to Business Measures
Based on the input from the team questionnaire, the five business measures with the strongest influence from the training program were

- increase sales of capital market products
- improve customer satisfaction
- improve employee satisfaction
- new business from existing clients
- new relationships established.

The two measures with the least influence were decreased employee turnover and deposit growth.

Although these ratings are very subjective, they reflect the potential from use of the skills to generate improvements in specific measures. The manager and team ratings closely parallel each other with the manager ratings showing a slightly higher influence overall. The influences reflected here are also reflected in the actual impact data presented later.

Trend-Line Analysis

Although trend-line-analysis data were explored, the effort turned out to be fruitless. The data for the four major products were erratic, making it difficult to develop a trend line or use the performance data to depict performance. Also, there were several other influences acting simultaneously on the variables, which caused upward and downward movements. Finally, some data originated from reporting systems that were not very accurate. Team members and managers did not record all the data if they were not meeting the threshold values for incentives. When they did meet the threshold, all the data were entered. This helped to explain the tremendous swings on the data. Consequently, a trend-line analysis was not feasible in isolating the amount of the improvement related specifically to training.

Customer Input

Customers were asked to provide specific information regarding the impact of the training on the business. Sixty-eight percent of customers responded that First Union bankers added value to their business. Customers rated the change of performance from moderate to significant with the average leaning toward a significant change in performance. Because the customers were selected by bankers for this particular survey, positive responses were expected.

However, the ratings were better than expected because they reflect important changes in performance. According to the customers' reports, the top five skills in terms of the change in performance were
- presenting a recommendation that is most aligned with customer preferences, goals, and strategies

- demonstrating knowledge of the bank's products and services
- identifying possible opportunities to obtain capital or reduce the cost of capital
- offering alternatives when addressing customer needs
- exploring the customer's business and personal goals and success measures when considering financial solutions to meet customer needs.

The overall ratings indicated a change in a broad range of skills that were visible to customers. The survey also asked customers to provide specific values if they could. Seven customers provided values for a total of $2,635,000. Although this was a difficult question, it showed that there were some specific cases of improvements linked to a change in behavior.

ROI

The return-on-investment for Project XXIV was developed only on the basis of participants' input. Their responses to questions, as shown in table 1, provided an opportunity for participants to specify what accomplishments were undertaken. Specific results were converted to annualized dollar values. Confidence levels are also provided. The percent of the improvement related directly to the Project XXIV training is captured in the question in table 1. An example from table 3 illustrates how the benefit is calculated. Item 1 in the table shows an annual contribution of $75,000 at a 70 percent confidence level:

$$\$75,000 \times 0.7 = \$52,500$$

Project XXIV training contributed 40 percent (participants' estimate) to the business result, for

$$\$52,500 \times 0.4 = \$21,000.$$

In all, 21 team members provided usable data for this series of impact questions. Table 3 presents a summary of the data. Individuals who did not provide data in this series of impact questions often indicated that they were unsure of the results or did not think the program had achieved results.

The total Level 4 benefits for the program were $1,028,250, which were derived by adding the total value in the last column of table 3. The actual return-on-investment was calculated using the Level 4 benefits value and the costs of the program for the 92 Virginia participants.

Table 3. Business impact data from participants.

Accomplishment/ Improvement	Profitability	Annual Con-tribution ($)	Basis	Confidence Level	Training %	Adjusted Value
1. • Better sales planning • Identifying needs • More focused on calling efforts	• New loans	75,000	• Net interest income + fees	70%	40%	21,000
2. • Identified cash management opportunities • Structured credit around opportunities	• Using package and materials, become sole bank for $80 mm middle market customer	114,500	• 7.3 mm credit @150bp 64,500 Cash manage-ment fees 50,000	80%	30%	27,480
3. • Improved ability to understand and offer multiple financing alternatives and help customer evaluate each approach	• Improved performance has increased fee income	500,000	• Fee income from two capital markets deals alone—one public debt offering and one syndication	90%	20%	90,000
4. • Ability to concentrate more on the customers' needs	• Increased sales	110,000	• Additional profits	60%	40%	26,400

Table 3 (continued). Business impact data from participants.

	Accomplishment/ Improvement	Profitability	Annual Contribution	Basis	Confidence Level	Training %	Adjusted Value ($)
5.	• Produced several models to confirm or modify relationship • Set up proposal referral system • Sought win-win agreements	• Cash management referrals • Capital management referrals • Loan terms and structure • Capital planning with customers at renewal time	300,000 R (90,000)	CSTS credits (30% margin)	70+%	30%	18,900
6.	• Analyzed customers' needs using financial consulting skills	• Solidified existing relationships • Established new relationships	150,000 I	• First-year profit on new customers	100%	10%	15,000
7.	• Both selling and financial consulting skills enabled identification of needs and close of sales	• Increased sales	90,000 I	• Profit from increased sales	60%	33%	17,820
8.	• Better understanding of customers' strategic goals has helped offer solutions	• Increased sales on all product lines • Enhanced position in bidding	100,000 I	• 25% improvement over previous year	20%	15%	3,000
9.	• More focused on customer needs	• Increased sales on existing relationships	250,000 I	• Fee income increases	80%	45%	90,000

Table 3 (continued). Business impact data from participants.

Accomplishment/ Improvement	Profitability	Annual Contribution	Basis	Confidence Level	Training %	Adjusted Value
10. • Improved calling and proposal efforts	• New relationships	400,000	• Profit from new relationships	75%	50%	150,000
11. • Improved strategic assessment of needs and objectives	• Better prepared to prospect and make calls	300,000	• New customers	70%	40%	84,000
12. • Spin selling techniques have helped get additional information	• Improved sales	25,000	• Actual cash management sales	100%	10%	2,500
13. • Use of spin model helped to uncover problems and develop solutions	• Increased cash management sales • Increased capital market sales	100,000	• CSTS calculations	75%	40%	30,000
14. • Explored customer needs	• Time savings	7,200	• 5 hr. per week savings	90%	20%	1,300
15. • Gained better understanding of nonfinancial management demands	Increased capital market sales	87,500	• Capital markets	50%	30%	13,125

Table 3 (continued). Business impact data from participants.

Accomplishment/ Improvement	Profitability	Annual Contribution	Basis	Confidence Level	Training %	Adjusted Value
16. • Took small company through hypergrowth with new facilities • Introduced capital markets for public offering	• 66% of annual goal achieved in six months • Leading in revenue generation	$480,000 I	CSTS reports	90%	30%	129,600
17. • More planning for sales calls • More cost-benefit analysis of options	• Identifying problems for prospects • Improved demonstration of cost benefit of customer solutions	100,000 I	• Estimation	70%	40%	28,000
18. • Call planning improved productivity	• Improved loan structure • Increased loans • More options	150,000 I	• Profit from new customers and cross-selling existing customers	80%	50%	60,000

Table 3 (continued). Business impact data from participants.

Accomplishment/ Improvement	Profitability	Annual Contribution	Basis	Confidence Level	Training %	Adjusted Value
19. • Improved presentations to customer • Communicated proactively	• Helped prospects define needs and increased sales	75,000 I	• Additional profits	70%	25%	13,125
20. • Improved presentations • Shifted from advisory role to sales • Used strategic questioning approach • Gained deeper under-standing of client strategy	• Increased sales • Increased loans	1,500,000R (450,000)	• Loan growth, fee growth (30% margin)	80%	45%	162,000
21. • Shifted from sales to consulting	• Increased capital market solutions • Increased fees	500,000 F (150,000)	• Additional sales (30% margin)	75%	40%	45,000
				TOTAL		**$1,028,250**

Notes: "I" represents Interest and "R" represents Revenue.

The three revenue factors presented (5, 20, 21) were converted to income factors using a 30% margin (an acceptable standard). Some of the revenues were actual fees that would have a higher margin, and others would have a lower margin.

The total fully loaded cost to train all the participants in Virginia was $698,725. When this amount is combined with the benefits in the standard Level 5 ROI formula, the ROI becomes

$$ROI = \frac{\$1,028,250 - \$698,725}{\$698,725} = \frac{\$329,525}{\$698,725} = 47.2\%$$

Although this value may be lower than anticipated, the return is much higher in reality. The 47.2 percent ROI value is an understatement of the actual return because of the following reasons:

- The value omits the potential improvement of the other 32 relationship team members.
- The value excludes the input of the 33 managers although some of the improvements reported may include a portion of their actual work on the project.
- The improvements reported in this analysis are very narrowly focused. Often there are other potential benefits not reported. Thus, even from the participants reporting data, there are usually additional benefits from the training.
- The participants indicated that on average 32.5 percent of the improvement was attributed to training. At the same time, they indicated that 8.8 percent of the improvement was through the coaching of the manager. Because the coaching module was a part of the training program, the influence of the overall training is actually greater.
- Only annual benefits were used in the calculations, limiting the improvements to first-year values. This program should have lasting benefits beyond the first year.
- The confidence levels for estimates were used to adjust the benefits downward, which is a conservative approach to adjust for uncertainty.

When these factors are combined, the actual ROI could easily approach a value in the 100 percent to 200 percent range. Overall, it appears that this program has had an appropriate and sufficient ROI.

Intangible Benefits From Project XXIV Training

Numerous write-in comments as well as the quantitative results of the study support the following intangibles as a result of the training:

- A change in thinking occurred that is important to the culture shift desired by First Union National Bank. Two specific examples follow:
  — The training has influenced job performance that has helped to improve the strategic assessment of clients' needs and objectives.

— The training has influenced job performance that has resulted in a more consultative approach with clients.
- The sales force and deal teams are more market sensitive.
- The sales force and deal teams feel that the training provided important tools that put them on an even keel with the competition.
- The training provided a common language for discussing the planning and execution of sales calls. This common language likely extends to other activities as well and probably contributes to an improvement in overall communication regarding business issues.

Recommendations From Participants

Along with input concerning barriers to successful implementation, participants were asked to make recommendations for improving Project XXIV methodology or to remove some of the barriers. The top five recommendations from both team members and managers are
- need more ongoing reinforcement
- put more emphasis on long-term horizon rather than short-term objectives
- recognize that the spin selling model is inappropriate for some situations
- need improved coaching
- provide refresher courses periodically.

Conclusions and Reactions to the Evaluation

Many participants felt that Project XXIV training was not only applicable to their jobs, but also was the best training they had ever had. They also acknowledged the bank's investment in them. Members of the Commercial College Advisory Board and Virginia's senior leadership were very interested in the Level 3 results of the evaluation. They had the data queried by market segment, job family, and job function. The evaluation was briefly presented to the HR Committee of First Union's board of directors. They responded favorably to the ROI process as a way to justify training and felt that the process was useful for a program the size of Project XXIV.

Questions for Discussion

1. What are your observations about the needs assessment for Project XXIV training?
2. What do you think about the decision to reassess the organization change initiative.

3. What do you think about the process for converting data to a monetary value to calculate the ROI.

4. What do you think about the process for isolating the effects of Project XXIV training.

5. How credible are the estimates used in this evaluation?

6. How could the evaluation process be improved for Project XXIV?

7. What tool or tools could be used as a part of Project XXIV training to enhance the application of skills? How would you implement the tool so that it could also function as a Level 3 data collection tool? As a Level 4 data collection tool?

The Authors

Ronnie D. Stone is vice president and chief consulting officer at Performance Resources Organization (PRO). In this capacity, he consults on numerous evaluation projects with a broad range of national and international clients. He also conducts public, in-house, and certification workshops on the return-on-investment process. Before joining PRO in 1995, he had 27 years of experience in human resources development in the aerospace and electric utility industries. He served in a managerial capacity for 18 years. Stone received his B.B.A from Georgia State University. He is a certified change consultant and is certified in PRO's return-on-investment process. He may be contacted at Performance Resources Organization, Box 380637, Birmingham, AL 35238-0637.

Doug R. Steele is senior vice president and director of the Commercial College in First Union's Corporate University (First University) located in Charlotte, North Carolina. The Commercial College has responsibility for delivering learning solutions required by Commercial Bankers to improve their performance. Steele has a B.A. in economics and accounting from Grove City College in Grove City, Pennsylvania. He has 20 years of banking experience, principally with First Union. For the past two years, he has served in his current position, prior to which he spent 18 years in various line management and leadership roles in commercial banking.

Debbie M. Wallace is a learning specialist and assistant vice president with First Union's Corporate University (First University) located in Atlanta, Georgia. She manages learning-related projects for the Commercial Bank including major process reengineering initiatives and strategic learning system initiatives, and she leads the business administration functions for the Commercial College. Wallace has a B.S. in accounting from Clemson University in Clemson, South Carolina, and is an experienced performance consultant. She has 10 years' experience in banking with NationsBank and First Union National Bank.

Wes B. Spurrier is a commercial bank training coordinator for the Commercial College in First Union's Corporate University (First University). He is primarily responsible for assisting in the performance of evaluations, managing the training registration process for the Commercial College, and auditing the monthly financial reports. He received a B.S. in accounting from Clemson University in Clemson, South Carolina. A month after graduation he started with First Union, where he has been for the past two years.

Computer-Based Training for Maintenance Employees

Bell Atlantic Network Services

Toni M. Hodges

Computer-based training is growing significantly in its application in a variety of training programs. This case shows how the return-on-investment (ROI) is developed for a computer-based training program for maintenance employees. The case illustrates a variety of innovative approaches to isolate the effects of the program and convert data to monetary values.

Organizational Profile

Bell Atlantic Network Services (hereafter referred to as Bell Atlantic) provides advanced voice and data services and directory publishing in the mid-Atlantic region. Nationwide it provides network integration and management services. Headquartered in Philadelphia, Pennsylvania, the company has offices throughout the region and employs over 60,000 people. Bell Atlantic is the premier provider of local telecommunications in the region, serving 29 million people in 11 million households in six states and Washington, D.C. Lines of business include network operations, consumer services, small-business services, large-business services, carrier services, directory services, public and operator services, and federal systems.

The Bell Atlantic Learning Center, part of the Bell Atlantic Human Resources Department, provides training services to each of the lines of business. The Learning Center conducts needs assessments; designs, develops, and delivers training programs; and evaluates the re-

This case was prepared to serve as a basis for discussion rather than to illustrate either effective or ineffective administrative and management practices.

sults of the programs. Learning Center personnel work closely with their clients to ensure that expectations are clearly identified and measurable.

Background

In 1995, the Bell Atlantic Learning Center, in partnership with the company's Network Operations organization, developed SLC/ Pair Gain computer-based training (CBT). The subscriber loop carrier (SLC) system technology reduces the number of facility requirements to a particular geographical area by introducing loop electronics into the facility. Loop electronics allows multiple simultaneous conversations over limited facilities. The system decreases cable pair requirements, which is referred to as a pair gain. Maintenance administrators and repair service clerks are responsible for handling trouble reports (customer calls) on telephone lines fed through SCL facilities. The purpose of the training, introduced in 1995, is to teach maintenance administrators and repair service clerks to recognize a SLC trouble type and to correctly interpret test results. An advantage of the CBT is that the participants can receive the training in the Learning Center performance labs at times most convenient to their work schedules and avoid traveling to different locations for a centralized instructor-led course. This arrangement would reduce the cost of training.

Initially, it was envisioned that the maintenance administrators and repair service clerks would be able to take full advantage of the skills acquired in training. However, business needs changed. At the time the course was being used and at the time of this analysis, the focus for the group being analyzed moved to other customer needs. As a result, trouble calls were referred to another group.

Evaluation Strategy

In August 1996, the Learning Center conducted an evaluation to determine what benefits participants had derived from the SLC/Pair Gain training and what benefits can be reasonably expected for its use in the future. If the participants better diagnosed SLC trouble calls, the following benefits would accrue:
- Increased customer satisfaction in having the trouble taken care of the first time and not requiring a repeat call.
- A reduction in repeat calls because the maintenance administrators or repair service clerks are able to correctly diagnose the SLC problem the first time the customer calls. Fewer repeat calls

reduce the amount of time spent by the maintenance administrators or repair service clerks on the phone, rediagnosing the problem.

- A reduction in the number of dispatches made. If a maintenance administrator or repair service clerk sends or dispatches a technician out to a customer's premises to repair a trouble and the technician discovers that the trouble has been misdiagnosed and cannot determine what the problem is, unnecessary technician time is spent.

Isolating the Impact of Training

Initially two methods were considered for isolating the impact of the SCL/Pair Gain training. One method would be to compare the number of repeat calls and misdiagnosed dispatches made by those who were trained and those who were not (control group). A second method would be to compare the number of repeat calls made by the trained participants three months before and three months after they took the training.

To obtain the call and dispatch data, the Mechanized Trouble Analysis System (MTAS) would be used. MTAS logs the numbers and types of calls each maintenance administrator and repair service clerk receives. It was discovered that MTAS only links a maintenance administrator and repair service clerk to the SLC trouble report that the individual closes out. If a repeat call occurred because of a misdiagnosis, the repeat call could only be linked back to the maintenance administrator or repair service clerk who received it and not to the maintenance administrator or repair service clerk responsible for misdiagnosis. And a link could not be established between the participant who effectively dispatched calls because if the call had been dispatched correctly, it would be the technician who would close it out and not the maintenance administrator or repair service clerk.

So the evaluation strategy used to isolate the impact of the training was to obtain the participants' estimation of the impact of the training. A perception questionnaire was developed and administered to a sample group of 45 trained participants to gather postprogram data. Individuals in the sample group were from maintenance centers in Wilmington, Delaware, and Charleston, West Virginia, and had completed training at least three months prior to postprogram data collection.

MTAS was used to determine the average number of repeat trouble

Figure 1. Follow-up evaluation questionnaire.

Bell Atlantic Learning Center
SLC/Pair Gain Training
Follow-up Evaluation Questionnaire
August 1996

Directions: Please read each question and circle the number which most accurately reflects your opinion. Please feel free to offer your comments. Thank you very much for helping us to measure the effectiveness of our training.

1. As a result of using the SLC/Pair Gain computer-based training, I have felt better prepared to do my job.

STRONGLY DISAGREE				STRONGLY AGREE
1	2	3	4	5

_____

2. The content of this course accurately reflects what happens on the job.

STRONGLY DISAGREE				STRONGLY AGREE
1	2	3	4	5

_____

3. I have had the opportunity to apply what I learned in the SLC/Pair Gain training.

STRONGLY DISAGREE				STRONGLY AGREE
1	2	3	4	5

_____

4. To what degree (percent) do you believe the SLC/Pair Gain training has increased your ability to effectively dispatch calls?

0%	25%	50%	75%	100%

_____

5. To what degree (percent) do you believe the SLC/Pair Gain training has increased your ability to reduce repeat calls?

0%	25%	50%	75%	100%

_____
_____
_____

reports made in each center per month, and the following formula was applied to determine a cost benefit:

amount saved = average no. reports per month x percent reduction
where
percent reduction = number of calls saved x value of each call
and where
value of each call = (combined) loaded hourly rates of maintenance administrator or
repair service clerk and technician

An average of 99 repeat calls per month was calculated for Wilmington and 93 for Charleston.

Performance Data

The questionnaire that was used for the postprogram data analysis appears in figure 1.

For questions 1, 2, and 3, values ranged from 1 for strongly disagree to 5 for strongly agree. For questions 4 and 5, the values ranged from 0 percent to 100 percent. Monetary values were assigned to the results from question 5, the degree to which the participants believed the SLC/Pair Gain training increased their ability to reduce repeat calls.

A total estimated training population of 100 was derived for the year based on the number of participants completing the training from December 1995 to August 1996.

Cost Data

The following program costs were used to calculate a return-on-investment (ROI):

CBT design and development costs	$96,759
Labor cost for participants using the training (average 4 hours' training time x $29/hour x 100)	$11,600
Evaluation costs	4,000
Total	$112,359*

*The average operating costs (using the computer and facilities) are currently under analysis and have not been included in the program costs.

The cost data used to determine monetary benefits of the program were the savings resulting from reduced repeat calls. The client (network operations) calculates each repeat call to cost Bell Atlantic $96.90, which reflects the combined loaded hourly rate for a maintenance administrator or repair service clerk and a technician.

Table 1. Postprogram survey results.

Survey Question Number	Mean Scores Wilmington	Mean Scores Charleston
1	2.92	1.83
2	2.5	2.0
3	2.33	2.06
4	33%	18%
5	29%	15%

The scores in Table 1 were used to calculate tangible and intangible benefits.

Analysis Results

Of the 45 questionnaires distributed, 30 were returned. Eighteen were from Charleston, and 12 from Wilmington. A mean score was calculated for each question. For questions 1, 2, and 3, a value was assigned to each response option and averaged across the number of responses for each item. For questions 4 and 5, the mean percentage was determined. Table 1 lists the mean scores for each question.

Tangible Benefits

Using the data generated by question 5 (perceived degree that SLC/Pair Gain training has reduced repeat calls), the following annual savings were derived:

Annual savings = average calls x calls saved x cost of a repeat report x 12 months/year.

For Wilmington, the annual saving is

99 x 29% = 28.71, or 29 calls saved x $96.90 = $2,810/month x 12 = $33,720

For Charleston, the annual saving is

93 x 15% = 13.95, or 14 calls saved x $96.90 each = $1357/month x 12 = $16,284

The combined annual saving for these two centers is $49,999. The total expected population to be trained for the year is 100. The returned questionnaires represent 30 percent of that population. We can reasonably predict a total annual saving of approximately $166,680.

There are several ways in which a cost-benefit analysis or ROI analysis can be conducted for these data. Because we will not see the recurring cost of the initial training design and development ($96,759) each year, perhaps the most meaningful way to assess it is to amortize the cost over a period of years. To obtain a reasonable estimate of the overall value, the following assumptions were made:

- The CBT cycle is three years, and the course has a residual value of $48,380 at the end of year 3.
- The greatest amount of depreciation (25 percent) will occur in the first year; depreciation is 12.5 percent in year 2 and 12.5 percent in year 3.
- Years 2 and 3 each have one-half the number of participants as year 1.
- Course revisions are required at the end of year 3, not to exceed $48,380.

Amortizing one-half the value of the design and development cost of $96,759 over three years and allocating 25 percent ($24,190) for year 1, and 12.5 percent ($12,095) for each of years 2 and 3, the following ROIs are calculated as follows:

$$\text{Year 1:} \quad \frac{\$166,680 - \$39,790^*}{\$39,790} \quad = \quad 3.19 \text{ or } 319\%$$

$$\text{Years 2 and 3:} \quad \frac{\$83,340 - \$17,895}{} \quad = \quad 3.66 \text{ or } 366\%$$

*The one-time evaluation cost of $4,000 was included in year 1 calculations only.

Intangible Benefits

The perception of the participants was that the SLC/Pair Gain training increased their ability to effectively dispatch calls (survey question 4) an average of 26 percent and their ability to reduce repeat calls (survey question 5) an average of 22 percent. We can assume these increases to have a positive impact on customer satisfaction.

Conclusion

The average score for question 1, the participants' perception of the degree to which they feel better prepared to do their job as a result of the SLC/Pair Gain training, was low (2.38). However, this may be a result of their perceived limited opportunity to use the skills taught as reflected in the ratings of question 3 (2.20). Based on their written comments, it appears that the low average score (2.25) for question 2, the participants' perception of the degree to which the course accurately reflects what happens on the job, may also be due to the limited opportunity. Changing business needs were apparently the reason the participants did not feel they had the opportunity to use the skills taught. Nevertheless, the SLC/Pair Gain training realized a positive ROI. We can expect, therefore, to see an even greater ROI for the future use of the SLC/Pair Gain training when used by an audience that has an increased opportunity to use the skills provided by the training.

Questions for Discussion

1. Was perception data appropriate for this analysis?
2. Was amortizing the cost of the CBT over a three-year period the best way to conduct the ROI analysis?
3. Why was the evaluation cost used for calculation for year 1 only?
4. How might the client (network operations) use these results?
5. How can the Bell Atlantic Learning Center use these results?

The Author

Toni Hodges has 15 years of experience working in the behavioral analysis, systems engineering, and communication environment. Her work has included designing corporate process flows for behavioral programs; conducting needs analyses that have defined training, operational, and system design requirements for the United States Department of Defense (DoD), the British Military of Defence (MoD) equipment and systems, and the Federal Aviation Administration (FAA) communication equipment and systems; and conducting pilot program evaluations, performance assessments, and return-on-investment analyses.

She currently manages measurements and evaluations for the Bell Atlantic Human Resources Organization and is establishing corporate standards and policies for Bell Atlantic Learning Center program evaluations. She may be contacted at Bell Atlantic, 1300 Columbia Pike, B-32, Silver Spring, MD 20904.

Replicating a Performance Management ROI Evaluation

Speedy Telecommunications Company

William Wurtz

This case illustrates the use of participants' estimation not only to provide information on the impact of the program but also to isolate the effects of the program on the improvements. The case describes the return-on-investment development for a comprehensive performance management system in a large global company. The case replicates the process presented in volume 1 of this casebook (Zigon, 1994). The results are impressive, and the case provides for insight into the value of participant estimation.

Background

The telecommunications industry has become extremely competitive since the court-mandated breakup of the Bell system. This change has opened the way for new entrants into the long-distance phone market (and, more recently, into the local telecommunications market). The move from being part of a highly regulated industry to competing in the open marketplace has spurred phone companies to place greater emphasis on aligning organizational efforts and managing employee performance. Concurrent with this greater emphasis has come pressure on human resource development (HRD) departments from their telecommunications executives to demonstrate the value of the departments' performance improvement programs through established means of evaluation. This case describes the implementation of

This case was prepared to serve as a basis for discussion rather than to illustrate either effective or ineffective administrative and management practices. All names, dates, places, and organizations have been disguised at the request of the author or organization.

a new performance management system in the Speedy Telecommunications Company and the evaluation of that system using a previously documented method for collecting data and deriving ROI.

Organizational Profile

Speedy's roots date from the late 1800s in a rural prairie town. The Amalgamated Telephone Company (ATC), as it was known then, grew steadily, if not spectacularly, for many years. Its growth was accomplished by buying up small, adjacent telephone companies and then wringing out the redundancies to drive up revenue margins.

In the 1950s new aggressive management came to the fore that extended this strategy across the nation. ATC began acquiring a number of non-Bell local operating companies in different regions of the country. These companies had histories similar to that of ATC, and like ATC, they served mostly small towns and rural areas. The process of consolidating operations was repeated throughout the expanding company. However, as the company's operations became more geographically dispersed, top management reluctantly granted greater latitude to each of the operating units to run its own business.

By the 1980s, ATC was composed of nine local operating companies—several of which were among the most profitable in the industry—and a corporate staff operation. However, as good as the situation appeared, management foresaw the need for substantial change in the way ATC did business. First, with deregulation on the horizon, the company would have to grow even faster if it was to achieve the critical mass necessary to deal with huge potential competitors like AT&T. Second, new technologies—particularly fiber optics and digital switching—offered an opening for the company to get into the long-distance market with a distinctive edge.

Third and finally, Speedy's chief executive officer (CEO) recognized that the technological edge would be short-lived. Thus, a long-term emphasis was placed on developing human resources to provide a competitive edge. Major commitments were made to implementing a quality management process and establishing a corporate university.

The building of the company's advanced fiber-optic long-distance network was a monumental effort and achievement. Unfortunately, the glory of this achievement was short-lived. As one executive put it, "We had a plan to build to a network but not to run a business." Among the key mistakes the company made was a calculated gamble to rely on an existing billing system for the new network. The billing system was unable to handle the demands of the new long distance network, resulting in inaccurate bills, lost revenue, and dissatisfied customers. As the losses mounted, the company went through several rounds of layoffs, a process that left the surviving employees demoralized. The company also sought to achieve economies by centralizing more functions, which caused resentment in the once ...independent local companies.

In this increasingly chaotic environment, the vice-president of the corporate university, Karen Smith, decided to launch a new company-wide performance management system that came to be called LINK.

The Program

The development of LINK grew out of the need to support the implementation of the company's quality management process. The goal was to fundamentally change how the organization managed human performance. LINK combined a number of methods—including means to link organizational goals, both vertically and horizontally (hence the name), competency-based planning tools, "360-degree" feedback, individual development plans, and a career planning process—into a single integrated performance management system.

The original design was conceived by the company's organization development consultant. Looking at the design, Smith saw perfor mance management as a means to address some key organizational issues—and make the university's reputation as well. She assigned a task team within the corporate university, which took the design from there and developed the first version of the system. In her determination to see the project through, Smith did not hesitate to replace task team members whom she perceived were not fully committed to the project. Ultimately, the vice president assigned responsibility to Donna Brown, the university's employee development director.

In its final form, the main vehicle for implementing LINK during the pilot phase was an eight-hour training course for managers. In full implementation, there was also a companion course for employees, detailing their role and responsibilities in the performance management process. There were other courses, such as a coaching course, which were provided as supplements to the basic LINK training course. The training course covered the philosophy behind LINK and the form-based procedures for planning and discussing performance improvement efforts and for appraising performance. The pilot phase was conducted in five of the company's business units.

Karen Smith's goal was to get the training out to as many people as possible. As a result of her pressure, the university's trainers began negotiating with business unit leaders, who were not all necessarily enthusiastic about spending time learning the new LINK process. These negotiations frequently led to customized versions of the original course. The course was presented in two- and four-hour versions as well as the original eight-hour version.

Level 1 results (reactions to the training) were closely monitored. Results were below five on a six-point scale. In assessing these results, university staff attributed these below-average results to a variety of factors, including resentment to having mandated training, an extensive self-study requirement, and the trainers' inability to answer some of the participants' questions (on compensation policy, for example). This last factor was caused by the training being implemented before certain policy issues had been fully decided. Under the circumstances, the university staff concluded that the training was satisfactory.

No Level 2 evaluations (measuring the amount of learning that occurred) were conducted during the pilot phase. The university's new policy, requiring a Level 2 for every course, was not in place at the time.

The university's assessment staff conducted an extensive evaluation of the on-the-job application (in effect, a Level 3 evaluation) of the LINK skills and practices. The results of this assessment showed that the skills and practices were being used to an acceptable extent and that participants generally considered the LINK practices more effective than the performance appraisal processes they had been using.

Research and Evaluation Unit

The university confronted increasing demands by executives throughout Speedy to demonstrate the value of its various programs and interventions. In response to these demands, the university established a new research and evaluation unit (R&E). The first major task for R&E was to conduct the Level 4 evaluation (organizational impact) for LINK.

In determining how to proceed, the head of the new R&E unit knew his group's first major study would be carefully scrutinized by business unit and university executives and university staff. Moreover, LINK represented a substantial investment by Speedy: More than 14,000 employees had invested over 90,000 hours in training classes. So it was critical that the evaluation design be one that had a track record and could be easily defended. Through a literature search, he came across a case study that met the need. Titled "Performance Management Training: Yellow Freight System," the case study set out a simple but effective design.

The R&E head contacted the editor of the case study volume, one of the world's leading authorities on HRD evaluation, to gain more details. The editor was eager to assist. The editor counseled that because HRD evaluations often produce surprisingly high benefits, it was imperative to collect and calculate the data very conservatively to make it more credible to upper management. In effect, every effort should be made to bias the results against the program.

Using the case study and the editor's advice as guides, the R&E head outlined the following steps for arriving at an ROI figure for LINK:

1. A sample of managers would each be asked to estimate in dollar terms the expected gain—revenue or savings—likely to be realized from one of their LINK objectives. (Allowing the choice of only one objective per manager is in itself an attempt to keep the figures conservative.)

2. Then each manager would be asked what percent he or she believes LINK contributed to the expected gain (the contribution estimate).

3. The manager would next be asked to list a "confidence estimate" (in percent), that is, how much confidence he or she places in that estimate.

4. That expected gain is multiplied by both the contribution estimate and confidence estimate to produce an "adjusted gain estimate."

5. The adjusted gain estimate is reviewed with the manager's supervisor. The supervisor is asked to either confirm or adjust the figure, based on his or her (the supervisor's) knowledge of the situation.

6. R&E staff review the two estimates (from steps 4 and 5) and select the lower figure as the one to be included in the final tabulation of LINK results. (R&E also later adjusted the revenue estimates to account for that percent which would be taken to the bottom line.)

7. Individual estimates are tabulated together and then calculated with program cost data to produce an estimated return-on-investment figure.

The proposed design, set out in early summer, called for data to be collected through the rest of the year with results to be reported early in January of the next year.

In assessing the overall design, the R&E head concluded that the built-in conservative bias in the data collection would lessen any concerns people had about the design's subjectivity. Besides, he reasoned, the estimates that a manager provided to a researcher are presumably the same ones the manager would report through his chain of command.

Consideration was also given to conducting a comparative study of results from the other performance appraisal processes that LINK was replacing. Ultimately, this idea was dropped. R&E couldn't identify any populations within the company that would survive challenge as equivalent to the ones included in LINK. And asking managers in the LINK study to estimate what they thought the differences were was rejected as carrying subjectivity beyond reason.

The R&E head reviewed the design with Donna Brown, the university's employee development director. Feeling the pressure from Karen Smith to demonstrate results quickly, Brown demanded that steps 4 and 5 be eliminated as too time consuming. She also ordered that the study timetable be moved up so that the report would be available by October to coincide with department budget reviews. To help move the data collection process along, she directed that her staff assume responsibility for gathering the data.

R&E worked up a sampling plan involving 85 managers and turned it over to the employee development staff, which conducted interviews in person and by phone. Despite a valiant effort, the staff was unable to complete the suggested number of interviews in the allotted time. However, this didn't hamper the study from arriving at some spectacular results.

Results

The total adjusted gain estimate from 69 reports came to an impressive $50 million. The university's finance group provided these cost estimates for the program:

Description	Amounts ($)
Course development (salaries)	131,000
Training (trainers salaries and material and administrative costs)	1,117,000
Trainees' salaries (@ $17 average hourly wage)	1,546,000
360 instrument development	240,000
360 administrative costs	26,000
Training video	50,000
Total	3,110,643

A benefit-to-cost ratio was calculated using these data ($50,000, 000/ $3,110,000). The result is 16.08 to 1, or about 16 to 1. In other words, according to this method of valuation, there has been an economic benefit to the corporation of at least $16 to every $1 invested in LINK.

Using the return-on-investment formula—net program benefits (program benefits less costs) divided by program costs multiplied by 100—resulted in a valuation of over 1,500 percent, a result comparable to the original Yellow Freight study.

It is worth noting again that these calculations are biased against LINK. The cost figures include all identified costs from the initiation of the development of LINK, a period of two years. The benefits are limited to those realized in one year by a small sample of participants.

Conclusion and Recommendations

Replication is important in the scientific approach because it helps to prove or disprove that a subject has been understood and brought under some measure of control. To the extent that HRD and HRD evaluations are applied sciences, replication is important for the same reason. It is exciting to note the similar (and huge) ROI that new performance management systems appear to achieve in two different industries. In addition, using a replicated method in an evaluation provides additional credibility to the conclusion. Thus, replication can become an important strategy for building an effective evaluation practice.

Questions for Discussion

1. What impact does offering different versions of the basic course have on the validity of the evaluation?
2. How would you critique the merits of the evaluation's focus on performance outcomes given the multidimensional aspects of the performance management system?
3. What cautions would you suggest to use when communicating the results to management?
4. How important is the eight-hour course for managers in this process?
5. Would the results have been different with a Level 2 evaluation in place?

The Author

William ("Bud") Wurtz has more than 16 years of experience as an organization development practitioner and manager with three Fortune 500 companies. Currently, he is a member of the change management practice within NCR Corporation's organization development team, based in Dayton, Ohio. He holds the designation of Registered

Organization Development Consultant through the International Registry of the Organization Development Institute.

Wurtz is a past president and long-time board member of the Kansas City Chapter of the American Society for Training & Development. He is a national board member of the American Creativity Association and is coleader of an effort to establish the HRD-ROI Network, an association of experienced HRD practitioners committed to advancing the art and science of ROI evaluation. Bud Wurtz can be contacted at NCR Corporation, 1611 S. Main Street, Dayton, OH 45479.

Reference

Zigon, Jack. "Performance Management Training: Yellow Freight Systems." *In Action: Measuring Return on Investment,* volume 1, Jack J. Phillips, editor, 1994. Alexandria, VA: American Society for Training & Development.

Evaluating Leadership Training for Newly Appointed People Managers

Global Technology Company

Jack J. Phillips

This case illustrates the difficulty in evaluating a program that was not originally designed to contribute directly to the bottom line. With the request of management, an evaluation was conducted on leadership training designed for newly appointed managers. The case tackles the difficult issues of isolating the effects of training and converting data to monetary values, two key ingredients in the return-on-investment (ROI) process. The results were impressive and, more important, were accepted by the senior management team.

General Information

Industry and Company

Global Technology Company (GTC) is a global company with significant manufacturing and marketing facilities in North America, Europe, South America, and Asia. The industry it serves continues to face rapid transformation through deregulation, increased competitive pressures, and changing technology. This situation has forced equipment suppliers to focus on technology, cost control, and customer service. For years, GTC has enjoyed a tremendous edge in technology, having developed a significant research and development (R&D) capability with its research organization. In recent years, GTC has undergone significant changes to focus on controlling cost while providing excellent customer service. As part of this transformation, GTC is downsizing or restructuring in some parts of the company while growing in others. One critical group for this transformational activity is the first-level manager (sometimes labeled supervisor, team leader, or project leader). He or she must manage and lead a team through the constant change and challenges. This study involves a program known as Management Leadership Program (MLP), directed at this group, which is one of several global leadership programs targeted at various audiences.

Background and Rationale for Review

Although the reactions to MLP and the global leadership development programs have been very positive, senior management must ensure that the investment in leadership development has maximum impact on the company, which is essential in today's competitive environment. Consequently, GTC Training and Education Department initiated this study as part of a major assessment into the business impact of the global leadership development programs for the company worldwide. Performance Resources Organization, a leading firm for ROI studies, was selected to conduct the impact study.

The study had three specific objectives:

- to assess the specific impact of the MLP in measurable contributions to the extent possible, up to and including the calculation of the return-on-investment
- to identify specific barriers to successful program implementation and utilization
- to recommend specific changes or adjustments in the program.

Management Leadership Program

The Management Leadership Program is designed for newly appointed managers in people management positions. The program teaches them the basic tools for success before they are actually appointed to the job of people manager. The program provides an overview of GTC's global vision and presents critical people management policies and skills necessary to achieve this vision. First-time managers are required to attend the program one to three months prior to their promotion. Upon successful completion of this program, the participant will be able to

- explain a manager's critical role in managing change effectively

- explain a manager's role as a team leader
- identify competencies and skill sets, tools, and resources critical to successful management
- discuss strategies for using the Performance Management System effectively
- evaluate his or her personal leadership and management strengths and weaknesses
- develop an on-the-job action plan to assess areas for personal growth.

The program has been operational for four years. Ten sessions are presented each year with an average of 25 in each session.

Several issues surrounding the MLP made the project more difficult. A comprehensive needs assessment was not conducted before the MLP was implemented. Without a defined need, an economic benefit may not be realized. Initially, the program was not designed to deliver a measurable ROI. Consequently, in the design stages, key performance measures were not identified as being linked to the program and specific objectives were not developed to improve performance. Data collection systems were not refined to link with MLP. Performance data were scattered throughout the company and, in some cases, not readily available.

Even with these difficulties, there was a need to measure ROI utilizing the most appropriate processes. Consequently, this project would attempt to connect the programs with a specific measurable return.

Model for Impact Study

Levels of Evaluation

An evaluation can be conducted at five different levels, as table 1 shows (Phillips, 1995).

Data had been collected at the first two levels. For Level 1 evaluation, participant reaction questionnaires were collected for each MLP. For a Level 2 evaluation, in the MLP, learning was assessed in role plays, skill practices, exercises, simulations, and subjective assessments from the program faculty. The evaluation data for the two levels were considered to be successful.

At Level 3 evaluation, on-the-job behavior change is monitored. For MLP, this type of follow-up evaluation was not planned or implemented prior to this study. For Level 4 evaluation, the specific business impact of the program is measured. For MLP, there were no attempts to measure business impact prior to this study. At Level 5, ROI, the

Table 1. Evaluation levels.

Level	Measurement Focus
1. Reaction and planned action	Measures participants' satisfaction with the program and captures planned actions
2. Learning	Measures changes in knowledge, skills, and attitudes
3. Job applications	Measures changes in on-the-job behavior
4. Business results	Measures changes in business impact variables
5. Return-on-investment	Compares program benefits to the costs

monetary benefits of the program are compared to the costs of the program. No Level 5 evaluations were developed for the MLP, prior to this study. This study focused on Levels 3, 4, and 5.

ROI Process

To understand the ROI process, it is helpful to examine the key steps involved in developing the ROI (Phillips, February 1996). Figure 1 illustrates the process and highlights the issues addressed in the study. The first step is the collection of data after a program has been conducted. A variety of postprogram data collection methods are available.

Perhaps the most important step in the model focuses on the issue of isolating the effects of training. In every training and development program, a variety of factors influence the output measures of business impact. Training is only one of many influences that will drive a particular measure.

The next step in the ROI model is converting data to monetary values. Output measures must be converted to dollar values so they can be compared to the cost of the program to develop the ROI. Another essential step is to tabulate the program costs to determine the specific investment. All fully loaded costs that are related directly or indirectly to the training program are included.

Finally, the costs and benefits come together in an equation for the ROI that shows the net benefits, which are the program benefits

Figure 1. ROI model.

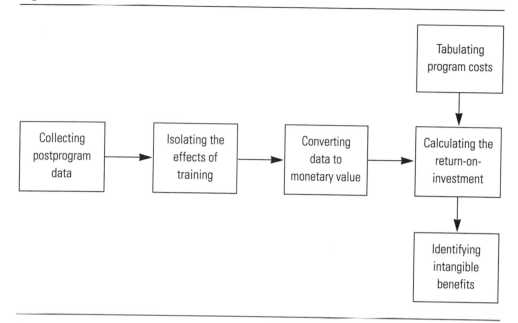

minus costs, divided by the total investment in the training program. This process provides an ROI formula comparable to ROI calculations for other investments that typically show the net earnings divided by the average investment. A final step lists intangible benefits that are very important but not translated into monetary values for the program benefits.

This model provides a framework to measure the return-on-investment in any type of training and development program and is the model used in this study. The key decisions for the study involve selecting specific methods to collect data, isolate the effects of training, and convert data to monetary values. These three most difficult and critical steps in the process are described in more detail below. Figures 2 and 3 show the completed data collection plan and the ROI analysis plan for this study.

Data Collection Methods

In this impact study, four methods were used to collect data. A questionnaire was administered to a variety of target audiences to determine the extent to which participants have utilized the training and have achieved on-the-job success. Also, focus groups were conducted to explore the same issues. Focus groups included both the participants

Figure 2. Evaluation strategy: data collection.

Program:_____   Date: _____

Evaluation strategy: Data Collection

Level	Objective(s)	Evaluation Method	Timing	Responsibilities
I. Reaction, Satisfaction, and Planned Actions	• Favorable reaction • Suggestions for improvement • Planned action	• Generic questionnaire	• End of program	• Program coordinator
II. Learning	• Skill acquisition • Knowledge of management policies	• Skill practice • Written tests	• During program • End of program	• Facilitator
III. Job Application	• Use of skills • Frequency of skills • Action plan implementation	• Interviews (small group) • Focus group (small sample) • Questionnaire • Action plan	• 6–12 months after completion of program	• Evaluation consultant
IV. Business Results	• Performance improvement	• Focus groups • Questionnaire	• 6–12 months after completion of program	• Evaluation consultant

and their immediate managers in separate groups. A third data collection involved interviews with a variety of key managers and executives to determine their perceptions of the success of the program and to identify important issues and needed changes. A fourth method of data collection was a documentation review.

Isolating the Effects of Training

Although there are several strategies available to isolate the effects of training, most of the methods were not appropriate in this situation. Participants' direct estimates were the most appropriate techniques.

Figure 3. Evaluation strategy: ROI analysis.

Program:: _Managerial Leadership_   Responsibility: _____   Date: _____

Evaluation Strategy: ROI Analysis

Data Items	Methods of Isolating the Effects of the Program	Methods of Converting Data	Cost Categories	Intangible Benefits	Other Influences/ Issues	Communication Targets
Variety of measures	Participant's estimate	Participant's calculation and estimate	• Program fee • Travel and lodging • Participant salaries and benefits	• Job satisfaction of participants • Job satisfaction of direct reports • Stress reduction	• Many variables influencing performance • Participants may have difficulty estimating values	• Top executives • Business unit presidents • Managers of participants • Participants • T&D staff

Their estimates of the impact of training can be a reliable indicator, although they are subjective. The participants are the individuals closest to the performance improvement and are often aware of the other influences that have an impact on the performance measures. In studies where participants' estimates have been compared to the differences obtained from control group experiments, their estimates were found to be very reliable (Phillips, March 1996).

Conversion of Data

There are many ways in which data can be converted to monetary values, but the primary strategy used in this study was to ask participants to make estimates of the value of improvements in their work units. In some cases, participants used accepted standards and conversion factors to arrive at monetary values.

Data Collection Strategy

Timing of Data Collection

The MLP is designed to have a long-term impact, but the specific improvements from training programs are difficult to capture years after the program is completed. Although the connection between a training program and an action plan or specific improvement may exist, it is very difficult for the participants and the managers of the participants to make the connection. In addition, for longer periods of time, additional variables will influence output measures, thus complicating the cause and effect relationship between training and performance improvement. Because of this, the evaluation was limited to programs conducted in a period of six to 18 months from the time of this study. With a few exceptions, participants' input was limited to these time frames.

A standard practice in ROI evaluation for short-term training programs is to capture the first-year benefits after the program has been conducted. This, in essence, limits the benefits to one year of improvements. Although this could slightly overstate the results in some cases, it represents a conservative approach because the benefits obtained in subsequent years are not used in the analysis. This practice is used in this study.

Interviews With Executives

Interviews with senior managers and executives were a rich source of input about the effectiveness of the MLP. The interviews obtained information from them about program effectiveness, program support, and recommendations for improvement. More specifically, each executive was asked about his or her level of involvement in the program, the perceived need for the program, specific feedback received about the program, perceived impact of the program, and recommended changes. The interviews provided a helpful insight into their perception of the program's importance and success and, more specifically, their recommendations for changes.

Focus Groups

MLP develops soft skills, and the focus group process is an effective way to capture their application. As participants develop and apply soft skills on the job, they may be unaware of their application and frequency of use. Consequently, a one-on-one interview or questionnaire may miss some important application data. The focus group process allows participants to interact with others and to discuss specific applications of the program on the job. The data from the initial interviews provided input to frame the issues for the focus groups.

In all, 10 focus groups were conducted for MLP, involving participants and their immediate managers from North America and world trade groups. Five groups of MLP participants and five groups of managers of MLP participants were conducted in Toronto; Ottawa; Dallas; Raleigh, North Carolina; and London. The data collected from the participants in focus groups revolved around the following five questions:

1. How useful or relevant was the program to your job?
2. How did you and your job change as a result of this program?
 • perceptions
 • behaviors
 • action plans
3. What specific accomplishments/improvements are linked to the program?
4. What barriers to improvement and change (2 and 3) did you encounter?
 • support
 • time
 • environment
5. How could this program be improved?

In addition, each focus group participant completed a questionnaire designed specifically for focus groups. Collectively, the questions that were discussed and the answers on the questionnaires provided an important source of input.

Questionnaire

The focus group discussions identified several issues that were fully included in a detailed impact questionnaire that explored the extent to which participants have applied what they have learned and the success they have achieved with the application. In addition, another important point of view about the success of the program was heard from in the responses to the questionnaires for participants' managers. Overall, 440 individuals were identified to receive a questionnaire either as participants or as managers of participants.

The questionnaire focused on the impact of training and the barriers to successful implementation as well as potential changes needed in the program. The key areas addressed in the participant questionnaires included

- success with objectives
- accomplishments and impact
- relevance to job
- barriers to implementation
- usefulness of program
- manager support
- knowledge and skills increase
- metrics linked to programs
- actions taken
- recommended changes.

Because of the need to have data on the impact of the training, the questionnaire provided significant detail to gauge the impact as it was applied. Figure 4 shows a series of questions asked of participants in an attempt to capture that data.

The key areas covered in the questionnaire given to participants' managers included

- familiarity with program
- perception of program
- quality of feedback
- level of involvement
- knowledge and skills change
- metrics linked to program
- performance improvements
- recommended changes
- administrative issues.

Figure 4. Key impact questionnaire.

What has changed about you or your work as a result of your participation in this program? (Specific behavior change, action items, new projects, etc.)

_____

_____

_____

Please identify any specific accomplishments/improvements that you can link to the program. (Job performance, project completion, response times, etc.)

_____

_____

_____

What specific annualized value in U.S. dollars can be attributed to the above accomplishments/improvements? Use first-year values only. While this is a difficult question, try to think of specific ways in which the above improvements can be converted to monetary units. Along with the monetary value, please indicate the basis of your calculation. $ _____ Basis:

_____

_____

_____

What level of confidence do you place on the above estimations? (0% = No Confidence, 100% = Certainty) _____ %

_____

_____

_____

Other factors often influence improvements in performance. Please indicate the percent of the above improvement that is related directly to this program. _____ % Please explain.

_____

_____

_____

Do you think this program represented a good investment for GTC?
Yes ☐   No ☐   Please explain.

_____

_____

_____

Documentation Review

A final and important aspect of this study involved a review of a variety of documentation to determine the effectiveness of MLP and the potential linkages to a variety of business metrics. The following material was reviewed:

- all of the course materials to determine the degree to which link-

Figure 5. Data integration process.

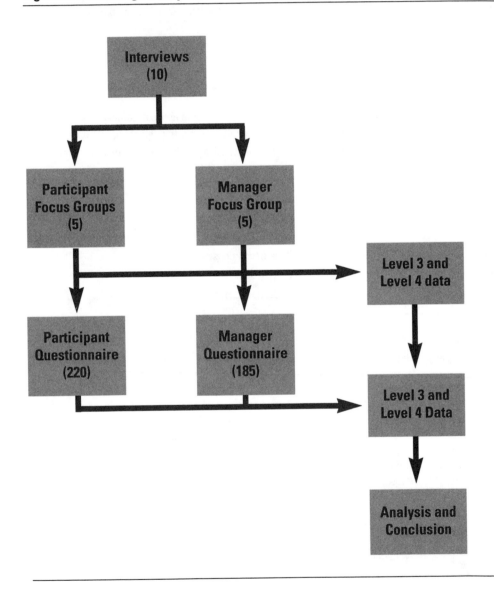

age existed and follow-ups were planned

- previous reviews and assessments of the data, including Level 1 evaluation data and other metrics on the effectiveness of the programs
- specific follow-up evaluation conducted previously showing the success of the program
- other business metrics that could be related to the MLP.

The variety of data collection strategies provided comprehensive input to make important assessments about MLP. Figure 5 shows the data integration process.

Program Costs

Cost Components

When the return-on-investment is developed, a tabulation of the costs for each program is necessary. A fully loaded cost profile was used in this study. This approach accounts for all of the costs of training so that senior management will fully understand the total costs of the MLP. The 10 cost elements considered in this analysis included

- Management Leadership Program
- average per program per participant
- ongoing cost of materials (handouts, purchased materials, use fees)
- conference facilities (hotel)
- conference facilities (GTC)
- consultants and external trainers (fees and expenses)
- training and education salaries and benefits (for direct work with programs)
- training and education direct travel expenses
- development and revision costs (prorated)
- training and education overhead (prorated)
- participant salaries and benefits (average daily salary x benefits factor x number of program days)
- travel and lodging for participants.

A participant fee has been utilized to charge the department for an employee participating in the program. For the most part, the fee is intended to represent the first eight categories of cost items. It captures all of the direct expenses and has a slight margin to cover the training and education overhead related to the program. Thus, this figure is utilized for the cost of those eight items for each participant in the program. This appears to be a reliable process under the assumption that the initial fee was based on an analysis of costs at that time.

Also, these costs appear to be reasonable when compared to costs of similar programs in other organizations. The cost of participants' salaries and benefits was estimated using their estimated average salary and benefits. These estimates were derived with input from the team leader for the program, the account prime. Travel and lodging expenses were estimated with input from each account prime based on estimates of a percentage of individuals who traveled to the program and their specific travel costs.

The cost estimates based on these assumptions and the corresponding costs appear in table 2. It shows the per participant charges for the program, salaries and benefits, and travel and lodging, yielding a total cost per participant per program.

Impact of Program

Because the main thrust of this project is to determine the impact of the MLP, every attempt has been made to uncover specific results linked to the program. Although the program was not designed to produce measurable, quantifiable results, it did produce significant changes and have a business impact, as outlined below:

Skills and Knowledge Application

Participants and their managers rated improvements in skills and knowledge since taking MLP. They explored 20 skills. The most significant changes occurred with the following skills:

- personal development planning
- developing teamwork
- valuing diversity and human rights
- conflict management

Table 2. MLP cost estimation.

Cost Item	Cost Per Participant
Charge for program	$1,200
Salaries and benefits	1,140
Travel and lodging	1,200
Total cost	$3,540

- team leadership
- objective setting
- coaching
- developing employees
- performance review
- providing rewards and recognition.

     Low to moderate changes were noted in the following skills:
- managing change
- implementing the corporate vision
- managing time
- ethical decision making
- strategic planning
- employee selection
- orientation/inducting a new employee
- performance improvement
- cross-functional communication
- GTC Global Focus.

     Strategic planning skills showed the least amount of improvement.
     Participants had little opportunity to use several skills, including
- employee selection
- orienting/inducting a new employee
- performance improvement.

     The top five skills that participants have used the most are
- providing positive feedback
- coaching
- teamwork
- delegating responsibility
- listening.

     Overall, MLP is a very serious skill-building program with reports of important and significant changes in skill levels after the program. Participants' managers were even more optimistic about skill changes, reporting higher levels of change than the participants.

Linkage With Metrics

     Participants and their managers reported linkages between the applications of skills and several business metrics. Conclusions are as follows:
- moderate influence on productivity
- moderate to low influence on employee turnover
- moderate to low influence on absenteeism
- moderate to significant influence on employee satisfaction

- moderate to significant influence on customer satisfaction
- low to moderate influence on quality control, cost control, and customer response time.

Overall, the program has influenced some very important metrics in the organization.

Business Impact

In an effort to calculate business impact, participants were asked to provide annualized dollar values representing specific improvements related to the training program. In all, 45 percent of the participants provided usable data expressed in dollar values. Participants were asked to provide the level of confidence they placed in their estimate. The value, ranging from 100 percent for certainty to 0 percent for no coverage, reflects the perceived error in the estimate. In addition, participants were asked to indicate the percent of the improvement that is directly related to the training program. Their responses are depicted in table 3.

Two adjustments were made to the data. First, the confidence level estimate, expressed as a percent, is multiplied by the dollar value to adjust for the uncertainty of the data as perceived by the participant. Second, the percent of the improvement related to training is multiplied by the dollar value. These two adjustments yield an average per participant of $20,500 for those reporting data. Table 3 presents typical data taken from the participants' questionnaires. Because 45 percent of the participants provided data, on average, 11.25 participants in a program of 25 furnished measurable data. This yields for a typical program a value of $230,625, a significant impact for a five-day leadership program. A word of caution is needed here. These are subjective values, although adjustments have been made to make them closer to the real values and possibly understate the results. From the perspective of the target audience, it is better to understate than overstate the results.

ROI

The final step in the impact equation is to calculate the ROI, which is perceived to be significant for this program. Two questions provided qualitative input on this issue. MLP was a good investment according to 85 percent of the participants and 94 percent of their managers. In addition, 47 percent of the participants' managers felt that MLP should not be required to show a measurable return.

Although MLP was not specifically designed to show a bottom-line impact, or ultimately a measurable return, the ROI was calculated.

Table 3. Sample of input from participants.

Participant	Annual Improvement Value ($)	Basis for Value	Confidence%	Isolation Factor ($)	Adjusted Value ($)
11	36,000	Improvement in efficiency of group. $3,000 month x 12 (group estimate)	85	50	15,300
42	90,000	Turnover Reduction. Two turnover statistics per year. Base salary x 1.5 = 45,000	90	40	32,400
74	24,000	Improvement in customer response time. (eight hours to six hours). Estimated value: $2,000/month	60	55	7,920
55	2,000	5% improvement in my effectiveness ($40,500 x 5%)	75	50	750
96	10,000	Absenteeism reduction (50 absences per year x $200)	85	75	6,375
117	8,090	Team project completed 10 days ahead of schedule. Annual salaries $210,500 = $809 per day x 10 days	90	45	3,279
118	159,000	Under budget for the year by this amount	100	30	47,700

Using a benefit of $230,625 for each program and considering each program had an average cost of $88,500, the estimated ROI becomes:

$$\text{ROI} = \frac{\$230,625 - \$88,500}{\$88,500} \times 100 = 160\%$$

Based on these assumptions and calculations, MLP yields a very high estimation of ROI. In addition to this ROI, additional value can be attached to the improvement in business metrics, outlined above, as well as the change in skills experienced by the participants.

Other Findings

In addition to the foregoing impact data, other useful evaluation information was uncovered and is presented here:

OBJECTIVES. MLP is designed for individuals who manage other people. However, 15 percent of those who attend the program are not in a people management role. This situation is causing some problems with the applicability of many of the skills taught in the program.

The questionnaire captured the participants' perception of the degree to which objectives were met. Overall, the participants felt the program had been

- generally successful in explaining a manager's critical role in managing change effectively.
- very successful in explaining a manager's role as a team leader.
- generally successful in identifying competencies/skill sets, tools, and resources critical to successful management.
- generally successful in discussing strategies for using the performance management system effectively.
- generally successful in evaluating personal leadership and management strengths and weaknesses.
- unsuccessful in developing on-the-job action plans to assess personal areas for growth. Sixty-eight percent of the participants indicated they did not develop and implement an on-the-job action plan.

USEFULNESS AND RELEVANCE. As a whole, the program appears to be both very useful and relevant to their jobs. The interactive activities in the program were very relevant as was the executive involvement. Group discussions were the most helpful and useful part of the process, followed closely by networking opportunities which many participants strongly valued. The reading materials did not appear to be very relevant, but the program content seemed to be relevant.

TRANSFER. This program had moderate success with transfer, although there is still ample opportunity for improvement. Thirty-five percent of the participants said they have not used the materials since they participated in the program. Also, there are not enough linkages from the program to the job, and there is a lack of follow-up to ensure that the material is used.

BARRIERS. The primary reason participants have not utilized the materials is the lack of time. Multiple priorities and time pressures kept participants from implementing many of the skills. Lack of management support was also a major barrier to implementation. The environment was another problem because the culture and work climate did not always support the use of the concepts or materials. Also, many of the participants did not view the concepts as useful and did not apply them.

MANAGEMENT SUPPORT. Management support for this program is seriously lacking. Almost two-thirds of the participants reported that their managers did not make any reference to the program or only casually mentioned the program and with no specifics. This assessment differed from the input of their managers who indicated they had supported the program very actively and discussed the program in detail after the participant attended. The discrepancy appeared in both focus groups and questionnaires.

Recommendations

Following are recommendations for changes in the MLP to address the issues raised in the focus groups, questionnaires, and interviews:

- Implement a results-based approach for the MLP. This will require a focus on output issues and measures instead of input. Among the recommended actions are the following:
  - Link the program more closely to business unit objectives, company goals, and strategic plans.
  - Revise course objectives to be more closely aligned with business goals and strategies. Consider adding objectives in each session that reflect bottom-line measures important to the specific group.
  - Build in manager follow-up as an important process in the program, shifting the responsibility for results to participants and their managers.
  - Implement an action plan process with specific instruments and requirements.
  - Increase the current level of management involvement at all levels to

ensure that there is adequate support and reinforcement.
— Regularly communicate program results and status to managers and senior executives.

- Involve senior managers in key decisions and actions regarding the MLP. Many of them have been left out of previous planning sessions. They need to be involved in establishing the direction, providing input, assisting with presentations, serving as a sponsor, and ensuring that the process is adequately supported throughout the organization.

- Revisit the issue of timing of participation in the program to determine whether it is best to attend this program before or after assuming people management responsibilities. Many participants indicated that attending after they have assumed responsibilities is more helpful because they can see a logical application of the skills.

- Consider dividing this program into two different sessions with an opportunity to practice some of the skills between the two sessions. A three-day session followed by a two-day session would be appropriate. Although logistically this creates problems, it would enhance the application of the material.

Collectively, these recommendations provide helpful suggestions for improving the MLP in an attempt to connect leadership training more closely to bottom-line measures.

Lessons Learned

Although the ROI was positive and significant, and the program shows important connections with business results, there is still much room for improvements, as suggested in the recommendations. Several important ingredients must be in place for the program to enhance business measures:

- There must be a comprehensive assessment conducted to determine needs at Level 4 (business impact) and Level 3 (on-the-job behavior and environment). Without this, it becomes extremely difficult to evaluate the programs at Levels 3 and 4.

- Programs need to have specific objectives at Levels 3 and 4 to provide direction to program designers, facilitators, and evaluators as well as a focus for the participants as they attempt to use the skills and knowledge on the job.

- A follow-up mechanism should be an integral part of the program instead of an add-on activity. This enhances the quality and quantity of the data obtained in a follow-up evaluation.

- Evaluation should be a carefully planned process in which the results are carefully communicated to target audiences.

Questions for Discussion

1. Should this type of program be subjected to an ROI evaluation? Please explain.
2. What are the advantages of collecting data from multiple sources?
3. How would you critique the methods used to isolate the effects of training and to convert data to monetary values.
4. How credible is the business impact and ROI data? Explain.
5. Critique the overall strategy for the evaluation project.

The Author

With 27 years of corporate experience in five industries (aerospace, textiles, metals, construction materials, and banking), Jack J. Phillips has served as training and development manager at two Fortune 500 firms, senior human resources officer at two firms, and president of a regional federal savings bank.

Phillips has been author or editor of *Accountability in Human Resource Management* (1996), *Handbook of Training Evaluation and Measurement Methods* (2d edition, 1991), *Measuring Return on Investment* (volume 1, 1994), *Conducting Needs Assessment* (1995), *The Development of a Human Resource Effectiveness Index* (1988), and *Improving Supervisors Effectiveness* (1985), which won an award from the Society for Human Resource Management. He has also written more than 75 articles for professional, business, and trade publications.

Phillips consults with clients in manufacturing, service, and government organizations. His clients are located in the United States, Canada, England, Belgium, South Africa, Mexico, Venezuela, Malaysia, Indonesia, South Korea, Australia, and Singapore.

Phillips may be contacted at Performance Resources Organization, Box 380637, Birmingham, AL 35238-0637.

Measuring the Impact of Leadership Training

LensCrafters

Patricia Zigarmi and Frank Baynham

The following impact study features a management development intervention conducted by LensCrafters. The intervention strategically supported LensCrafters' business objectives to build market share and increase company earnings by improving leadership effectiveness. More than 1,500 LensCrafters managers participated in the change effort. Using qualitative and quantitative data, LensCrafters evaluated the intervention over a two-year period on four levels.

Background

From its start in 1983 to the close of the decade, LensCrafters enjoyed swift growth, high sales, solid earnings, and the leading market share position in the burgeoning full-service optical retailing category.

By the beginning of the 1990s, however, new and significant threats loomed for the retailer. An economic downturn, precipitated by the Gulf War, was hurting consumer optimism. Retail sales began to decline, with the optical category hit among the hardest. LensCrafters' revenues turned lackluster, and company earnings spiraled downward, declining 72 percent in a single year.

Exacerbating the situation was the company's growth frenzy during the 1980s. In particular, hundreds of novice managers were promoted or hired to support the growth spurt, and a core training program to support them was inconsistent at best.

This case was prepared to serve as a basis for discussion rather than to illustrate either effective or ineffective administrative and management practices.

"The successive years of rapid-fire new-store openings led to dozens of battlefield promotions," said Frank Baynham, senior vice president of operation services. "If you were a good optician, lab tech, or frame stylist, and had enthusiasm and staying power, the system pulled you to the top."

Marta Hollis Brooks, director of management training, added: "Unfortunately, our previous training efforts had been fragmented, with little or no skill building. Company conferences emphasized operational issues, leaving the regional directors on their own to build their managers' skills in developing people and cultivating a customer service mentality."

Baynham explained: "Being competitive and profitable in these new, more demanding times meant reevaluating and, in some cases, reengineering a number of our business practices. Leadership training was among our top considerations and, by January 1992, we were ready to take action."

Starting at the Top

As 1992 began, LensCrafters was committed, at the very top level of the organization, to implementing a management development intervention in the form of a companywide training program.

It was agreed that the intervention's emphasis would be on skill building, including developing managers' abilities in important areas such as goal setting, coaching, and providing feedback. Managers would become accountable for knowing and using the skills, which would be a factor in their performance reviews.

A partner was needed to help design and launch the intervention by early March. "We looked for a partner who could offer us the building blocks," Baynham explained. "We knew we needed a common-sense management model and a practical training methodology that would work for every level of corporate and field management."

Selecting a Partner

After reviewing several resources, LensCrafters selected as its partner Blanchard Training and Development (BTD), a San Diego-based consulting company.

BTD's widely known Situational Leadership II (SLII) model, originally conceptualized over 20 years ago by Ken Blanchard and Paul Hersey, had been updated through the years. It was the common-sense model for which LensCrafters was looking.

Through SLII, LensCrafters' managers would learn how to use

four core leadership styles (that is, directing, coaching, supporting, and delegating), in response to the individual needs of their associates. In addition, they would become more skilled in goal setting, observing and monitoring performance, and providing feedback on results.

The SLII training materials would be customized by BTD for LensCrafters. Plus, BTD would guide LensCrafters as it made the SLII model an important part of the company's total culture. "It was apparent that SLII could be easily understood and applied, Baynham said. "Plus, it would provide the core approach and common language we had been sorely missing."

Launching the Intervention

For several weeks, BTD studied LensCrafters' inner workings to design a meaningful intervention that would support the retailer's business objectives.

By March 1992, a team of BTD associates had presented a customized, two-day program to more than 700 LensCrafters managers. Training began with LensCrafters executives and senior managers. Then, through a series of regional conferences, all regional directors and general store managers were trained. Eventually, retail managers and lab managers were trained, and BTD later taught a group of LensCrafters trainers and managers to present the concepts to newly hired managers.

These best practices, which worked together to support the LensCrafters intervention, are worth noting:

- GETTING COMMITMENT AND INVOLVEMENT FROM SENIOR MANAGEMENT. At the top of the organization, Baynham was a critical champion. He was involved throughout the process, from assessing needs and defining objectives to selecting resources and supporting curriculum design. In addition, he attended each of the regional conferences, often doing role-playing exercises in front of the attendees.
- CUSTOMIZING DESIGNS AND MATERIALS. Patricia Zigarmi, a top BTD associate and codeveloper of SLII, traveled to several store locations to develop a complete understanding of how the stores operated and then led an intensive customization effort back at BTD.

A customized 70-page participant's workbook, including dozens of case studies, games, and lab experiences, made SLII training more relevant for all the managers, whether they worked in the optics, manufacturing, or retail area. In addition, the BTD associates were able to enrich the training experience by giving real-life examples and appropriately using LensCrafters terminology.

- PROVIDING MANAGERS WITH FEEDBACK FROM SUBORDINATES. Through two different instruments, the Leader Behavior Analysis (LBAII) and the Leadership Skills Assessment (LSA), LensCrafters managers received important feedback from their subordinates. Both instruments were computer scored by an independent company, providing anonymity to subordinates and, in turn, an honest portrayal of their skills to the LensCrafters managers.

  The LBAII was administered once, at the time of the initial training. It provided the LensCrafters managers with different scores relative to their use of four leadership styles and their flexibility and effectiveness.

  Of particular importance was the LSA. Because it was administered twice (at the time of initial training and then six months later), it was used as a pre- and posttest assessment of the skills of the Lens-Crafters managers in applying all four SLII leadership styles and in goal setting, observing performance, and providing feedback. In other words, did managers actually change their behavior after training, as perceived by the people who work with them everyday?

  The nine-page LSA Scoreboard provided LensCrafters managers with their scores relative to 24 different situations and, after the post-training assessment, a comparative look at the pre- and posttest scores. General norms were also provided to give the managers a big-picture look at where they stood in comparison to other LensCrafters managers, as well as other companies in the data base.

- ESTABLISHING BASELINE DATA. As noted above, the LSA administered during the initial training provided LensCrafters with important baseline data. As a result, the posttraining LSA results were highly relevant, as they would provide managers with before and after feedback and help the company determine if their investment was beginning to pay off.

- INTEGRATING BELIEFS INTO THE CULTURE. Fueled by its top-down commitment, LensCrafters incorporated the SLII concepts into its culture, ensuring that the intervention was a long-term strategy versus an "event."

  Measures were taken to integrate SLII into the performance management system. This had a profound impact on the managers, both during the initial training and in the months thereafter. Because they understood that their reviews, and their compensation, would be affected by how they were applying the SLII concepts, the managers were motivated to listen and learn during the training and consistently apply their new skills back on the job.

Managers were also given a variety of tools, each one reinforcing that SLII was an important part of the LensCrafters culture. Laminated inserts, customized for the managers' daily planners, were distributed, and posters for back-room meeting areas in the stores were provided. These and other aids reinforced the four leadership styles and when to use them, plus reaffirmed the company's overall commitment to the approach.

Although these best practices were important, they had to lead to results for the intervention to be considered successful. Thus, Lens-Crafters and BTD set out to systematically evaluate their efforts.

Evaluating Results

From the onset, LensCrafters and BTD agreed to evaluate their efforts on four successive levels:

1. AFFECT. Did the managers feel good about what happened?
2. KNOWLEDGE. Did the managers learn?
3. BEHAVIOR. Did the managers change their behavior?
4. OUTCOMES. Was measurable progress realized in one or more business areas?

The first two levels, affect and knowledge, could be evaluated immediately and qualitatively. The feedback was overwhelmingly positive.

"Across the board, managers responded to the training with enthusiasm and appreciation," said Ulrich Koenig, a LensCrafters regional director. "Everyone enjoyed the experience itself and, more importantly, they were pleased to finally have a core model for developing their people."

"The managers felt nurtured and supported," according to Brooks, the director of management training. "Many of them thanked us for the 'real training,' saying they felt more confident already." "The practicality and clarity of the SLII model was a big plus," said Regional Director John Jordan. "All the managers felt they could start putting it to work as soon as they returned to their stores."

According to Baynham, managers began using "the language" immediately. "The common knowledge allowed us to get to the heart of management matters quicker than ever before." Indeed, the apparent success at the first two levels of evaluation was rewarding. It was clear that all the managers liked the training, and during the months immediately following the program, most showed important signs of increased knowledge.

After six months' time, the next two levels of evaluation could begin. LensCrafters and BTD began to look for the intervention's positive results in leadership effectiveness, employee turnover, and customer satisfaction, as well as sales and earnings. The team acknowledged that other economic and business factors would influence results, including companywide marketing shifts and all new store designs.

The findings were highly positive, and LensCrafters and BTD celebrated the results. Here are the specific findings:

- THE LEADERSHIP SKILLS ASSESSMENT RESULTS PROVED THAT LEADERSHIP EFFECTIVENESS GREATLY IMPROVED. A comparison of the results from the pre- and posttraining Leadership Skills Assessment (LSA) showed that LensCrafters managers had improved in all seven skill areas measured by the LSA, according to their subordinates. In five of the managerial skill areas, supporting, delegating, goal setting, observing performance, and giving feedback, the managers showed improvements at a statistically significant level. In other words, the odds of the increased effectiveness occurring by chance were highly improbable, or less than 50 in 1,000. Table 1 provides detailed information about the pre- and posttest scores, including their statistical significance.

- THE ASSOCIATE OPINION SURVEY RESULTS SHOWED THAT EMPLOYEES WERE MORE SATISFIED. Distributed biannually to its 10,000 employees, the LensCrafters Associate Opinion Survey (AOS) helps LensCrafters determine if it is living up to its vision, mission, and core values. The survey includes 65 questions within 17 different categories, providing the company with important feedback in areas such as managerial practices, performance feedback, quality, customer orientation, and technology. Associates are ensured confidentiality (the AOS is administered by an independent company), which may attribute to the high 79 percent participation rate.

Two AOS categories, "Performance Feedback" and "Managerial Practices," represented 14 percent of the total questions and were considered especially relevant to evaluating the management development intervention. Improvements from the 1992 to 1994 surveys were hoped for, with gains or losses of 5 percent or more in "favorable" and "unfavorable" ratings being noted as statistically significant by the survey administrator.

In 1994, favorable ratings within the "Performance Feedback" category rose eight full percentage points from 1992, a statistically significant gain. Based on the questions in this category, these ratings showed that associates felt positive about their managers' abilities to give useful feedback, recognize good performance, and evaluate them fairly.

Table 1. Summary of means and probability levels for pre- and posttest Leadership Skill Assessment scores for LensCrafters managers.

Skill	Pretest Mean	Posttest Mean	P Level
Directing	24.83	25.61	.067**
Coaching	26.32	26.96	.125
Supporting	25.48	26.32	.055**
Delegating	26.31	27.63	.001*
Goal setting	16.76	17.43	.022*
Observing performance	15.89	16.53	.012*
Giving feedback	16.51	17.32	.007*

The increases in the posttest mean scores proved that the LensCrafters managers had become more effective, as evaluated by their subordinates, and did so to a degree that is considered "statistically significant." (The last three skill areas shown above report lower scores for the managers than the previous four skill areas solely because the mean scores are calculated from a lower base.)

A statistical tool, the probability, or P level, helped LensCrafters to see real improvement versus chance improvement. A statistically significant change, marked here with *, is less than .050, signifying that the probability of the improved rating occurring by chance is less than 50 in 1,000. Thus, a P level of .001 is optimal because it confirms an improvement in leadership effectiveness so great that it had only 1 in 1,000 odds of happening by chance. Items marked with ** denote a noteworthy probability, though they do not meet the criterion of being statistically significant (.050).

(Note: Central region data, representing 402 subordinates and 98 managers)

In the category of "Managerial Practices," favorable ratings rose two full percentage points from 1992 to 1994. The positive trends here indicate that associates believed their managers were doing a good job overall, especially as it related to accessibility, fairness, and managing diverse people and issues.

Results in all other AOS categories were positive as well. In fact, LensCrafters exceeded retail norms on 89 percent of all survey questions by an average of 11 percent, according to Carolyn Slager, director of human resources.

- EMPLOYEE TURNOVER DECREASED. LensCrafters employee turnover data, comparing the period through the second quarter of 1992 with the same period in 1993, revealed that employee turnover decreased by nearly 8 percent companywide. Overall, the compa-

Table 2. Summary of percentage increases in posttest mean scores and probability levels of LensCrafters customer satisfaction ratings.

Variable	Percentage Increases in Posttest Mean Scores	P Level
Friendly service	3.2	.002*
Overall satisfaction	3.8	.001*
Glasses < one hour	1.9	.172
Likely to return	3.2	.004*
Personnel	16.4	.001*
Quality control	14.9	.002*
Pricing	5.5	.251
Product options	9.0	.016
Faster service	11.1	.079**

The gains in customer satisfaction were evidenced by an increase in mean scores on nine different scales of service. The probability, or P level, allowed LensCrafters to determine improvement that is statistically significant (the lower the P level, the more significant the improvement). The P levels noted with an * confirm statistically significant improvement, as they fall below .050. Those marked with ** show noteworthy improvement.

(Note: Central region data)

ny remains substantially below retail norms related to employee turnover.

- CUSTOMER SATISFACTION RATINGS ROSE. Customer satisfaction surveys are mailed to customers' homes after their visit to a LensCrafters store. Customers rate their experience on nine different scales and mail the completed survey to an independent company for scoring.

  Surveys administered six months after the management development intervention revealed positive results on nine scales. Seven of the nine areas showed statistically significant improvements with gains in the areas of "Friendly Service," "Overall Satisfaction," "Likely to Return," "Personnel," and "Quality" especially noteworthy. Table 2 provides more details.

- TOTAL AND COMPARATIVE STORE SALES INCREASED. Since the intervention, LensCrafters continues to dominate its category and surpass national averages for comparative sales increases. At $660 million, total sales for 1992 increased 5.6 percent over the prior year. In 1993, sales rose 5.9 percent to $699 million, and sales for the 10 months ending November 26, 1994, indicate a banner year, up 13.3 percent.

- EARNINGS REACHED AN ALL-TIME HIGH. In 1992, earnings totaled $40.4 million, a 21.7 percent increase over the prior year. With $43.6 million in 1993 earnings, a 7.9 percent increase was realized. And, for the nine months ending October 29, 1994, earnings reached $57.4 million, an overwhelming 77.2 percent increase against the same period in 1993.

Another recent study revealed an important, direct correlation between profitability and the management development intervention at LensCrafters. The company was once again affirmed that its investment in developing its managers was paying off, and in this case, on the all-important bottom line.

This study examined LensCrafters stores within the company's central region according to the net profit increases during comparative business periods between 1992 and 1994. Stores with above average increases during this period were distinguished from stores with below average increases. Then, the posttraining Leadership Skills Assessment scores for the managers of both groups of stores were compared. The results were significant.

The managers from the stores with above average increases in net profit were found to have significantly higher scores on the Leadership Skills Assessment than the managers from stores with below average increases in net profit.

In all seven skill areas measured by the Leadership Skills Assessment, the differences between the "high profit" managers and others were profound. Their scores for the four SLH styles—directing, coaching, supporting, and delegating—were higher to a statistically significant degree, as were the scores related to their skills in goals setting, monitoring performance, and providing feedback. (As noted earlier, the managers' scores on the assessment tool reflect direct feedback from the people they manage on a daily basis.) In fact, the probability, or P levels, an important statistical tool, showed odds as low as 2 in 1,000 that the differences in scores between the two groups of managers could have happened by chance alone.

Summing It Up

On all four levels of evaluation, the LensCrafters management development intervention was a short- and a long-term success. Managers stated that they had a chance to learn and they liked the experience. Then, as documented by thousands of satisfied employees and customers, they put those learnings to work to influence sales and earnings.

Today, LensCrafters remains a vibrant company with a promising future. Healthier, stronger, and more competitive than ever, the company continues to prove that investing in people pays the biggest dividends of all.

A Footnote

LensCrafters did not make a conscious decision to calculate its return-on-investment (ROI). It should be noted, however, that the investment for the program and results as described here totaled $253,694, including the cost for all trainers and materials. With 650 participants, the per-participant investment was $390.

Questions for Discussion

1. How would you critique the best practices as noted? What other practices should have been considered?
2. How would you critique the methods used to evaluate the program at each of the four levels?
3. How credible are the business results? Explain.
4. Without the benefit of an ROI study, did the company make good on its reported expense of $253,694? Why? Why not?
5. What follow-up strategies would you recommend?

The Authors

Patricia Zigarmi is vice president of business development for Blanchard Training and Development. An expert in leadership and developing excellence, she consults and trains in the United States and abroad with a host of Fortune 500 and fast-track companies. Her client list includes AT&T, Boise Cascade, General Electric, Inter-Continental Hotels, and Zenith Data Systems. She is co-author of *Leadership and The One Minute Manager* and codeveloper of Situational Leadership II. She received a bachelor's degree in sociology from Northwestern University and a doctorate in leadership and organizational development from the University of Massachusetts, Amherst. Zigarmi may be contacted at the following address: Blanchard Training and Development, Inc., 125 State Place, Escondido, CA 92029.

Frank Baynham is senior vice president of operations for LensCrafters. He joined the company in 1987 as marketing manager. He was soon promoted to director of marketing and then director of retail operations for the southern division and became senior territory operations director in 1990. He rose to vice president of operations in 1992 and in 1994 assumed his current role. He holds a bachelor's degree from Murray State University.

Workforce Transition Project

Pitney Bowes

Rãndi Sigmund Smith

Many organizations are going through significant transitions to adjust to changing market forces and workplace demands. This case describes a workforce transition project undertaken by Pitney Bowes and a variety of human resource interventions that contributed to the bottom line. The case illustrates the difficulty in isolating the impact of a variety of influences on the output measures.

Background

This unique use of criterion-referenced validation was developed to measure the return-on-investment (ROI) to Pitney Bowes of the multiple human resource activities associated with the Workforce Transition (WFT) Project activities. This project was initiated because the senior management at Pitney Bowes, in its strategic planning process, identified several critical external and internal issues. The external issues were

- growing U.S. and international competition, with increasing numbers of competitors and the potential of a decreasing market share
- customer demand for high (total) quality and for corporate flexibility and responsiveness to rapidly changing customer requirements
- customer demand for customized products, produced rapidly and without traditional manufacturing delays around materials and processes.

This case was prepared to serve as a basis for discussion rather than to illustrate either effective or ineffective administrative and management practices.

The internal issues were the need for dramatically increased work-force skills to ensure the required productivity and to meet quality demands, and an absolute requirement to lower overhead and other costs to bring competitively priced products to the global marketplace.

Senior management further concluded that responding to these issues successfully depended upon the accomplishment of the following formidable tasks: a significant increase in the efficacy of Pitney Bowes' manufacturing processes; a substantial upgrade in the performance capacity of Pitney Bowes' manufacturing workforce; and a revolutionary change in the way in which Pitney Bowes manufacturing employees accomplish work and interact with one another. It was also recognized that it would be impossible to achieve one without the others, and that the future of Pitney Bowes depended upon meeting these challenges.

Corporate strategists, manufacturing experts, marketing and financial personnel, and human resource specialists concluded that only an extensive workforce transition would address the following five performance issues associated with the three tasks identified above:

1. Pitney Bowes must create an assembly process that transitions from the existing batch-type assembly line to a continuous flow, "pull inventory" process. This requires dramatic changes in labor requirements. Also, a major culture change must be fostered, with both professional staff and hourly workers reconsidering their expectations about their work responsibilities and those of the other groups. In the Pitney Bowes manufacturing environment, workers must take greater responsibility for productivity and quality. Manufacturing engineers must implement new techniques that ensure the workers' high involvement in the redesign of the work flow.

2. A new materials requirement planning data system must be installed to tie multiple locations together around centralized scheduling and to combine that system with localized production schedule planning. All classifications of factory workers must acquire new planning and scheduling skills and take on increased responsibility for product demand and the impact of defective materials.

3. The assembly lines and fabrication operations must be conducive to a worker's completion of an entire task (assembly of machine, fabrication of part) rather than one segment of a task. Pitney Bowes future manufacturing will be based upon a sociotechnical systems model, at the core of which are high-performance, self-managed work teams. Workers will have to become multiskilled and take new responsibility

for completion of entire subassemblies, components, or finished product.

4. The Pitney Bowes factory compensation plan had been an individual-oriented, piece-rate incentive pay program, which provides merit pay increases based on performance appraisals and annual general adjustments. This compensation plan must change to a pay-for knowledge, or skill-based system in which performance criteria will be based on both quantitative and qualitative standards of competency. This will require extensive current and future task analyses for all manufacturing operations in all Pitney Bowes manufacturing facilities. The future pay delivery mix will be balanced toward individual effectiveness and skills acquisition, with group-based gainsharing or a team-oriented bonus program.

5. Management has communicated with employees through videos and group meetings regarding future downsizing expectations and the anticipated changes in workplace design and processes. In the factory selected as the pilot location, small group meetings have been held and more detailed information regarding the change processes has been shared.

Target Audience

The personnel affected by the human resource interventions are manufacturing employees; manufacturing supervisors; technical and support staff, including engineers; and plant management. One unusual factor is that the manufacturing employees have an average tenure of 10 years, with good performance ratings. Therefore, a significant number will not comprehend or accept the need for such radical changes in their competency requirements.

The manufacturing employees were the first to be involved with the human resource (HR) initiatives and measure of ROI. There were a total of 1,373 manufacturing employees who worked at the following facilities:

- Barry Place Assembly Plant (pilot facility), Stamford: 189 employees
- MMP Assembly Plant (new product pilot facility), Shelton: 65 employees
- MSU Assembly Operations, Stamford: 349 employees
- Plastics Fabrication Operation, Danbury: 84 employees
- Components Fabrication Operations, Stamford: 627 employees
- Mid-Range Assembly, Stamford: 27 employees
- Other: 32 employees
- Total Manufacturing Employees: 1,373

Table 1. Human resource development program activities.

1. Task analyses/development of constructs

2. Job classification/skill cluster levels matrix for implementation of a pay-for-knowledge program

3. Development of employee assessment instruments
   - Literacy/math
   - Operational (technical knowledge, skill and ability) assessment
   - Performance (interpersonal/administrative/cognitive) assessment

4. Design and delivery of employee communications
   - Brochures
   - Song
   - Videos
   - Communication meetings

5. Development and implementation of employee assessment protocols

6. Development and provision of employee feedback protocols, including individualized training plans

7. Design and development of original PC data processing software
   - Assessment System
   - Educational Tracking System
   - Task Analysis System
   - PC Workwords Analysis System

The HR initiatives are outlined in table 1.

Issues

Three major issues exist regarding measurement of ROI. First, is the so-called new ground issue. This human resource program is unique overall in that it developed an assessment and selection process for an in-place workforce with a demonstrated history of competency in order to retrain that workforce. Historically, assessment and selection processes are used primarily with job applicants and candidates for promotion. Testing of in-place employees is done for developmental purposes, and this project has employee development as one of the objectives. Also job redesign and restructuring are a part of it.

Second, because of the number of activities included in this program, the criteria traditionally associated with measurement of program results are insufficient. For example, such commonly accepted criteria as objectives, duration, participants, cost calculations, program content, frequency, method of delivery, demographics, and expected

Table 1 (continued). Human resource development program activities.

8. Design, development, and implementation of training and certification
- Literacy/math
- Operational (technical)
- Performance/cognitive
- Facilitator/diversity
- Technical/support staff
- Work/new product teams
- World class manufacturing
- Task analysis
- Instructional design
- Assessor training
- Feedback provider training

9. Development of training activity guides

10. Development and implementation of certification protocol

11. Learning contracts for corporate employees: concept and implementation

12. Development and implementation of learning contract training programs

13. Design of production specialist learning contracts: operational and performance

14. Design and implementation of validation protocols
- Content
- Construct
- Criterion referenced

15. Design and implementation of methodology for rollout of employee teams

16. Definition of performance measurement criteria and performance appraisal protocol

---

results are suited to evaluation and determination of ROI for a *single* human resource (training) program, or one where multiple components exist, but each is a variation on a single theme and there is an integrated mode of delivery. In this case, these criteria are not the same for each of the workforce transition activities, and different combinations of criteria are applicable to each activity. To analyze these criteria in the traditional manner would be to throw apples and oranges onto the same scale and to assume that the overall weight and number of pieces of fruit provide new data for cost assumptions and calculations, as well as "hard data" that describe results.

Third, interrelatedness and interdependency of the multiple performance interventions make it difficult to link measured results with any single program activity. Most results are attributable to a combination of HR interventions or to simultaneous implementation.

Models and Techniques

Rationale

Given these issues, a new conceptual framework for evaluation of business results was designed. Return-on-investment, the ultimate business barometer, remains the corporation's focus. The human resource program had to show that it was necessary and financially justifiable. However, most existing methodologies for a cost-benefit analysis, or calculating ROI for human resource programs, are difficult and sometimes imprecise. They focus only on self-limiting or subjective factors such as employee skill enhancement, productivity, and customer satisfaction measures as outputs. The same limitations apply when ROI is determined using only traditional inputs, such as costs for consulting, training hours, research and development, and/or standard (or utilization) hours.

None of these measurements affords even an estimate of the overall, long-range cost benefit due to the organizational changes, culture changes, and new products or services facilitated by most contemporary HR programs. The selected approach to determine such critical cost benefit is to expand calculation of ROI for HR initiatives to include concrete definitions of "outcome(s)" as well as the traditional "output(s)."

Design Process

The challenge was to design an ROI model for a multifaceted HR program, with many highly interdependent components, that was implemented to achieve both short- and long-term employee skill acquisition and comprehensive organizational reengineering.

Prior to the implementation of any HR activity, success criteria are defined in the form of outcome statements. Depending on the definition of each criterion and the evidence that directly links its achievement to the HR intervention, it is feasible to

- determine the cost benefit or ROI to the organization resulting from the achievement of the outcome
- establish a direct correlation between this cost benefit (or ROI) and the HR activity responsible for the successful outcome
- calculate ROI for the HR activity by a traditional comparison of the cost of that activity (input) with the cost benefit to the orga-

nization as a result of the outcome (output).

The first and most critical design choices were the selection of the outcome categories that would provide the most comprehensive description of desired results. In addition, the (design) model needed to provide a systematic and manageable taxonomy of outcomes to segment the human resource and organizational variables, establish the relationship between the human resource activity and the outcome, and simplify the required data collection. Three major classifications were selected to represent the scope and diversity of desired outcomes: effectiveness, efficiency, and transformational.

In this model, effectiveness outcomes are qualitative. They represent observable, documented results of human resource activities, such as changes to or elimination of existing work processes, implementation of any new work processes, changes to existing procedures or the introduction of new ones, and training. Examples of effectiveness outcomes include culture change, employee attitude, new employee accountabilities and skills, and customer satisfaction.

Efficiency outcomes are quantitative. Measurement of such results are statistically reliable, such as traditional productivity and quality measures. These outcomes describe the quantitative results of such human resource activities as employee assessment and training, organizational reengineering, changes to existing procedures, or the introduction of new ones.

Transformational outcomes may be either qualitative or quantitative. They describe the anticipated results of the organization moving from the current (present) state to the desired (future) state. These outcomes show that the human resource initiative did "transform" the organization in the long term, and can include changes to the basic ways in which an organization operates on a daily basis and results that alter the nature of the business enterprise.

The second critical design decision established three subcategories within each of these three major outcome classifications. This allows important, independent calculations of ROI for each of the three most common organizational components affected by human resource programs: people, product, and process. This organizational component delineation ensures a more precise definition of the outcomes in each classification, the further separation of human resource and other variables, and the accuracy and efficiency of the calculation of ROI for multifaceted human resource endeavors.

The third design decision identified those organizational variables that affect the achievement of desired outcomes. These organizational variables are methods to obtain (proof of occurrence of result); value statements (organizational); frame of reference (population); and assumptions (description of what the organization will look like when the measurement is made).

The next step was to define the threshold event or catalyst that would pinpoint the start of the evaluation timeline—one year and three years. What is documented is, "What event initiates the human resource activity(ies) that must occur to produce the anticipated result(s)?"

At this time, it is reasonable to define the one-year benchmarks that provide both an initial analysis of results to date from the human resource program and a first cut at short-term ROI for those results that are measurable after one year or while the program is ongoing.

Within the context established by the above, it now is feasible to define specific three-year outcomes in whatever number is necessary to describe the anticipated results fully. The extent to which achievement of these can be linked to the human resource program determines the use of each in calculating ROI.

The final step in the design of the model is to operationalize the outcomes through a list of behavioral and result descriptors that closely parallel the output in traditional calculation of ROI. Each output should describe one facet of the outcome, make the anticipated outcome results observable, ensure common perception of what the outcome statements represent, set up indices to measure the accomplishment of the outcome, and set up indices to measure the benefit to the organization of achievement of the outcome. (Space does not permit the printing of an actual model here. See tables 2, 3, and 4 for examples of efficiency outcomes for product, effectiveness outcomes for people, and transformation outcomes for process.)

Use of the Model

To develop a completed version of the model, the following steps were followed:

1. During the planning of the Workforce Transition (WFT) Project, the stakeholders and the human resource practitioners (the Pitney Bowes/Smith and Associates team) met, brainstormed, and reached consensus on a first draft that included definition of all elements. The only exception was that the letter x was used to indicate percentages and other indices that only could be provided by operating management. This draft was circulated to subject matter experts (SMEs) within the corporation for feedback and recommendations.

2. Upon receipt of the SMEs' comments, the project team met again

Table 2. Efficiency outcomes for product.

Method to Obtain	Value Statements	Population	Assumptions	Threshold Event
Track, record, and report quantitative measurements.	Manufacturing product in the most efficient manner will result in increased production flexibility, higher product quality, decreased product cost, and greater customer satisfaction.	Mailing Systems Operation	• Thresholds established are attainable in 3 years. • Producing quality product in less time results in decreased product cycle rates. • Decreased product cycle rates will effect increased production flexibility. • Increased production flexibility will result in decreased cycle times for customized products. • Efficient production will result in achievement of process yield goals set for the manufacturing operation. • Achievement of process yield goals for manufacturing operations will result in delivery reliability and consumer satisfaction. • Productivity indices will be reported within 3 working days of the end of the reporting period. • All employees will have received training in their Work Teams to interpret report data. • Increased product quality will result in less production scrap. • Product and process improvements will result in 100% process yield.	The establishment of Work Groups in a Section.

Table 2 (continued). Efficiency outcomes for product.

Method to Obtain	Value Statements	Population	Assumptions	Threshold Event
			• 100% average outgoing quality will result in increased reliability. • 100% average outgoing quality will effect a decrease in filed returns by 100%. • 100% average outgoing quality will effect a decrease in customer product complaints by 100%. • Quality indices will be reported within 3 working days of the end of the reporting period. • All employees will receive training in appropriate quality techniques.	

Table 2 (continued). Efficiency outcomes for product.

Results

1-year Benchmarks

- 3-year outputs replaced with 1-year percentages.
- Customer satisfaction increased by X%.
- Number of customer returns decreased by X%.

3-year Outcomes

- Efficient production of high-quality product to increase reliability and achieve greater customer satisfaction.

3-year Outputs

- Scrap reduction of X% per year.
- Process yield to reach 100%.
- 100% average outgoing quality.
- Decrease in field returns by 100%.
- Decrease in customer product complaints by X%.
- 100% customer satisfaction.
- Reduction in standard hours per product by X%.
- Product quality to be improved by X%.
- Schedule attainment at 100%.
- Product cycle time reduced by X%.
- Resources (defined by facility; example: machine, equipment, computers) downtime reduced by X%.
- Machine per person per hour should be trending favorably.
- Process yield achievement at 100%.
- Customer satisfaction increased by X%.
- Number of customer returns decreased by X%.

Table 3. Effectiveness outcomes for people.

Method to Obtain	Value Statements	Population	Assumptions	Threshold Event
Track, record, and report qualitative improvements in the competence of the Pitney Bowes manufacturing workforce.	Development of the full potential of employees is critical to the achievement of World Class Manufacturing objectives.	Mailing Systems Operations	• Thresholds established are attainable in 3 years. • Systems, policies, procedures, and resources are in place that encourage and support employee development. • Employee and team development requirements are defined and understood at all levels. • Employees are desirous of fully developing their skills. • Managers, supervisors, and technical support staff recognize the need and support development of employees.	Start of individual and/or Facilitator-assisted training for Work Team members.

Table 3 (continued). Effectiveness outcomes for people.

Method to Obtain	Population	Value Statements	Assumptions	Threshold Event
			• Flexible Work Teams and multiskilled employees require constant development in order to participate in and succeed in continuous process improvement. • Enhancement of skill leads to greater effectiveness for individuals and groups in achieving objectives.	

Table 3 (continued). Effectiveness outcomes for people.

Results

1-year Benchmarks

- All employees are in Work Teams with Pitney Bowes-trained Facilitators.
- All support personnel are trained in their roles and responsibilities and in effective interaction with Work Teams.
- A minimum of three randomly selected employee focus groups respond favorably to questions regarding improvements in workplace effectiveness.

3-year Outcomes

- Demonstrated application of multiple skills in a self-managed Work Team environment.
- Demonstrated efforts to develop higher level technical skills and/or leadership skills.
- Demonstrated participation and contributions to achievement of Team objectives, utilizing interpersonal skills.

3-year Outputs

- Minimum of Level 2 operational and performance skill level achieved and demonstrated in self-managed Work Team environment by all assigned members.
- Documentation of Work Team activities indicates full participation by all Team members in discussions, decision making, problem-solving activities, rotation of duties in operational and Team tasks.
- 100% of Work Team members are cross-trained within their defined levels of operational and performance skills.

Table 4. Transformation outcomes for process.

Method to Obtain	Value Statements	Population	Assumptions	Threshold Event
• Track, review, and evaluate the extent to which WFT protocols are fully implemented in all business units. • Track, record, and report the presence of WFT language throughout the organization. • Track, review, and evaluate the extent of organizational and process changes initiated by WFT activities, and any improvements/problems that result.	• Continuous organizational refinement and manufacturing process improvement is central to success in a World Class competitive environment. • Continuous improvement in processes directing workforce activities and facilitating employee development is central to success in a World Class competitive environment.	Mailing Systems Operations	• Thresholds established are attainable in 3 years. • The WFT initiative is the correct process to attain improvements required for success in a World Class competitive environment. • WFT will not be simply a transitional process, but rather the way in which MSO conducts all work activities at all organizational levels. • WFT processes will be supported by adequate staffing and budget on a go-forward basis. • Organizational and employee commitment to WFT is demonstrated through use of WFT vocabulary and implementation of WFT processes.	• Introduction of WFT initiatives to business unit. • Formation of Work Teams. • Initiation of individual skills training.

Table 4 (continued). Transformation outcomes for process.

Results

1-year Benchmarks

- Initiating WFT events, such as task analyses, instrument development, employee assessment, formation of Work Teams, training module development, scheduling of employee training. Certification tracking and implementation of a Pay-for-Knowledge Compensation system either are completed or within 2 years of completion.

3-year Outcomes

- WFT ceases to be designated a "transition." All WFT activities that are ongoing will be given new organizational titles and/or integrated into the organization's standard work processes and infrastructure.
- Continually increasing competency and collaboration of the manufacturing workforce, technical/support staff, and operating management results in (a) improved workforce/staff utilization, (b) increased productivity, (c) improved product quality, (d) integration of manufacturing processes, (e) decreased infrastructure, and (f) reduction in time and cost of New Product Development and Introduction.

3-year Outputs

- WFT processes (without the "transition" designation) are a priority component of the Pitney Bowes Mailing Systems 5-year plan and annual budget process.
- WFT processes (without the "transition" designation) appear in the organization's vision and strategic plan.
- Public statements (internal and external to Pitney Bowes) by senior staff mention/discuss specific WFT processes a minimum of (X) times a year.
- All manufacturing employees, technical/support staff, and operating management employ the WFT vocabulary in all planning and daily work activities.
- All manufacturing employees, technical/support staff, and operating management practice the WCM principles, using the WCM vocabulary, in all planning and daily work activities.

Table 4 (continued). Transformation outcomes for process.

Results (continued).

3-year Outputs (continued)	• Manufacturing employees, technical/support staff, and operating management take responsibility for continuously reconceptualizing and improving upon WCM principles. • Causal links are documented between implementation of WFT processes and (a) increased competency and collaboration of the manufacturing workforce, technical/support staff and operating management, (b) improved workforce/staff utilization, (c) increased productivity, (d) improved product quality, (e) integration of manufacturing processes, (f) decreased infrastructure, and (g) reduction in time and cost of New Product Development and Introduction.

and reached consensus on a more complete version, again with the exceptions noted above. This version was provided to the management steering committee for its approval, along with a brief presentation to ensure the committee's understanding of how the model would be utilized to determine both the efficacy of the HR activities and ROI.

3. Following approval of the outcomes (and output) by management, a copy of the model was provided to the operating managers in each facility so that they would insert the appropriate percentages and other indices wherever x appeared. This allowed for any differences between the manufacturing facilities based on function, start date, and other conditions, and it ensured that the measurements would be reality-based.

4. This completed version of the model then was submitted again to the management steering committee, both for their information and for feedback.

5. A validation group was formed to collect the requisite data at the planned dates and to participate in the data analysis. The recommendation was to train these staff members in this new use of criterion-referenced validation to determine ROI and data collection methodology, such as behavioral interviewing and observation.

6. It was necessary for the validation group to determine which data collection methods were best suited to each category of outcome and to establish a schedule for collection of the data and a plan for analysis of the data.

7. The validation group and management needed to reach consensus regarding to whom the results of the data analysis would be communicated and the format for the communication.

8. Once the entire action plan was finalized, the data collection methods, the schedule, the degree of employee participation required, and the communication format were shared with management and the employees to encourage complete cooperation.

9. The data collection and data analysis were initiated.

10. ROI could be calculated for the human resource activities by a traditional comparison of the cost of each activity (input) with the cost benefit to the organization as a result of the outcome (output). The initial results were published.

Linkage

A critical consideration in determining the ROI produced by HR programs is the requirement to demonstrate a causal link between the HR intervention and the outcome. This often is a perplexing and inconsistent endeavor, primarily because of two issues. First, as discussed previously, most contemporary HR interventions are designed with multiple activities. The measurement criteria usually are not the same for each activity, and the activities may be so interrelated and interdependent that it is not possible to link results with any single program. Second, no HR program is executed in a vacuum. Existing or new environmental and business factors may have an impact on outcome. There is a need to isolate these factors and account for them to ensure that a result used to calculate ROI is attributable directly to a HR activity.

The model uses a systematic and manageable taxonomy of outcomes to segment the HR factors from other environmental and business factors, and thereby establish a link between the HR activity and the outcomes. This linkage is strengthened by the design process, which requires SMEs to define the following:

- the assumptions used to predict that a human resource intervention will cause the desired result
- any value statements underlying the assumptions
- the initiating or threshold event out of multiple, interrelated, interdependent HR initiatives
- the employee population that should be affected
- the method most likely to obtain data that demonstrate both the linkage between an HR program and the outcome, and the extent to which the desired result has been achieved based on the one-year benchmarks, three-year outcomes, and three-year output.

Using this design process, traditional quantitative criteria like quality and productivity allow the measurement of such human resource factors as changes in employee knowledge, skill, and ability; changes in employee responsibility and accountability; redesign of work processes; and redesign of the work environment.

Quality and productivity are linked to all relevant HR results and are distinguished from environmental and business factors by the specificity of the outcomes and outputs.

The exactness with which the model isolates environmental and business factors creates a context in which to establish whether or not each is a causal agent. The calculation of ROI depends upon an analysis of the data to determine if environmental and business factors are more instrumental than the human resource program in producing the result.

Table 5 provides an example of how to determine the effect of environmental and business factors on each indicator, using schedule at-

Table 5. Mailing products and systems 1992 work group performance, The Elms Products.

Schedule Attainment	M/P/H	Process Yield	Problem/Causes	Safety
January 100%	4.9	97.4%	6 identified 4 solved	No accidents
February 100%	5.04	97.5%	3 identified 1 solved	1 accident
March 100%	4.85	98.6%	5 identified	No accidents
April 100%	4.89	97.5%	1 identified	No accidents
May 100%	5.31	97.2%	1 identified	No accidents
June 100%	5.14	97.6%	New format established	No accidents
July 100%	5.18	98.6%	New format established	No accidents
August 100%	4.53	98.4%	9 identified 8 solved	No accidents
September 100%	4.92	98.0%	None identified	No accidents
October 100%	4.57	98.6%	None identified	1 accident

tainment to measure productivity. The number of machines per hour (m/p/h) to achieve 100 percent schedule attainment decreased from 5.04 in February to 4.85 in March. Knowledge of manufacturing suggests that this is due to the business factor of diminished customer demand. (High inventory levels might be the contributing environmental factor.) Logically, an organization could attribute the 100 percent schedule attainment achieved in March to this business factor because workers had a lower, less difficult goal to achieve.

However, schedule attainment also remained at 100 percent when the number of machines per hour increased from 4.89 in April to 5.31 in May. If the business factor of decreased customer demand and the resulting easier schedule caused the 100 percent schedule attainment in March, what accounts for schedule attainment of 100 percent when customer demand increased and the schedule became more difficult?

The answer to that question (and other similar questions) demonstrates that the cause actually is the human resource program implemented to establish work teams and upgrade individual skills.

Another illustration is the measurement of three components of quality: process yield, average outgoing quality (AOQ), and installation quality. Process yield and installation quality exceed the objective, and AOQ is below the objective, as shown in table 6. To ensure the integrity of the measurement of ROI for human resource programs, environmental and business factors should always be considered as causal agents, and either established as the most important variable or eliminated.

One such result is the disappointing AOQ. In this instance, a business factor rather than a human resource activity was the cause. Industry experts agree that the trend is for customer expectations to increase each year. Quality no longer is a competitive issue. Rather, it is a "must have" as customers refuse to accept products with even minor, cosmetic defects. This generates pressure to upgrade internal quality standards to match those of the customer. Until this is accomplished, customer complaints and returns hold down the rate of outgoing quality.

The remaining two results are positive. Again, the causal role of human resource must be established. Industry experts agree that one-half of all quality improvements come from the workforce understanding what is required and what to avoid to produce unblemished products. Therefore, process yield and installation quality results are attributable to the human resource initiatives that downloaded indirect tasks, such as quality inspection, to the work teams. Awareness was increased, and accountability was assured. Even the environmental factor of poor incoming materials was overcome through the workforce having new authority to refuse any defective material or parts delivered by vendors.

A final example is the traditional manufacturing indicator of space utilization. The business and environmental factors are very influential with this outcome. Vertical integration or the synchronization of manufacturing processes causes manufacturing operations to fold subassembly lines into final assembly lines and integrate product assembly with components manufacturing, resulting in a decrease in the space required for a single line or an entire operation. The Workforce Transition human resource interventions allowed Pitney Bowes to consolidate seven manufacturing facilities into one, and still increase operating efficiencies.

Both better space utilization and an increase in output per square foot of manufacturing space are impossible in most instances without

Table 6. Mailing products and systems operating results, October 1992 status.

Responsibility	Indicator	Objective		Current Month	Year to Date
Product supply	Master production schedule	100%		100.5%	99.6%
	Linearity	Line 4 R150	5.0%	75.0%	21.5%
		Line 3 62XX	16.3%	35.4%	22.5%
		Line 5 E20X	5.0%	1.8%	0.8%
		Line 2 5650	5.0%	0.0%	35.4%
		Line 2 61XX	19.5%	49.8%	33.4%
		Line 1 56XX	7.4%	10.0%	19.6%
Quality	Process yield	ELMS 97.5%		97.8%	98.2%
		62XX 67.5%		71.0%	70.5%
	AOQ		3.2%	2.6%	1.8%
	Installation quality	2.3%		5.6%	2.35%
Budget attainment	Expense budget	98%		123%	108%
	Capital budget	100%		21%	50%
Assets	Day's supply	* R150 28		31	35
		62XX 20		19	17
		E20X 10		20	14
		61XX 27		18	20
		56XX34		31	33
	Inventory accuracy	In-stores	96%	57%	57%
		WIP	95%		57%
Safety	Total case rate	10.7 days		9.7	9.7
	Lost workday case rate	5.9 days		3.7	3.7
Human Renewal	ELMS Midrange 6200	Monthly operating reviews		See attached	See attached

* Includes 32XX

human resource intervention. For example, skilled professionals can reengineer a manufacturing environment so that it requires less space. The workforce cannot build product in the new environment, however, if workers do not have the knowledge, skill, and ability required to complete the redesigned processes or if the organization's culture does not reinforce the cooperation forced by the new work flow and increased proximity.

Results

Because of the long time frames unique to the WFT project and the different start-up dates at each facility, the evaluation process is ongoing. However, examples of some of the results to date that can be translated directly into bottom-line measures are

- Pitney Bowes manufacturing productivity increased 30 percent (15 percent per year for the last two years), which is highly significant—the industry average is 7 percent to 7.5 percent.
- The downloading of indirect tasks to the work teams is credited with a 26 percent improvement in overall quality.
- PB achieved a 50 percent rise in output per square foot of manufacturing space.

Pitney Bowes now has been measuring the ROI it achieved from its Workforce Transition Program from 1992 through the beginning of the third quarter of 1997. Although specific dollar amounts for the actual cost of the program and the monetary value of the Workforce Transition results are considered confidential and cannot be published, a Pitney Bowes spokesperson confirms that the overall payback is excellent.

The public financial record of Pitney Bowes for the first year that Workforce Transition results were measured is a public indicator of the return-on-investment. In 1992, Pitney Bowes' profit margin increased to 14.4 percent from 13.9 percent in 1991. This increase in profit margin was achieved despite the fact that PB's 1992 net income was $100,237,000 (adjusted for first year under FASB [Federal Accounting Standards Board] 106), which is down from $295,299,000 in 1991. The ability to increase profit margin, even when net income decreases, is directly linked to the increased individual employee and manufacturing team productivity and the consistent decrease in unit costs of manufacturing product that resulted from Workforce Transition.

Its most recent results for two significant metrics for manufacturing—process yield (all mailing machines) and audit rejection rate (all mailing machines)—appear in figures 1 and 2.

Figure 1. Process yield (all mailing machines) through second quarter 1996.

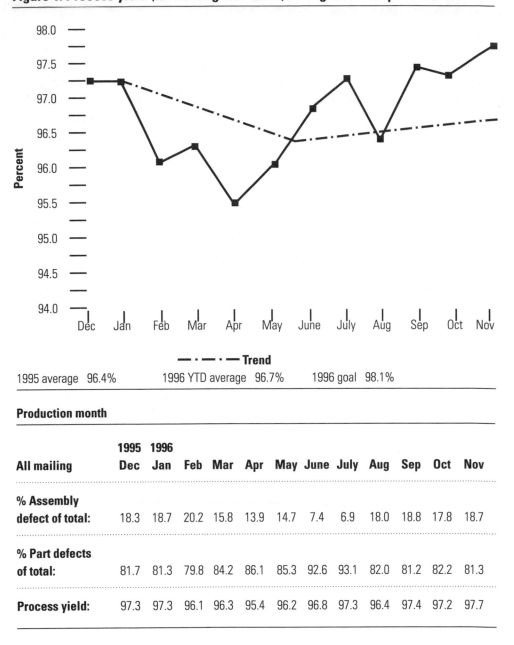

1995 average 96.4%   1996 YTD average 96.7%   1996 goal 98.1%

Production month

All mailing	1995 Dec	1996 Jan	Feb	Mar	Apr	May	June	July	Aug	Sep	Oct	Nov
% Assembly defect of total:	18.3	18.7	20.2	15.8	13.9	14.7	7.4	6.9	18.0	18.8	17.8	18.7
% Part defects of total:	81.7	81.3	79.8	84.2	86.1	85.3	92.6	93.1	82.0	81.2	82.2	81.3
Process yield:	97.3	97.3	96.1	96.3	95.4	96.2	96.8	97.3	96.4	97.4	97.2	97.7

Figure 2. Audit reject rate (all mailing machines) through the beginning of third quarter 1996.

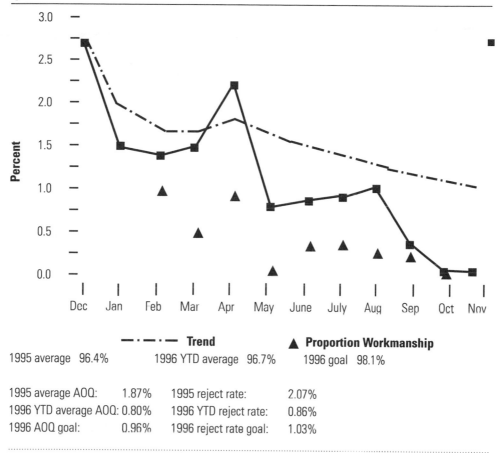

—·—·— Trend   ▲ Proportion Workmanship

1995 average 96.4%	1996 YTD average 96.7%	1996 goal 98.1%

1995 average AOQ:	1.87%	1995 reject rate:	2.07%
1996 YTD average AOQ:	0.80%	1996 YTD reject rate:	0.86%
1996 AOQ goal:	0.96%	1996 reject rate goal:	1.03%

Questions for Discussion

1. Would this criterion-referenced validation model for calculating return-on-investment for human resource activities work in your organization? What adaptations would be necessary to ensure its applicability to your organization's unique characteristics?

2. In order to gain some experience with the use of this model, write a definition for each element that would be reality based for your organization. Share these definitions with the group. Are major modifications truly required? How can some of the differences be reconciled?

3. Examine the interdependency of the various factors. For example, what types of assumptions could be changed?

Figure 2 (continued). Audit reject rate (all mailing machines) through the beginning of third quarter 1996.

All mailing machines Reject rate and AOQ:	1995 Dec	Jan	Feb	Mar	Apr	May	June	July	Aug	Sep	Oct	1996 Nov
Total produced	8,636	9,837	8,706	10,031	9,257	10,321	7,565	3,770	4,201	7,647	8,006	8,305
Quantity inspected	632	736	663	731	690	816	543	258	650	1,006	987	1,028
Quantity rejected	17	11	9	11	15	6	4	2	6	4	1	1
Proportion workmanship	59%	100%	78%	36%	40%	17%	50%	50%	33%	50%	0%	100%
Audit reject rate	2.7%	1.5%	1.4%	1.5%	2.2%	0.7%	0.7%	0.8%	0.9%	0.4%	0.1%	0.1%
AOQ	2.5%	1.4%	1.3%	1.5%	2.1%	0.7%	0.7%	0.7%	0.8%	0.4%	0.1%	0.1%

4. Assess the method utilized to isolate the effects of the WFT initiatives. What other approaches do you think would be feasible?

The Author

Rändi Sigmund Smith, president of Smith and Associates Inc., received her Ed.D. and M.A. in adult development from Columbia University and her M.A. in industrial psychology from Norwich University. She completed thesis research at Yale University. Publications include *Written Communication for Data Processing,* (published in 1976 by Robert E. Krieger Publishing Company and reprinted in 1981 and 1986 by arrangement with Van Nostrand Reinhold Company); "How to Measure and Assess the Psychological and Work Management Factors Associated with Introduction of New Technology in Workplace," a research paper published as master's thesis; "A Case Study of Data Processing Training within a Corporate Setting Utilizing Principles and Practices of Adult Education," Doctoral Dissertation, Columbia University and U.M.I. Dissertation Information Service, 1988; and "ROI for Knowledge Industries," research paper prepared for a consortium of client corporations. Smith's clients include Xerox Corporation, The Travelers Companies, The Aetna Life and Casualty, and

IBM. She may be contacted at Smith and Associates Inc., 87 Westmont, West Hartford, CT 06117. Phone: 860.521.9363; fax 860.561.4034; e-mail: rsmith@ smithinc.com; Web page: www.smithinc.com.

Measuring the Impact of Basic Skills Training

Otto Engineering

Edward E. Gordon and Boyd Owens

Many organizations are providing basic skills training in English, mathematics and reading. These skills are essential for growth and improvement. The payoff on these programs, however, is very difficult to capture. This case traces the efforts to evaluate basic skills training at a manufacturing company. It illustrates the potential impact from this type of training and the difficulty in arriving at the precise contribution of the program.

Background and Organizational Profile

Otto Engineering is a small manufacturing company in Carpentersville, Illinois. In 1961, Otto entered the switch market as a supplier of switches for military and industrial applications. Otto anticipated the downturn in the military market in the late 1980s and moved into commercial markets that required precision, highly reliable, snap-action switches and electrical assemblies for applications in such areas as aerospace, medical technology, construction, and agricultural equipment. Otto started producing complete electronic assemblies in the early 1990s.

By early 1988, Otto's management realized that the company was losing business because of poor product quality. Commercial markets proved more demanding in quality requirements than the military market, and Otto quickly realized that something must be done to retain commercial customers and Otto's reputation in the electronics

This case was prepared to serve as a basis for discussion rather than to illustrate either effective or ineffective administrative and management practices.

market. With four or five direct competitors and more than 100 other switch companies worldwide, Otto had to preserve product quality as a distinguishing company feature.

A statistical process control (SPC) training program was initiated but suspended several weeks later because of no improvement in quality. Otto's senior managers met with the frontline supervisors (group leaders) to discuss what had gone wrong. These group leaders knew that many of the employees either did not speak English or had not graduated from high school. An evaluation showed that 40 of the 80 employees in Otto's production department used English only as a second language. The average English proficiency level for this group was a third-grade level, but most workers had listening comprehension skills below that level. More than half of the hourly workforce who attended the SPC class did not understand what the instructor was saying.

The Training Initiative

Classes in English as a Second Language (ESL) were recommended for the 40 employees who were not native speakers. Those employees spoke a variety of primary languages. Spanish was the primary language of 50 percent of the group, and the other languages were Laotian, spoken by 20 percent; Korean, spoken by 15 percent; Vietnamese, by 10 percent; and Pilipino, by 5 percent. An instructor was identified who specialized in Pacific Rim languages.

Elgin Community College (ECC) offered classes four days a week, Monday through Thursday. The 40 employees were split into two groups, roughly by grade level. One group attended class on Monday and Wednesday, and the other on Tuesday and Thursday. Each class period lasted two hours, with Otto paying employees for one hour of class. One hour was on the employee's time. After six months of these classes, Otto started paying employees for both hours to eliminate attendance problems.

The Illinois Prairie State 2000 initiative is a grant program to help companies educationally upgrade their workers for increased competitiveness by modernizing management methods or teaching workforce skills. Otto applied for and received a $10,000 Prairie State 2000 Grant to help offset training costs.

Before the class started, each employee was assessed using the Test for Adult Basic Education (TABE), and reassessments were conducted every three to four months thereafter. The instructor from ECC met with the Otto SPC instructors to determine the specific skills that the employees needed to learn. A major focus of these ESL classes was to enable employees to apply SPC as a part of their daily jobs. This effort produced a dictionary of slang terms used at Otto Engineering as an educational tool for the ESL instructor. Additional training materials were produced from the company's handbook, policy and procedures manual, the SPC training material, and other common company forms.

Key Issues and Events

In conjunction with the ESL basic skills education program, Otto's management began work on a quality training effort. A SPC steering committee was established and charged with implementing an SPC program in manufacturing. This committee included the quality manager, engineering manager, manufacturing manager, and manufacturing engineering manager. In early 1990, the committee designed a SPC training course and an in-house SPC train-the-trainer program. A key component of Otto's plan for restructuring the business was to have the manufacturing department become the driving force for its quality improvement program.

HRD Program Description and Delivery

The SPC training program also focused on giving basic skills training that paralleled the ESL training to the native English speakers. Employees were given a pretest that covered the various math skills needed in SPC. The employees were then divided into groups based on math-skill levels so that the instructor could focus only on the math that each group needed.

An additional support for the SPC class was the training schedule in blueprint reading (BPR). These courses were taught by one of the authors and an engineer working in computer-assisted design (CAD). The BPR classes also covered gauge operations and basic measurement. Employees were chosen to take this class according to their department and job at Otto. Approximately 25 percent of Otto's workforce went through the BPR class. In all cases, everyone attended the math review classes before the SPC class.

To reinforce the importance of SPC to Otto's company culture, individual performance reviews were rewritten to include quality. They asked whether employees participated in the quality program and how well they performed the work. Performing SPC operations was made a part of all job descriptions. A detailed job description was written for Otto group leaders, which included responsibilities in the quality program. A subset of the leader's job description became a job description for the assistant group leaders. By including quality at so many levels, the company sent a message to all employees that SPC had become a part of Otto's culture and not just a short-term training fad.

When employees' skills in the ESL classes advanced to the sixth-grade level in reading fluency, they were automatically scheduled for a SPC class. The idea was first to enroll these employees in SPC training when they had sufficient knowledge of English so that they could complete the SPC training, and then to get them started using SPC on the job. Fifteen employees did not reach the sixth-grade reading level and were placed in a SPC class for one-on-one tutoring. Even though these employees completed the training, they were never able to perform SPC as part of their job.

In conjunction with this training program, Otto collected data about participating employees and their work performance. The information the company gathered included performance ratings, number of jobs that could be performed, pay grade of the job, pay rate, field returns (that is, defective products that were sent back) caused by human error, productivity rates, and the like. Otto encouraged and assisted employees to learn new jobs and advance to jobs with greater difficulty.

An effort was also made to cross-train employees within and between departments. Like other companies with modern industrial plants, Otto experiences monthly shifts in product mix. When one assembly line slows down, it is a common practice for supervisors to move employees from that line to another. Moving a person in this manner is tied directly to the number and type of jobs the person can perform. Otto's group leaders started creating a matrix of jobs and employees who could perform each job. This matrix allowed leaders to plan appropriate training, line staffing, and personal vacations and to have an adequate number of employees ready to perform a specific job.

Program Costs

Otto's costs for the training program changed as the source of the instruction changed from outside service providers to inside providers. Training costs for some of these programs are as follows:

English as a Second Language (ESL)
40 participants, 1.5 years

Instructors and materials	$152,000
Employee wages	80,010
Replacement overtime	48,000
Total	$280,010

Statistical Process Control (SPC)
85 participants, 2 years

Instructors	$ 25,200
Employee wages	12,801
Replacement overtime	7,680
Materials	1,600
Total	$ 47,281

Program Results: Quality Improvements

Otto began its workforce education program to improve the quality of its products, and quality improvement was the program's principal achievement. The workforce training allowed employees to learn the basic skills for successful implementation of SPC throughout Otto's manufacturing sections.

Field Returns

As the ESL class progressed, there was a dramatic drop in the number of field returns. Figure 1 shows the average dollar of field returns per year according to employee reading levels.

Figure 1. Annual dollars of field returns per employee over five-year period.

Average $ of Field Returns/Year/Employee

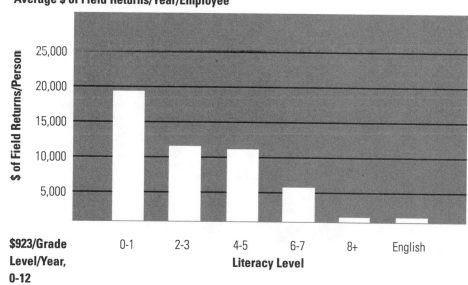

This graph includes only those field returns that can be directly traced to an operator error. It does not include returns that were caused by poor machine capability or bad parts from suppliers. Based on this information, Otto saved $923 per year in field returns for each grade level in reading gained by an employee through the workforce education program.

Scrap

Scrap data (that is, the defective products that Otto must discard) from 1990 through 1994 were analyzed and correlated strongly with the data on training dollars spent on basic skills. However, dollars of scrap did not correlate to total training dollars or to training dollars spent on quality training. The data showed that for the five-year period, each dollar invested in workforce basic skills reduced the dollars of scrap caused by human error by $1,656. The data could not be analyzed by individuals' reading-fluency level, but they indicated that the basic skills of the workforce were the main determinant for reducing scrap caused by employee errors.

Figure 2. Dollars of product shipped per year per employee.

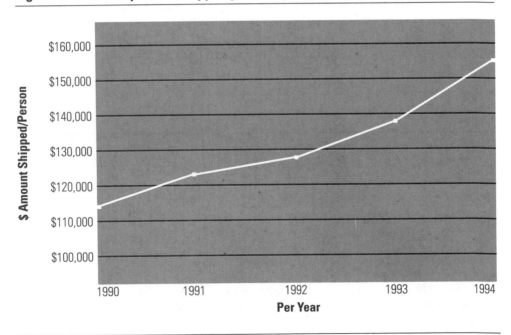

Productivity

Otto experienced a large productivity improvement over the five-year period. Productivity was measured as the dollars of product shipped per year, per employee. Figure 2 shows the trend from 1990 through 1994.

This productivity improvement resulted from training, capital investment, and management operational changes that took place within the organization. A statistical analysis of these productivity improvement dollars, training costs, and the capital investment costs revealed that 31 percent of productivity improvement came from training and 32 percent from capital investment; 37 percent can be attributed to all other changes that were not specifically tracked. During these five years, Otto Engineering spent $556,000 on all training and $8.5 million on capital equipment investment. A combination of investment in both training and capital improvements yielded the best results.

Over the five-year period, the results demonstrated a direct annual correlation between employees' educational gains and increased company profit. The National Center on the Educational Quality of the Workforce at the University of Pennsylvania designed a broad-based survey to document the degree to which education is directly linked to productivity. The study found that a 10 percent increase in the value of capital stock, such as tools, building, and machinery, produced a 3.4 percent increase in productivity, but a 10 percent increase in worker education (equivalent to one grade level of skill improvement) yielded an 8.6 percent annual increase in business productivity (as compared to Otto's more than 6.0 percent annual increase over a five-year period).

Number of Jobs

Otto also witnessed a growth in the number of jobs that individual employees could perform, enabling the company to increase its ability to adapt changes in product demands. In the late 1980s and early 1990s, Otto experienced instances when production lines were shut down because of employees' vacations or illness. Management also found it difficult to move workers between areas on an as-needed basis. The effort to cross-train employees through a workforce education program yielded interesting and positive results. Figure 3 shows the average number of jobs employees knew how to do. The three lines represent those employees with reading skills at the fifth-grade level or lower, employees at sixth grade or higher, and employees who were not assessed because they were native English speakers.

Figure 3. Average number of jobs known by literacy grade.

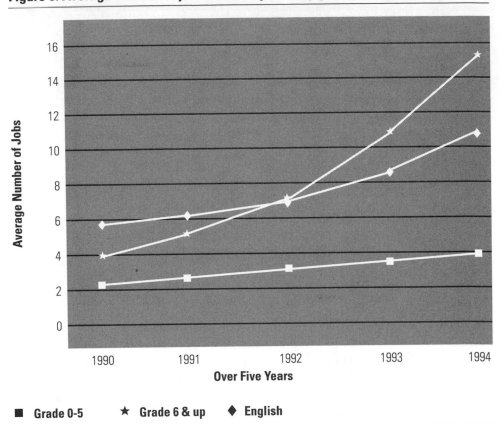

Over Five Years

■ Grade 0-5   ★ Grade 6 & up   ◆ English

As evident in figure 3, the fifth grade and under group could perform many fewer jobs than could the sixth grade and over and the native English-speaking. Otto's management also noticed a difference in performance between the two groups. Those employees functioning above the sixth-grade level proved more flexible in performing job assignments. In 1990, there were five instances when assembly lines were shut down because of an absence of operators. After cross-training was initiated in 1993-1994, however, no lines were shut down. The availability of backup operators on all jobs increased Otto's flexibility and reduced the incidence of late deliveries due to absences and illness.

It is important to note that even though the actual direct financial benefit from this training appears to be low (about $200 per day of shutdown), the indirect financial benefit from improved customer service and market penetration was much larger.

Reduced Training Costs

Workforce education skills training also improved the ability of employees to learn subsequent job skills. The company kept records on the time and costs for employees to learn specific job skills over the five-year period. For a given level of job difficulty (pay grades G1 to G5), it was found that increasing the reading-fluency level by two grades reduced the cost of training the person in that job skill by 50 percent. This is illustrated in figure 4.

Employees with lower reading comprehension abilities were also unsuccessful at learning the more difficult jobs. The authors believe that it is reasonable to assume that employees with higher reading comprehension skills were given greater opportunities to learn new jobs be-

Figure 4. Training dollars needed based on employee literacy level.

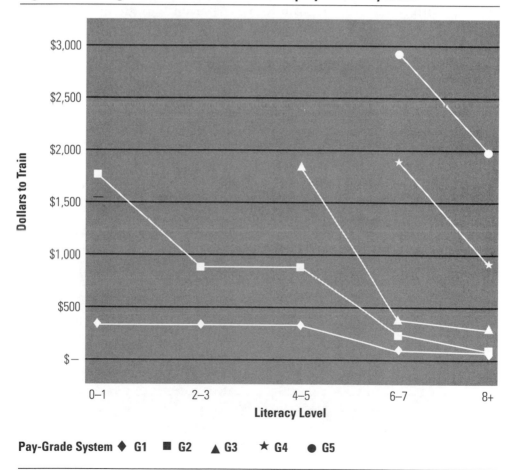

cause their participation in the workforce education program made them easier to train.

The costs of the workforce education program generally declined over the five-year period because of the changes that occurred over time. Figure 5 shows that program costs peaked at approximately $160,000 in year one and declined to about $40,000 in year four due to the increasing educational levels of the participants and the increased use of Otto employees as instructors.

Job Skills and Pay Grade

Otto has a five-tier pay-grade system. The levels are G1 to G5, with G1 being the easier, lower paying jobs, and G5, the most difficult and highest paying. It was found that people with a reading-fluency level of third grade or lower occupied the G1 and G2 level jobs. However, employees with reading levels from fourth to seventh grade had the ability to perform jobs at the G3 and G4 levels. The more complex G5 jobs

Figure 5. Dollars spent for training over five-year period.

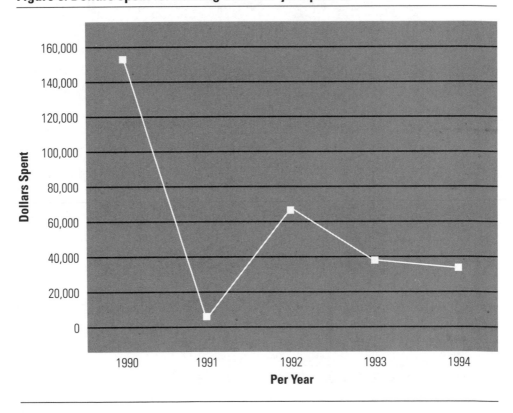

were almost exclusively held by employees who had attained an eighth-grade or higher level of reading fluency.

Employees at the fifth-grade or lower reading level seemed unable to advance after a certain point, but those who read at a sixth-grade or higher level continued to move up in pay-grade level (see figure 6).

The analysis further indicated that employees with sixth- and seventh-grade reading levels moved up more slowly in pay-grade levels than those with reading levels of eighth grade and above.

A clear relationship was established between the increased educational attainments of the employees and their ability to do more complex and difficult jobs. In addition, employees received higher pay and performance reviews, and the company's competitiveness and profitability improved because of this relationship.

Performance Improvement

Before the workforce education program began in 1990, native English speakers received clearly better reviews than the nonnative speakers. Many of the nonnative speakers received a small improve-

Figure 6. Pay vs. educational attainment during five-year period.

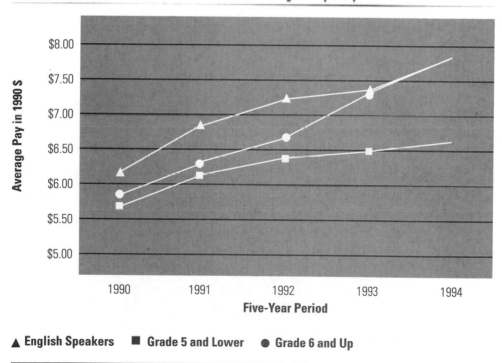

▲ English Speakers   ■ Grade 5 and Lower   ● Grade 6 and Up

ment in their performance review scores within a year after the start of the educational skills classes (see figure 7).

The nonnative speakers who ended the training program with reading levels under fifth grade saw no additional improvement in performance review scores even with additional job-related training. However, employees with reading levels of sixth grade or higher continued improving, and by 1993, were obtaining performance ratings equal to those of native English speakers. When the study ended in 1994, the native English speakers and the higher-educated nonnative speakers also received better performance reviews than employees with reading fluency skill under the sixth-grade level, further suggesting a correlation between personal educational improvement and better on-the-job productivity.

Employee Pay

The ability of an employee to be promoted to a higher-grade job has a direct impact on the employee's pay. Figure 8 shows the pay of native English speakers, nonnative speakers below sixth grade, and

Figure 7. Performance improvement during five-year period.

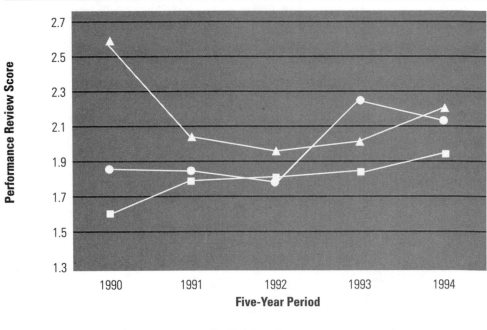

nonnative speakers sixth grade and up. The graph shows that nonnative speakers earned less than the native speakers in 1990. By 1992, the nonnative speakers whose reading level was sixth grade or higher distinguished themselves from those below sixth grade. By 1993, they were being paid at a level equal to the native English speakers. The employees with lower reading levels saw their pay start to flatten out by 1993 and 1994, and they were unable to move into the more difficult and higher-paying jobs.

With the help of Otto's Work Force Education Program, in as little as four years, some employees were able to close a gap in skills between the native and nonnative speakers.

Economic Value Added by Training

To calculate an overall economic payback from the study's data, the average training cost for all types of training was figured on the basis of per person, per year for instructor time, material costs, and costs for making up lost labor. The measurable financial benefits coming from the program are lower injury claims, field returns, and internal

Figure 8. Pay vs. educational attainment during five-year period.

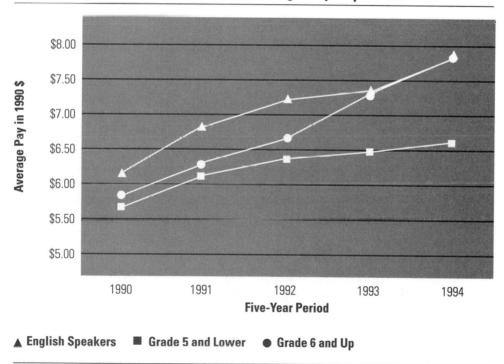

▲ English Speakers ■ Grade 5 and Lower ● Grade 6 and Up

scrap, and improved productivity, as these figures show:

Training costs into the program
 $1,877 per person, per year

Benefits from the program
 Reduced injury claims $625 per person, per year
 Reduced field returns $923 per person, per year
 Reduced internal scrap $3,097 per person, per year

Productivity profit
 Contribution (31%) $314 per person, per year

The economic payback to the company was as follows:

$$(\$1,877 \text{ per person, per year}) / (\$625 + \$923 + \$3,097 + \$314 \text{ per person, per year}) \times 1 \text{ year} =$$
$$(\$1,877 / \$4,959) \times 1 \text{ year} = 0.378 \text{ years payback.}$$
$$= 4.5 \text{ months}$$

These calculations do not take into account that education takes time, and therefore causes a delay in the payback a company can expect. Using Otto's average of four hours of class time per week, and an average time of 100 hours of contact time to advance an employee one grade level, the payback time becomes 10.3 months. This measurement corresponds closely to the amount of time following the inception of ESL classes that it took for production supervisors to begin noticing improvements in these employees' job performance on the factory floor.

Based on the evaluation of program results, most employees' improvement resulted from the basic skills training and not from other types of training. Educational skills, particularly in reading, are a major cost driver for business quality and productivity improvement. The success of other types of training, such as SPC, was largely the result of improved reading comprehension and vocabulary skills gained from the ESL workforce education classes. It is our belief that SPC will add future increased economic value as advanced manufacturing technology increases within the switching industry as a whole, and Otto Engineering in particular.

Conclusions and Recommendations

Many of Otto's experiences are typical of educational skill programs for U.S. production workers. Four final recommendations are of great importance. First, to maximize the success of any workforce education program for any group of employees, personal participation must become mandatory. Most programs begin as a voluntary effort. However, as technology becomes more complex, workforce education will become essential for employees to retain their current jobs and cope with continuous technology upgrades and new management systems (teams, quality, and the like).

Second, to help further ensure the success of these programs, Otto moved attendance from shared time to 100 percent company time. It is essential that adequate, guaranteed time in class be given to each worker. This is not meant to discourage employee attendance at local community colleges or universities for degree programs on their own time. However, employee tuition reimbursement programs are among the most underused personal benefits that U.S. businesses offer.

Third, the American-born production workers who did not participate in the workforce education skills program generally failed to advance in pay grades or to higher job categories at the same rate as the nonnative production workers. This is hardly surprising because most of the jobs at Otto require higher levels of reading and math skills. Employees who raise their educational ability levels will advance, and those who maintain a status quo will be left behind in job advancement and pay increases. The lesson to be learned is that all employees need to participate in educational programs to some degree to prosper in high-technology business environments.

Fourth, a better educational mix is required of small-group tutoring of a diagnostic and developmental nature, with standard large classroom instruction. The combined use of tutoring and teaching will dramatically accelerate adult learning and show even faster employee productivity increases on the job. In the long term, this proves to be the most economical training procedure for these skills training programs.

Questions for Discussion

1. What is your assessment of the mix of the output measures?
2. How would you critique the method used to isolate the effects of training?
3. How would you critique the method used to convert data to monetary values?
4. Is this a credible study? Explain.
5. What specific Otto economic-value-added (EVA) strategies can you use for your company?
6. Who are the managers in your organization whose help you need to quantify operational problems areas that training might improve?
7. How can your outside training vendors or internal training designers help determine the length of the "training effect" or "shelf-life" to

quantify potential depreciation schedules for EVA?

8. If your company does not offer employee training during work time, what quantified revenue improvements must the training offer to change this company policy?

The Authors

Edward E. Gordon is an internationally recognized authority on employee training and education in the workplace. He is the principal author of *FutureWork, the Revolution Reshaping American Business* (Praeger, 1994), *Closing the Literacy Gap in American Business* (Quorum, 1991), and *Workforce Education: Improving Educational Skills* (ASTD, 1993). Gordon is the author of numerous articles in *Training & Development* (ASTD), *Instruction and Performance* (NSPI), and *Workforce* (ICE-SA), and he is a columnist for *Workforce Training News/Corporate University Review*. He received a Ph.D. in psychology and history from Loyola University.

Gordon is president of Imperial Corporate Training and Development, a Chicago-based management consulting firm, and is an instructor at Loyola University of Chicago in the Adult Corporate Instructional Management Graduate Program. He can be contacted at Imperial Corporate Training and Development, 10341 S. Lawler Avenue, Oak Lawn, IL 60453-4714.

Boyd Owens is now the quality manager for Veeder-Root Company in Altoona, Pennsylvania. He was the assistant operations manager at Otto Engineering at the time of this study. He graduated from Valparaiso University in 1985 with a B.S. in mechanical engineering and has been a design engineer, reliability program manager, quality assurance manager, materials manager, and assistant production manager, in addition to his current position. Boyd has taught SPC, mathematics, blueprint reading, time management, English as a Second Language (ESL), and computer skills to his workforce.

Owens has spoken before the Chicago section of American Society of Quality Control, the Chicago Institute on Economic Development (CIED), William Rainey Harper College Work Force Training Conference, Illinois Adult and Continuing Education Conference, and for six consecutive years he was invited to address the Illinois Work Force Education Conference.

Other Books Available in the Series

The ASTD *In Action* series examines real-life case studies that show how human resource development (HRD) professionals analyze what worked and what didn't as they crafted on-the-job solutions to address specific aspects of their work. Each book contains 15–25 case studies taken from many types of organizations, large and small, in the United States and abroad. Choose from case study collections on the following topics:

Measuring Return on Investment, Volume 1

Jack J. Phillips, *Editor*

Who's going to support a training program that can't prove itself? This volume shows you case after case of trainers proving that their programs work—in dollar-for-dollar terms. Each of the 18 case studies shows you the best (and sometimes not-so-best) practices from which every trainer can learn. Corporations demand bottom-line results from all branches of their operations, including HRD. This volume hands you the

tools—the hows, whys, and how-wells of measuring return-on-investment—to mark that bottom line.

Order Code: PHRO. Published by ASTD. 1994. 271 pages.

Measuring Return on Investment, Volume 2

Jack J. Phillips, *Editor*

This volume contains even more case studies on return-on-investment. Authors, reflecting several viewpoints from varied backgrounds, examine their diligent pursuit of accountability of training, HRD, and performance improvement programs. The 17 case studies cover a variety of programs from a diverse group of organizations, many of them global in scope. As a group, they add to the growing database of return-on-investment studies and make an important contribution to the literature.

Order Code: PHRE. Published by ASTD. 1997. 272 pages.

Conducting Needs Assessment

Jack J. Phillips and Elwood F. Holton III, *Editors*

How can you fix performance problems if you don't know what they are? This volume gives you the investigative tools to pinpoint the causes of performance problems—before investing time and money in training. Each of the 17 case studies provides real-world examples of training professionals digging deep to find the causes of performance problems and offers real-world results.

Order Code: PHNA. Published by ASTD. 1995. 312 pages.

Designing Training Programs

Donald J. Ford, *Editor*

These days, training techniques must consist of much more than setting up flipcharts, handing out manuals, or plugging in audiovisual aids. Organizations are more frequently asking instructional designers to create innovative learning systems that use a wide range of methods and media to spark participants' interest and increase retention and use on the job. This volume showcases 18 real-life examples of customized and artful programs, which improve learning and staff performance. Computer-based training, distance learning, and on-the-job training are just a few of the many methods used by the organizations contributing to this book.

Order Code: PHTD. Published by ASTD. 1996. 340 pages.

Creating the Learning Organization, Volume 1

Karen E. Watkins and Victoria J. Marsick, *Editors*

It's time to take learning organizations out of the think tank and into the real world. This volume contains 22 case studies from a cross section of organizations—international and national, industry and service, government and private sector. They show you the hows and whys of creating the learning organization as HRD professionals move beyond theory and into practice,

transforming organizations into businesses that perform, think, and learn.

Order Code: PHCL. Published by ASTD. 1996. 288 pages.

Transferring Learning to the Workplace

Mary L. Broad, *Editor*

The 17 case studies in this volume cover a wide range of organizational settings. Specifically, the real-life training examples feature dramatic, large-scale knowledge and skill transfer applications that affect overall organizational performance, as well as smaller programs that affect individual employee effectiveness. As more training and HRD professionals struggle to

implement learning transfer support activities, this collection of field experiences will be an invaluable source of ideas and advice.

Order Code: PHTL. Published by ASTD. 1997. 331 pages.

Leading Organizational Change

Elwood F. Holton III, *Editor*

HRD is concerned fundamentally with change, which is traditionally in individual knowledge, skills, and abilities. Today, however, organizations face an ever-increasing rate of change and struggle to manage change processes. HRD professionals have the opportunity and challenge to become key players in leading organizational change efforts. Covering a wide range of organizational types, change strategies, interventions, and outcomes, the 14 case studies show dramatically that HRD professionals can and should lead change.

Order Code: PHLE. Published by ASTD. 1997. 260 pages.

ASTD

1640 King Street
Box 1443
Alexandria, VA 22313-2043
PH 703.683.8100, FX 703.683.8103
www.astd.org